THE FLIGHT OF
THE SMALL WORLD

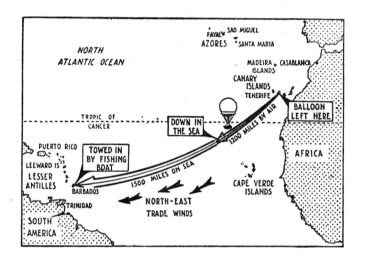

THE FLIGHT OF
THE SMALL WORLD

ARNOLD EILOART
and
PETER ELSTOB

With a Foreword by
The Rt. Hon. Lord Brabazon of Tara
(P.C.), G.B.E., M.C.

London
HODDER AND STOUGHTON

*Printed in Great Britain
for Hodder and Stoughton Limited,
by Richard Clay and Company, Ltd.,
Bungay, Suffolk*

TO

BRITISH INDUSTRY

THE FRIENDLY GIANT
WHO MADE IT ALL POSSIBLE

FOREWORD

BEFORE the advent of the aeroplane at the beginning of the century, the only way of getting up into the air was by balloon. The great Aero Clubs of the world were originally formed to foster the sport, and good fun it was. There were, of course, the great international Gordon Bennett balloon races in which enormous balloons were used, capable of staying up for two or three days and traversing vast distances, but in our own country, with its south-west winds, most trips started from London and had to finish in the Eastern Counties, usually Essex.

Fashionable and popular as the sport was, it all started to come to an end with the advent of power flight about 1908, and is now an almost forgotten pastime, nor would it today be so pleasant with high-tension grids traversing the country in all directions.

It came, therefore, as somewhat of a shock to us old balloonatics to hear of the extraordinary proposals to cross the Atlantic from East to West. We are, of course, familiar with the south-west trade winds that cross our country, but quite ignorant of the eastern winds with a touch of north in them that occur farther south.

An ordinary balloon flight as we know it was not envisaged, very wisely, as gas is wasted in ascending to increasing altitudes, but to cross the ocean at a low altitude governed as to height by a trail rope dragged through the sea was revolutionary and ingenious.

This book gives an intimate account of how the idea was born, and how after all difficulties were overcome a start was made, and all that happened *en route*.

One lives and learns, but few would ever have guessed that the project would fail after a gallant try, by virtue of powerful up-currents of air in the middle of the night irresistibly raising the balloon with its trail rope clear of all contact with the sea.

The sound planning and ingenuity of the car becoming a boat saved the occupants from a watery grave. Thank goodness for the car boat, for without it we should not have had the fortune to learn all about a great and splendid adventure, so admirably told in this book.

Brabazon of Tara

LIST OF ILLUSTRATIONS

LIST OF ILLUSTRATIONS

[1] Associated Newspapers Ltd.
[2] Martin Herzberg, Tenerife.

CHAPTER ONE

COLUMBUS, of course, was mad. Charles Lindbergh was mad too — and Thor Heyerdahl and Edmund Hillary and every man who ever fell in love with a wild idea the rest of the sober world thought impossible. 'Bushy' Eiloart is another of these rare madmen.

His three fellow balloonists must have all been touched with a little of the same divine insanity, but they are the first to admit that it was his drive, his single-mindedness, his complete disregard for all other commitments — theirs as well as his own — that resulted in them all finding themselves swinging gently beneath a silver-and-black balloon a thousand feet over the Atlantic and a thousand miles from land.

Three men and a girl in a balloon over the Atlantic — it might have been any time since the Montgolfier brothers sent the first fire balloon soaring over the heads of the astounded crowd in 1783, but it was Christmas 1958 and far above their heads the first man-made satellites were whipping around the world, a rocket was fired at the moon and huge I.C.B.M.s doubled the balloon's projected voyage in a matter of minutes. Between them two worlds touched: the robot-controlled, atomic-powered new age and the old but ever-present world of man-power — of mountain climbers, skin divers, channel swimmers, of men in gliders, tiny sail-boats, on rafts and in balloons.

How had it all happened?

On a grey evening nearly two years before, Bushy Eiloart sat in Colin and Rosemary Mudie's small London flat. All three were small-boat sailors, and they were talking of the boats they'd sailed in and the voyages they'd made. Outside there was a cold drizzle coming down from slate-coloured clouds, but inside that room the sun was shining out of a tropical blue sky and the warm trade winds were blowing.

"God, I wish I was there now!" Colin said dreamily. "Sitting at the helm in the sunshine with that lovely wind coming up astern, steady as a fan, pushing you on to the West Indies."

If you passed Colin in the street you probably wouldn't guess that he's the stuff adventurers are made of, for he's slightly built, has a great shock of hair that looks more than a little comic, and a deceptive air of diffidence. But a closer look reveals the wiry tautness, the nervous tension, the alert, humorous eyes, and the firm mouth behind the shy, boyish smile.

"How long did you take in *Sopranino*?" Eiloart asked. *Sopranino* was the tiny nineteen-and-a-half-foot sloop Colin and Pat Ellam had sailed ten thousand miles five years before.

"Twenty-eight days from Las Palmas to Barbados — nearly a month of sun and sea and not much else. A lovely, lovely month." He looked over to Rosemary and grinned. "Some day . . ." he promised.

"Yes," she agreed. "When we get our boat built we'll take a year off and go sailing in those nice warm waters."

Rosemary and Colin had met during a week-end's sailing and had married a few weeks later; since then they had put in a lot of time sailing in the cold, rough waters around the coast of Great Britain, and Rosemary had had to listen to Colin's stories of tropic seas, flying fish, phosphorous-bright water and warm sun until she finally decided that somehow, some day, they would sail those seas together.

"We took over a month in *Revive*, but it didn't seem that long." Eiloart lay back on the sofa and contemplated the ceiling almost as though he expected a gull to be hanging there like they do just over the mast. "It gives you time to think — I know I did. What about you? What did you think about all that time?"

"Oh, I don't know — thousands of things. The different boats I was going to build some day . . ." Colin is a designer of yachts and had, in fact, designed *Sopranino* for Pat Ellam. "Or how I could wangle it so that we could go on sailing around the world — or sometimes just how to go a bit faster."

"Don't we all?" Eiloart laughed, "when the wind drops and she starts to crawl. You look up at the clouds and wish that you could hitch on to one . . ."

Colin and Rosemary looked at each other.

"How strange that you should say that," Colin said.

"Why?"

"Because that's exactly what I *did* think, and one day, lying on my back looking up at the sky with Pat asleep below and *Soppers* sailing herself, I had a mad idea . . ." He looked quizzically at Rosemary.

"Yes," she said, "Bushy's a little mad too — you can tell him."

"Well, I thought, as I watched the clouds come up behind us and disappear ahead, how nice it would be, as you said, to hitch on to them. And then quite suddenly I realised how I could."

"With a sky hook?"

"No — in a balloon. A free balloon drifting with the north-east trades."

Bushy sat bolt upright in amazement. "Good God, what a bloody marvellous idea!"

The Mudies laughed. "We call it our mad scheme for getting away from it all," Rosemary said. "To blow up our little balloon and just drift off."

"Is it possible — from a technical point of view, I mean?"

"I don't see why not," said Colin. "Once you got it up, a balloon would travel with the speed and direction of the wind itself. Down there, at the right time of year, you'd drift about two or three hundred miles a day and get over in about ten days to three weeks."

"But will a balloon stay up that long?" Eiloart asked. "Won't the gas seep out?"

"I don't know, but I should think with modern materials that needn't be much of a problem."

"Well, why hasn't someone done it, then?"

"No one seems to have done much ballooning in recent years, and I suppose it seemed too dangerous to risk coming down in the sea in a wickerwork contraption."

"But it wouldn't have to be a wickerwork contraption, would it?"

"No," said Colin. "It could be a boat — a very light but very strong boat . . ."

For a moment there was silence in the little room as Bushy looked first at Colin and then at Rosemary. "By God," he said softly, "I'd like to have a shot at it!"

"You mean you don't think we're mad?"

"Of course you are, but what's that got to do with it? Are you really serious about it?"

"We haven't been up until now, because it never seemed possible. Even if it were possible, with modern materials, to make a balloon that would stay up long enough, it would cost a small fortune."

"Yes, I suppose it will. I can raise a few hundred pounds — what about you?"

"We haven't got tuppence."

"Well, we can raise enough to get started. I'll ask Pete tomorrow if he wants to come in, and if he does we can use the business to get credit. Anyway, if it's technically possible and we can somehow scrape up the money, do you want to have a shot at it together?"

Colin and Rosemary had talked half-humorously of floating across the Atlantic in a balloon for years, but it had not seemed likely that it would ever be more than a dream. Suddenly, here was someone who not only thought that it was possible but also wanted to get started immediately. They didn't hesitate.

"We're on!" Colin said. He crossed to the bookcase and came back with a little heap of books on ballooning, and the three of them pored over them for hours.

They hadn't known each other for much more than a year or so, and were still at the slightly unsure stage in their relationship. Bushy was much older than the Mudies, but a virile, active man who sailed his small Hornet class dinghy competitively every weekend down at Hayling Island on the English Channel. He had first got to know the Mudies when Colin did a series of eight drawings to be used as designs by our company. Since then they had sailed together and the acquaintance was growing into a friendship.

Each respected the other's abilities, and when Bushy made his sudden proposal, and they accepted, all three of them knew that it was no idle conversation. The Mudies had seen enough of Bushy working on something to know a little of what lay ahead.

They read about some of the famous balloon voyages and laughed together over the old prints. Colin read to them about other attempts on the Atlantic; about the famous American balloonist Wise, for whom a New York newspaper had raised the money in 1873 to build a monster balloon capable of lifting seven tons.

"He planned to go up to ten thousand feet to catch the constant east to west wind he believed was always blowing up there," Colin told them. "He'd have been damn cold, of course."

"How far did he get?" Bushy asked.

"It never left the ground — the fabric wasn't strong enough, and it just ripped when it was nearly full."

"Plastics!" said Bushy enthusiastically. "That's the answer — and all the other modern materials. The old balloons must have leaked like mad, but I'm sure that we could get one that would hardly lose any gas at all. I bet that no one has thought of using modern materials for ballooning! Come on — let's get started now. Have you got a pencil and paper?"

They were produced, and they made a list of the first things to be done and assigned some to each one. It was after two in the morning when Bushy left. It had been the first meeting, and there were to be hundreds of others at which they would exchange ideas, knock them down, deal with the latest good reason why they couldn't possibly succeed and plan the next steps. They knew that a lot of hard work lay in front of them, but not, of course, how much; for in the beginning they thought that they might do it in their spare time and holidays. In fact, it took them nearly two years, during the whole of which they gave all their spare time, and during the last few months of which all their waking hours and most of their sleeping ones were occupied by the balloon and its problems.

Colin and Bushy worked together very well, although they would not have been human if, from time to time, they hadn't become irritated with each other. I think that they both believe themselves to be primarily practical men with little time for dreaming and a scorn for the impractical artist who is proud of being 'all thumbs'. In fact, both of them are dreamers and artists in the wider sense first and practical men afterwards. Colin had served a full apprenticeship to a boat builder before becoming a boat designer himself, and works in wood or metal with great skill. Ingrained from his Scottish ancestors is a tremendous respect for good workmanship. Some of the temperamental difficulties in the early days of the project were caused by a different outlook on the task of making the balloon and the car. Bushy Eiloart, as the production half of our small manufacturing company, was well used to the innumerable difficulties that get in the way of making something new, and therefore budgeted his time generously. Colin met most of his doubts with confident assurance.

"We wouldn't have to find anyone to do a simple job like that, Bushy," he'd say. "We'd do it ourselves in half the time."

Bushy knew that Colin was a first-class boat designer — he had helped Giles to design the famous *Sopranino*, and he assumed that he must have access to a well-equipped engineering shop somewhere. So Bushy allowed himself to be persuaded that they could do most of the work themselves. It would mean that everything was going to be much simpler and, what was also very important, much cheaper.

Colin did not have access to an engineering shop, and all of the metal parts had to be made for them, and as they were 'one-off' jobs they took a great deal of time. Colin worked himself unmercifully, as did Bushy, but the project seemed to them to progress terribly slowly.

However, this was the first night, and the scheme was hardly more than a wild idea which had been pinned down for a moment. The next morning Bushy came into the office like a whirlwind. I could see that he was bursting with some new scheme, and let him lead me off to a corner of the factory where he could talk without being overheard. One of Bushy's traits is a feeling that any good idea will be stolen unless great precautions are taken to keep it secret. There had been many strange enterprises in the twenty years that we had been partners, and I wondered what it was going to be this time.

"You're pretty bored with Archives Designs, aren't you, Pete?" he asked. Archives Designs was a small business, making table mats and trays using modern designs and simple colours, which we had started about three years before. It was now fairly successful; we supplied all the most expensive shops and, as Bushy said, I was getting bored with it, but I knew from the question that he was going to try to sell me something. I agreed cautiously that I was bored and ready for a change.

"You've often said that you'd like to have a go at sailing across the Atlantic, haven't you?" He hardly waited for me to agree, "Well, how would you like to float across in a balloon?"

"To do *what* in a *what!*" I had been prepared for something unusual, but not quite that. Then he told me about his conversation with Colin and Rosemary the night before, and pointed out that hundreds of people had crossed the Atlantic in small boats but that no one had ever done it in a balloon. I murmured something about perhaps there was a good reason for that, but he was carried on the wave of his enthusiasm, and after twenty years as his partner I knew better than to try and stop him. I listened to the ideas bubbling out of him and finished up by agreeing to join them. Our two small companies, Archives Designs and Yeast-pac, which manufactured face packs, would be squeezed for the necessary money. All my spare time would henceforth belong to the yet unborn balloon.

Rosemary had most efficiently made a list of the first people to see, and among these was the author of the book which had started it all, Mr. Gibbs Smith, who, we learned, was one of the principal officials at the Victoria and Albert Museum. I wrote and asked for an interview, saying only that we had become interested in ballooning and picturing to myself an elderly and didactic theoretician.

But the man who greeted us next day at the Victoria and Albert was about the farthest thing from a benign and elderly fossil that could be imagined. Youthful, big and exuding energy like a sun-ray lamp, he seemed to delight in doing four or five things at once. His office was piled high with the most extraordinary collection of objects, among which, as he talked to Bushy and me, he roamed like a browsing animal; picking up some, staring thoughtfully at others and all the while breaking off to dictate a letter, make a note for another book or answer the telephone. In between these activities he gave forth to us the most valuable information.

"One thing, though," he warned us, "Never say 'gondola'; it's not done. It's always the 'car'. Remember that, you can never be proper balloonists while you say gondola." We promised, and he went on with details of drip flaps, thermals, equators, north poles, grapples, ripcords, ballonets and a dozen other equally mysterious things. I tried taking notes, but I knew that they would make little sense to me the following day.

"What it all boils down to is this: if you want to go a long way, you get the biggest damn balloon you can possibly afford and you take the maximum amount of ballast and precious little else. Gas and ballast — that's all, and as much of both as you can, for from the moment that you take off you will be dissipating one or the other, and when you haven't got enough of either left you have to come down."

"But why not just go up to a respectable height and stay there?" I asked.

"Because once you've started to rise you won't stop until you've let out gas, and once you've started to sink you won't stop until you've lightened her by discarding ballast, and so you go on. An expert can judge it so finely that only a little gas or ballast is lost, but there are other factors to upset your balance. An updraught of warm air, for instance, or a downdraught of cold; the sun going behind a cloud and cooling the gas in your balloon or coming out again and heating it up. Loss of gas through porosity; loss of gas out of the open neck . . ."

"Why not close it then?" I asked.

"Because," he said patiently, "as the balloon rises into thinner air the gas inside the envelope expands, and if it couldn't get out the balloon would burst." This started him off on a train of re-collections of most of the goriest balloon disasters he had read about, and we were entertained for some time with freezing at high altitudes, turning blue in the face from lack of oxygen and burning to death. After giving us a good lunch, he shook us both warmly by the hand as though for the last time.

"Well, the best of luck, anyway. You'll have to go to Holland if you actually want to go ballooning yourselves. I'd love to go with you, but I've never been up in a balloon in my life — I suffer from vertigo, you see."

"Well," said Bushy when we were outside, "we know a lot more about ballooning than we did an hour ago, anyway."

"I wonder what the symptoms are?" I asked.

"What symptoms?"

"Vertigo," I said. "If it's a sinking feeling in the stomach I've got it."

Bushy laughed. "The next thing is Bristol University, where they make the meteorological balloons," he said. "We'll find out how much one will cost."

Gibbs Smith had told us who to write to there: Professor Powell, the Nobel Prize-winner, and he had given us other names; a seventy-three-year-old French balloonist, Dollfus, the best-known American balloonist, Winzen, the head of the Dutch Balloon Club, and he had recommended that we write to the Lighter-than-air section of the Air Ministry at Cardington in Bedfordshire.

Meanwhile Colin had been finding out about different materials of which to make the balloon. Rosemary had taken advantage of her position in the London Press Exchange to find out the names, addresses and telephone numbers of the Secretaries of any of the official bodies they thought might be able to help them. A few days later we held a second council of war in Bushy's flat. Colin and Rosemary welcomed me to the crew, and I thought that if the idea of drifting over the cold ocean didn't worry her there was ob-viously no reason why it should me. None at all.

So far all we had learned had served to show us the extent of our appalling ignorance, but that is probably as good a beginning as any other. We didn't know yet where to get a balloon, what it should be made of, how big it ought to be, how much it would lift, whether its direction could be controlled at all or even if there wasn't a perfectly good reason why the whole plan was quite impossible.

"There's one thing I'm certain of," said Colin. "That I can build a two-hundredweight gondola — oops! I mean car — that will be capable of crossing the Atlantic under sail as a boat. Look here — I've done some sketches."

We pored over the sketches and suggested changes and improvements, but even then Colin had thought of most things. It would, he pointed out, have to be as light as possible, and with modern synthetic substances and glues he thought he could make a seaworthy hull, able to carry four people and emergency food and water, that would weigh no more than the basket cars of the old balloons.

I know next to nothing about the theory of boat-hull shapes, but I could see that Colin's ideas were unconventional. One of his old employers once told me that Colin's theory is that if you want to strengthen something you should lighten it, and so the problem he had set himself now was an ideal one for him. I watched him explaining points to Bushy, who had built his own racing dinghy in his living-room some years before and was well able to deal with the theory involved, and tried to remember how much I knew about Colin.

Scottish born ('my father was a Dundee man') and educated there and in England. At sixteen he was apprenticed to Power Boats Ltd., a Southampton firm, where he worked all through the war years, going through each department in turn as part of his training to become a floor executive. But the end of the war brought his job to an end, too. He was chosen to go to Harwell as a draughtsman on rocket design, but had suddenly realised that he wanted to work with boats and instead had gone along to a boat builder, whom he had long admired, and asked for a job. He had known that the pay wouldn't be as good nor the ultimate goal so high, but he would be designing things he loved, and this was important to him. He had spent the next five years learning the craft of boat building from one of its masters, and had responded wholeheartedly to the demand for fine workmanship and the challenge for original design.

The turning point in Colin's life came when Pat Ellam asked Giles to design him an ultra-small sloop for world cruising. Colin was given the job and produced *Sopranino*, which was only nineteen and a half feet long and weighed but three-quarters of a ton. It was built by a boat builder on the upper Thames who had never built a sea-going boat before. When it was finished the owner was so pleased he invited Colin on the maiden cruise to the West Indies, and his sea voyages began.

He had been interested in the sea and boats for as long as he can remember. He believes that this, like his ability to draw, is an inheritance; for his grandfathers were sea-faring men and his father, although earning his living as a Civil Servant, should have been, Colin thinks, a scene painter, for he loved doing that more than anything else. It was perhaps the memory of his father, working all his life at something he didn't love, that decided him to turn down Harwell and a future with rockets for the uncertainty of designing small boats.

Also that same evening we wrote letters to half a dozen people and divided up the next steps among us. It was after one in the morning when I got home with a long list of things to do, and I realised that I would have very little time for anything else until the balloon was launched.

A reply came from Professor Powell at Bristol University in a few days. He said that they made all their own balloons, and that if we would like to see them being made to come along. We jumped at the chance and on 19th February 1957 Bushy and Colin took the train to Bristol. They talked balloons solidly the whole way and thought of many brilliant ideas to make their task easier and, as usual, discovered that most of them were quite impracticable. They were to spend weeks, for instance, trying to devise a towed rudder or paravane which would enable them to control their direction, before they had to admit that it wasn't possible. There were many similar ideas that consumed valuable time.

At Bristol they climbed to the top of the Royal Fort, where the H. H. Wills Physics Laboratory stands, and asked for Dr. Heitler, with whom they had an appointment. They both felt their hearts beating a little faster at the prospect of getting to grips with actually making a balloon at last.

A blond young man, whom they mistook for an undergraduate, told them that Dr. Heitler was ill and Professor Powell had not yet arrived. He asked if he could help them. Bushy asked him if they could see Dr. Heitler's assistant.

"I'm afraid he doesn't have one, but my name is John Davis," he said diffidently. "He and I are sort of joint managers of the balloon department. Next to us are about a dozen or so people — some of them make balloons, some instruments, some inspect photographs and so on . . ."

They explained who they were, and he immediately asked them what they were going to do with a balloon. They had expected to be asked this, and they replied that they were thinking of making an attempt on the free-balloon distance record. John Davis was immediately interested.

"I should think you've got a very good chance. The record was probably put up with one of the old rubber-coated cotton balloons, whereas we make ours of polythene. I should think that by now we have made more *big* polythene balloons than anyone. Come along and I'll show you one being made."

"How big is big?" Bushy asked.

"Oh, from three hundred thousand cubic feet up." That was big all right, for we had worked out that with hydrogen lifting seventy pounds per thousand cubic feet we could have a shot with one thirty thousand cubic feet.

Following close behind him, they found themselves at the top of a wide stone stairway. The walls were almost covered with photographs of balloons: enormous balloons, lovely balloons, balloons of all shapes and sizes. Along one wall something was covered with sheets of pink polythene, and dropped casually in a corner was a parachute. Bushy and Colin fingered the polythene, and both suddenly felt a great jump nearer their goal. This was the stuff balloons were made of; this was the stuff their balloon would be made of — they were half-way across the Atlantic already.

Around the next corner and through a door they saw their first balloon being made. Four girls in white coats stood at a hundred-foot-long table sealing one immense sheet of pink polythene to another with great care. A gigantic balloon was slowly taking shape under their skilful fingers, and Bushy and Colin gaped enthralled, hardly taking in what John Davies was telling them.

"That apparatus is a hot-air sealing machine, and it seals about a hundred feet of vertical seam in ten minutes." He crinkled a sheet of the polythene between his fingers. "Unfortunately, it won't work on anything thicker than one and a half thou., and that's pretty flimsy. Then again it won't work on a horizontal seam — across the grain that is. For those we have another machine called a clicker." He went on explaining the difficulties of balloon making and answering their questions. They learned about loss of gas through porosity, change of altitude, sudden expansion from the heat of the sun — called superheating — and a number of new ones.

"What you have to do if you want to conserve your gas is not so much keep at a steady height as maintain your position in a density ridge," he told them earnestly and then laughed at their blank looks. Before he had a chance to explain, a quiet little man with bright, humorous eyes came in and they were introduced to Professor Powell, who had won the Nobel Prize for cosmic-ray research in 1948, the work for which he is still sending balloons up into the stratosphere. He asked the same question as John Davies:

"What are you going to do with this balloon if you get it?"

"Have a shot at the distance record," Bushy said.

"Oho, so that's it, is it? What's the present record?"

"Just under two thousand miles," Colin said.

"Then it will have to be an international event unless you plan to start in the United States or Russia?" They shook their heads.

"Australia perhaps? As a matter of fact, I should think that you'd get the best conditions over some nice stretch of warm sea away from the effect of land features on the wind. The lower latitudes of the Atlantic, for instance, so that you'd get the trade winds. I should think that the Canary Islands would be the best place to start from — a wonderful excuse to go there, anyway."

Bushy and Colin looked at each other. It was obvious, Bushy told me wryly later, that they don't give the Nobel Prize away for nothing. Professor Powell had guessed their whole plan very quickly, and he could be of the greatest help to us if he was sufficiently interested.

"As a matter of fact, that's the very place we'd thought of," Colin said.

"Well it's the logical place, but how will you make sure that there is a boat near by when you come down?"

"We shan't come down until we're over land again," Bushy said.

"But that means . . ." Professor Powell stopped, and they all looked at each other.

"An Atlantic crossing! What a marvellous idea," John Davies said.

"Now I *am* interested," Professor Powell said. "But I wonder if you know how many problems there are? How will you control your height, for instance? If you do it by the conventional gas and ballast method there is no reason why you should stay aloft any longer than anyone else — you'll have to devise some other way to check rise.

"You see, every morning when the sun rises you'll get at least an extra hundredweight of lift — it may well be much more, I should have to do some sums to tell you — and that is your first big problem. It occurs only once a day, but all day long you'll be either losing or gaining lift for a dozen and one reasons. When the sun goes behind a cloud, when it rains, when you run into a column of rising air and many others. You'll have to check rise and fall many times every day."

"The morning sun is the most serious problem," Colin said. "But the other minor ones are not so important, are they? After all, we don't have to stay at exactly the same height. If we go up or down a thousand feet or so it shouldn't make much difference."

"Ah, but it doesn't work like that. If a thermal starts you rising you'll keep on going up until something acts as a brake. You see, you've no friction, and once your craft, weighing one or two tons, is given a momentum, it will keep on going until something stops it."

"We did think of trailing a long length of rope in the sea," Bushy said. "Then as the balloon rose it would be checked by the extra weight of the rope coming out of the water, and as it fell it would be lightened by the water taking up the weight of the rope. Wouldn't that work?"

"Yes, it probably would, for it is a very well-known method, but I should think that to be effective you would have to have so much rope in the water that it would slow you down enormously. I don't think that you would want to drag a weight equal to the extra lift you'll get through superheating at dawn — anyway, those are your problems. Solve them, and I don't see why you shouldn't be the first to cross the Atlantic in a balloon. If there is any way in which we can help let us know. You will want a good altimeter, for instance, and we have devised one that will register as little as six inches of climb. John will show you films of our various launchings and tell you anything you want to know. Good-bye and good luck."

In the little projection room they sat like small boys at a cowboy picture and watched the gigantic, shiny polythene balloons rapidly rising in the bright early morning. They watched the careful procedure of inflating, of attaching instruments, and they saw balloons leave the ground one after the other and rise almost straight up until they were out of sight. It encouraged them and nearly made them forget the almost insoluble problems between them and their goal.

Bushy asked boldly if there was any chance of Bristol University making the balloon for them.

"I'm afraid not," John Davies told them. "We've been endowed for research, and that would hardly come under that heading. But why don't you make one yourselves? It's not difficult — the heat-sealing devices are quite simple things really."

"Do you think that I could come and stay here for about a week and learn how to make a balloon?" Eiloart asked.

"I don't know. I'll have to ask Dr. Heitler. When do you want to come?"

"The week before Easter," Bushy said promptly, as though he had not just made up his mind.

"Well, I'll write and let you know if it's on."

Back in London they told Rosemary and me of the meeting.

"We've seen that balloons aren't too horribly hard to make," Bushy said enthusiastically. "We've been told by a scientist that it can be done . . ."

"If we solve a few insoluble problems," Colin added dryly.

"Oh, there's always a solution waiting to be seen," Bushy said with confidence. "Some just take longer to find than others, that's all. If we all keep thinking about it we'll get it in the end. After all, if it was easy someone would have done it years ago. Now I'll bet that they do let me go up there and learn how to make a balloon, and by the time I've made one you'll have the craft built, Colin, and then we'll be well on our way. Now to work — there are a million things to do, so let's divide them up, and then each of us will only have a quarter of a million jobs."

I got home that night just before two with an even longer list than last time. All my spare time, and much of my working time, since Bushy had presented me with the idea, had been given to the balloon, and I had discovered a good deal about the practical problems involved, as had the other three. We now knew that to be ready in two years we would have to work very hard. It was a good deal longer than I had contemplated.

I had long since arranged to take a month-long holiday in Italy, during which my wife, who is a painter, would be able to see her fill of primitives and I would finish the war novel on which I had been struggling for years. Now it looked as though I ought to give up our month in Italy for the sake of the balloon, but after a great deal of heart searching I decided to go ahead with my plans.

Bushy didn't like it when I told him the next day, for when he throws himself into something he does just that, and he can't understand anyone else giving it any less. Whatever the problem is that he is thinking about, it takes all of his time, all of his energy, all of his interest. It has always been so, and no one knows it better than I, for twenty years before, when we started our cosmetic-manufacturing business on a few pounds, I learned to expect nothing from him but the problems of making and marketing a face pack for the sixteen hours a day that we worked together. Nevertheless, the business prospered against astronomical odds, and since then I had seen him throw himself just as wholeheartedly into a dozen other enterprises, from a London Theatre Club to a Mexican hotel. As soon as the problems were solved and the business running smoothly he lost interest and looked around for something else. We never got rich, but we had a lot of fun.

So I stood firm while he tried first sweet reason, then persuasion and finally bullying, and when all these failed he accepted the situation with good humour, which is also characteristic.

"What you can do in your spare time — and don't tell me that you'll be writing all day, because I know damn well that you won't — is to think about our big problem. How to avoid the balloon rising at dawn with the superheating? Just think about it several times a day and before you go to sleep at night. Perhaps with nothing to do but that you'll come up with a solution."

So we went to Italy, and I struggled with my novel and, as Bushy had requested, thought about our problem and the other problems. One night in Sicily I walked about the ruins of a Greek city until dawn, and the next day I wrote a long letter backing out of the first British Trans-Atlantic Balloon Crossing. I explained that I thought the chances of success were so remote as to be almost impossible, for it seemed to me that no amount of improvement of modern materials over old-fashioned ones could overcome the fundamental objection which had been put so cogently by our first expert, Mr. Gibbs Smith, when he had pointed out that from the moment of leaving the ground it is necessary to dissipate either gas or ballast, and that it therefore seemed impossible to get a balloon large enough to hold four of us and enough ballast for perhaps three weeks. It seemed to me that ballooning was a skill like gliding or skiing, and that to hope to beat the world's record at the first attempt — let alone doubling or trebling it — was madness.

I said that if I thought there was a sporting chance I would carry on, even though it meant doing nothing else for two years or more, and even though it obviously meant that it would take all our money, but that, as I thought the chance of success was practically non-existent, I was backing out. I went on to urge Bushy to drop the idea before it had used up all his money or, worse, resulted in his and the Mudies' death. I didn't really have much hope of persuading him to give up, but I thought that I should try. I added that if despite my reasoning he was determined to carry on that I shouldn't ever try to persuade him to stop (I couldn't foresee then how near I was to come to breaking that promise months later on a windswept beach in Tenerife), and that short of investing my money in it would help in any way that I could.

I don't even now know how much the simple fear of being killed had to do with my decision. It is true that I believed that it wasn't possible to cross the Atlantic in a balloon, and that therefore I believed that the craft would come down in the sea, and I thought it extremely unlikely that it would be in one piece and I had a vivid picture of hanging on to a bit of the boat until I could hang on no longer. I know that I felt a vast sense of relief that I was released from the tyranny of the balloon.

CHAPTER TWO

W HEN Bushy got my letter he called a meeting, read it to Rosemary and Colin and asked them what they wanted to do. Without hesitating for a moment they decided to carry on as long as possible — that is as long as the money, now halved, would hold out.

"Peter may be right," Colin said, "but it's too soon to give up. If we can't solve the problem of controlling our height without losing gas, then I agree that it would be mad to try the Atlantic, but I think that we can — as a matter of fact, I've got the beginnings of an idea and I expect that you have, too, Bushy, so let's carry on."

"I'm all for carrying on," Bushy said, "and that means acting just as though we've got that problem licked and getting on with making our balloon and the craft. I'm not worried about the objections Pete has raised — we'll get round those all right. It's the blasted money that has me worried, for now that he's backed out I shall have to find it all and I just haven't got it."

"What's the next big expense?" Rosemary asked.

"The polythene to make the balloon."

"What about getting into touch with the manufacturers of the polythene and telling them what you want it for? You never can tell, they might like the idea and let you have it a bit cheaper."

"It's certainly worth a try," Bushy said. "Most of these big companies are run by blokes with a good share of taking-a-chance in them. And, let's face it, if we get there they'd probably like to say polythene by so-and-so, nylon net by what's-its-name . . ."

"Now you're talking," said Colin. "There's no end to it. What about the whisky for the medicine chest? We couldn't take anything but the best Scotch."

"And Mrs. Mudie's dresses by Dior, of course," added Rose-mary.

"Sorry," said Bushy, "but this has to be an all-British effort — you'll have to pick a British dress designer."

One of the reasons the enterprise didn't founder on the obstacles it met was their ability to clown and see the lighter side always. They were to need it many times in the next two years.

A week or so later Bushy reported to the University of Bristol as an apprentice balloon-maker and was taken along the same stone corridors and introduced to the four girls.

"Mr. Eiloart is going to try to learn to make a balloon in a week," John Davies told the head girl, Sylvia Lawrence. "See if you can teach him each operation."

Bushy says that it was one of the pleasantest weeks in the whole project. The girls were lively, intelligent and pretty, and very nice to him. Sylvia Lawrence, like most girls in England, had left school at fifteen, but it was obvious that she would have been well able to cope with a University education and it should somehow have been made possible for her to become a physicist as she had wanted to.

She took him patiently through each of the operations and pointed out the snags. He found that he could work the mechanical heat-sealers without much difficulty, but he couldn't master the electric iron used to seal long seams, for its proper use depended upon feel. It was a question of judging the temperature of the iron and deciding how long to hold it on the polythene, and it was the kind of delicate balance that comes with long practice. At the end of the week he knew how to make a balloon, but he wasn't satisfied that he could do it himself — at least not well enough for all their lives to depend upon his seam.

Once again it looked as though they were stumped, but Eiloart had learned from talking to her that Sylvia was getting married in August and leaving her job. Why, he thought, shouldn't she leave two weeks earlier and come to London and make them a balloon in his flat? He had a living-room thirty feet long for the table — there didn't seem to be any objections.

Of course there were rules and regulations about manufacturing in private flats, safety regulations about electrical equipment, his landlord would no doubt object, Bristol University might well not like the idea of letting her go two weeks earlier, the young man she was to marry might not like the idea of her going up to London for two weeks and indeed Sylvia herself might not be enthusiastic about the idea.

I don't think that any of these objections carried much weight with Bushy. What was important was to get the balloon made — surely anyone could see that? With complete confidence he approached the University and Sylvia, and to everyone's surprise, except his, it all worked out. Sylvia Lawrence would leave her job two weeks early, travel up to London and make an enormous balloon in the fifth-floor Kensington flat. Why on earth not?

Bushy had, of course, told Sylvia what it was all about and it was probable that that had persuaded her, for what girl wouldn't want to make the first balloon to float across the Atlantic Ocean?

Bushy had two months to get everything ready for her. It wasn't too long, for he had to get the polythene, the heat-sealers and a table twenty-five feet long by five feet wide smuggled into his flat, as well as carry on with all the other jobs. Gradually, as the idea progressed from talk to paper planning to actual construction it took more and more of his time until he was doing little else but snatching quick meals and a few hours of sleep at night.

Colin and Rosemary, too, were getting caught up by the Atlantic balloon and finding less and less time for anything else. It had all come at a peculiarly bad time for them, for they had been working towards Colin's becoming a full-time free lance, which would mean his working very long hours until he was established. Colin had resigned himself to giving up most other activities anyway, but had not, of course, allowed for the demands of the Atlantic balloon. Now he found himself working until two and three in the morning most days of the week.

While Colin worked away at his plans for the hull he also kept turning over in his head the basic problem — how to overcome the sudden lift at sunrise without letting off gas and how to check a sudden fall without discarding ballast. If you could pull yourself up by your boot-straps, he thought humorously to himself, that would do it. Or to stop a rise you could lean over the side with a huge fan and push yourself down. It was the sort of idea that many of the old-time balloonists had tried in their vain attempts to alter the direction in which the balloon was drifting. They had tried paddles like a paddle-steamer and things shaped like birds' wings, and fans, but nothing had had the slightest effect. They had even tried propellers, but, of course, propellers weren't efficient then, for no one really understood the principle on which they worked. Today's propellers, he remembered reading somewhere, were ninety per cent efficient . . .

A few minutes later he was dialling Bushy's number. It was after one in the morning, and it had to ring for a few minutes before it woke Bushy up.

"Why shouldn't we use a propeller?" Colin asked without pre-amble. "A man-powered propeller mounted to give us vertical lift or downward thrust if we turn it around? Modern propellers are ninety per cent efficient."

Eiloart was wide awake now. "Of course — that's it! Some sort of a crank that we could all turn to make it spin fast. Even if the four of us got only a hundred pounds lift, think of the difference it would make. We'll get down to the actual plan first thing to-morrow morning."

It was more difficult than it had appeared at first to drive a pair of contra-rotating propellers inside the car.

Bushy's son, Tim, a chemical engineering student at Cambridge, was in London and looked at some of their sketches. He seemed a bit dubious.

"I should think that if you're going to depend on man-power you should use your legs," he said. "No one could possibly turn a propeller by hand fast enough to lift himself."

"We don't expect to lift ourselves," Bushy said testily. "But two of us could certainly turn a winch that would raise three hundred pounds or so, and if a propeller is ninety per cent efficient why can't we raise a hundred pounds?"

32

The Small World on its first test flight at the Ministry of Supply Research and Development Establishment at Cardington, Bedfordshire, November 1958.

The crew. *Left to right:* Colin Mudie, designer of the balloon and boat, the navigator; Rosemary Mudie, the photographer and in charge of food supplies; Tim Eiloart, radio operator and meteorologist; Bushy Eiloart, Captain and pilot of the balloon.

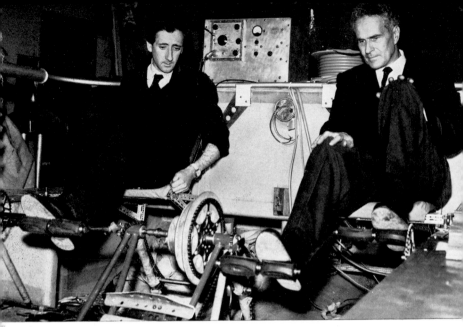

Colin and Bushy trying out the pedal apparatus at City Display's workshops.

The crew in their positions ready to take off in their first test flight.

"I don't know," Tim said carefully — he is used to his father's sudden enthusiasms. "First I should like to know about this ninety per cent efficiency — ninety per cent of what?"

"Ask Colin," Bushy said, but Colin was busy. "Better still, find out for us — you're the engineer, aren't you? Well, find out all about propellers."

"Right," Tim said, and not believing in unnecessary work, sat down and wrote to a leading firm of propeller manufacturers asking them for all the technical details.

Meanwhile, Bushy and Colin recalled their school physics and worked out their own formulas. They decided that a conservative estimate would be a twenty-pounds lift from each propeller, which should certainly solve most of their problems.

It was the kind of encouragement that they needed just at the right time, but, of course, it added tremendously to the work that had to be done, for the entire apparatus had to be designed, the working drawings made, the parts ordered and the whole thing assembled and tested. It meant modifying the internal arrangements of the craft, too. But they were satisfied that they had found the answer to their biggest problem, and this more than compensated for the extra work.

Bushy had got to know John Davies well while working at Bristol learning to make balloons, and had learned a tremendous lot from him about the problems of flight in free balloons. He had never actually seen a balloon take off, though, because all flights had to be made from Cardington and were under the control of the Air Ministry. When Bristol's cosmic-ray research team were ready for another set of experiments they notified Cardington and got permission. John Davies promised Bushy that next time he would ask for him to be allowed to come along and actually help in the inflation and watch the ascents, but he found it impossible to persuade officialdom to give the necessary permission. He wrote and told Bushy this and at the same time gave him a valuable lead.

"Last week," he wrote, "I spoke to Mr. Long, who works for the Research and Development Establishment here and is one of the very few licensed balloon pilots in this country. He pointed out that you would have to have a licence for any flights here, and probably anywhere else in the world. He has flown in balloons made of synthetics, but he doesn't like them very much. Anyway, he would be glad to talk to you and give you advice about ballooning, valves, etc."

Eiloart wrote and asked Mr. Long for his help, and a reply inviting them all to come and see him the following week-end came back almost by return. Bushy, Rosemary and Colin drove there the next Sunday.

Sixty-five-year-old Gerry Long joined the Navy in 1910, but he has the alert bearing and springy step of a young man. Balloons have been the business and pleasure of his whole life. He had gone into 'Lighter than-air' at the beginning of his service life and had remained in it ever since, flying in almost every famous British balloon. He had been one of the crew of the *R101*, and had luckily missed going on her last tragic flight when she crashed in France with the loss of all on board. He had held a balloon pilot's licence for forty years, and the walls of his house were covered with photographs and pictures of famous balloons. They spent the first half-hour or so just looking at his collection. He was the first practical balloonist any of them had ever met, and they had many questions to ask. He answered them all cheerfully.

The most ballast he had ever had to let go at once? Forty pounds — and that was to clear some high-tension wires that had suddenly appeared in front of him. What had happened? He'd shot up like a lift. They smiled at each other, for they were convinced that they could get that much lift from their man-powered propellers. They had decided to keep their propellers secret for the time being, and so they asked him what he thought of their chances of staying up long enough to drift across the Atlantic Ocean. They waited anxiously for his answer, because if anyone knew of some good reason why their whole scheme was impossible it would be this man.

"Well, balloons can be made to stay up indefinitely these days, for there need be no leaks and only an insignificant loss of gas through seepage. If you husband your gas and ballast carefully

34

it should be some time before you're down to your rock-bottom emergency ballast. When that happens and you start to go down, if you use a good long trail rope to relieve you for weight I don't see why you shouldn't trail the rest of the way."

"Hooray!"

"Wait a minute though," he said with a smile. "All this depends on two things that I don't know about. One is that the wind really does blow steadily day in and day out in the right direction . . ."

They assured him that it did.

". . . and the other is that you don't meet an electrical storm."

They had wondered about that one. They asked if balloons got struck by lightning. He hadn't actually heard of one, but all the aeronauts he had ever met or ever heard about had come down quickly when an electrical storm came up.

"Even in the *Graf Zeppelin*, which flew the Atlantic for eight years, they always steered around them," he said, "But you won't be able to do that — you might be able to change direction a bit with towing a hydrofoil and a sail, but you will certainly not be able to dodge a storm. If you see one ahead the best thing to do is to come down."

"And give up the whole thing?" Rosemary Mudie asked.

"Better to give up alive than be killed. You probably wouldn't get hit by lightning, but your balloon would be torn to pieces by the turbulence inside a storm. I don't think you'd stand a chance if you tried to stay up in a severe electrical storm."

They were all gloomily silent for a few moments.

"What are the chances of meeting one?" Bushy asked. Gerry Long didn't know, but it was obvious that they would have to find out.

"One last thing," Bushy asked. "Will you come to the Canary Islands and take over the launching?"

"Of course I will," he agreed enthusiastically.

They learned much more about the technique of ballooning, from the best way to inflate the balloon evenly to the final landing and a hundred and one other tips. They took many notes, and left elated by the help they had received and at the prospect of

Gerry Long, with his vast experience, supervising the very tricky business of the inflation and launching when the day came to take off.

But the question of electrical storms was serious. The obvious thing to do was to find out the time of year when there were least of them, and then to find out what the odds were in the period they were likely to be in the air. They agreed that if the chances of meeting one were worse than one in five they would call the whole thing off.

"Will you find out about that, Colin?" Eiloart asked.

"Right," Mudie said readily.

"No, this time I mean it, Colin. You always agree, but you know you haven't been getting the jobs done." They were in the car travelling back to London, and it was obvious that Eiloart was annoyed.

"Go on, Bushy," Mudie said quietly.

"It's just that I'm getting fed up with doing all the pushing and shoving on this thing. I'm spending most of my time at it — I know that you can't do that, but if you can't manage a job you shouldn't take it on. Time and time again you say that you'll do something, and then just forget about it — no, I admit that's not fair — you don't forget, but you don't get it done. Damn it, Colin, we can't treat this like a hobby or a spare-time occupation! There's such an enormous amount for the three of us to get through in the next eighteen months. There are so many things to be made — at first I got the idea that you could make most of the things . . ."

"I think that I can . . ."

"I expect that you can, but where, for God's sake?"

"We'll need a workshop, of course."

"We haven't got one, and we haven't the slightest prospect of getting one. For this job we'd need a fully equipped machine shop, and we just haven't got that kind of money. But, Colin, it's not that sort of job I mean — we'll get the things made for us by someone else all right — but all the other little jobs that take an hour or two of telephoning or running about. You take them on, but you don't get them done."

"I've been unusually busy lately," Colin said slowly. "I've been trying to clear the decks so that I could give more time to the balloon, but it's been difficult. I know that you're giving it more time than we are, but you've got your own business and can afford to — you knew when we started that Rosemary and I have full-time jobs to do as well."

Rosemary wanted to weigh in on this argument and point out what she knew — that Colin seldom went to bed before one or two in the morning, and put in hours at his drawing-board, and that any social life they had had no longer existed, but she held her tongue and let Bushy and Colin talk it out.

During the two years that they worked together, from the first evening when it was a casual after-dinner plan to the end in Barbados, they had remarkably few quarrels. But they were all sensitive, highly strung people, and it would have been a miracle if, seeing each other some part of every day, giving up almost all other interests, always talking or thinking about the flight, they hadn't sometimes become heartily sick of the whole thing. When Rosemary and Colin agreed to have a shot at the Atlantic crossing they hadn't realised what an all-consuming monster they had taken into their lives.

Bushy, on the other hand, welcomes an interest that will override everything else in his life. He is really only happy when devoting all his intelligence and energy to whatever has captured his interest. He has an enormous capacity for sheer hard work, and is one of those people who thrive on it. Right from the start, he decided that it would take complete dedication to get a passenger-carrying balloon across the Atlantic Ocean. In their differing attitudes were the ingredients of a conflict, and it came to a head on the ride back to London from Gerry Long's when the project was about six months old.

"Never mind about the past," Bushy said after each had reminded the other of mistakes and omissions. "Recriminations accomplish nothing. What about the future? Are you going to be in this thing heart and soul to the exclusion of everything else, or aren't you? I can't pull it off by myself, I need your help — as much as you can possibly give. It's no good for you just to be in it verbally. What do you say?"

"Of course we're in it heart and soul. I need ten days to get rid of the back-log of work, and then all my free time will be given to the balloon," Colin promised.

"Right," Eiloart said. "I'll wait to hear from you — I'm tired of pushing and nagging, and I shan't get in touch with you first. When you're ready to get down to it, telephone me."

They drove in silence for a bit and then, because all of them are too big for sulkiness, they talked about sailing for the rest of the way to London. Bushy dropped them off at their flat and drove home. He waited the ten days but heard nothing. It became two weeks, three and stretched into six without any word. Bushy, too, did little or nothing on the balloon project all this time, for he had decided that if Colin didn't ring he would give up the idea. After six weeks he had just about called the Atlantic Balloon Crossing off, when one day his phone rang and it was Colin.

"Do you remember the American we wrote to asking if one of us could go over there and do some flights with him?" Colin asked. One of the things we had done in the early days was to write to the great American balloonist Winzen and ask him if there was any way we could get ballooning experience. We had not had a reply.

"Yes," Bushy answered. "Is there an invitation from him?"

"No, just a non-committal letter saying that some day perhaps, you know."

"I see." Bushy waited, but Colin said nothing more. "Look — does this mean that you are still in on this, Colin, or not? If you've decided, too, like Pete, that it's impossible, tell me so."

"No, I think we can do it. I'm still keen — what about you?"

"Of course I am. Right, then we'll start again. Now where were we — oh, yes, electrical storms. Will you find out about those, because if we can't avoid one, then it's off anyway. If the odds against meeting one are better than five to one we'll go — agreed?"

"Agreed," said Colin and marvelled at the way Bushy's mind was able to pick up the thread where it had broken six weeks before.

He finally tracked down the information they needed from the International Weather Bureau, who told him that in November the average incidence of electrical storms was five, each lasting from one to two hours. Bushy was jubilant.

"Look — let's say six storms of two hours each in the thirty days. That's twelve hours of storms in seven hundred and twenty hours, so that the odds against our being in the same place as one is sixty to one. Right, Colin?"

"Well, it's better than five to one, anyway," Colin agreed.

And so after faltering for six weeks the project got moving again, and from then on they all devoted more and more of their time to it. Colin immediately got down to doing the final working drawings for the making of the balloon. This meant deciding the size and shape of the panels and working out the co-ordinates.

Bushy made sure that Sylvia Lawrence could still come as she had promised, and then he ordered the polythene. Before she arrived he would have to make a table twenty-five feet long by five feet wide somewhere — in sections so that it could be taken into his flat. Bushy never hesitates to ask his friends for help, and this time he turned to one who is the Managing Director of City Display Ltd., a large firm making window displays and exhibition stalls. His name is Freddy Keil, and as soon as he heard of the plan he was immediately enthusiastic.

"What a marvellous idea — do you want anyone else to come?"

"No, thanks, Freddy." Eiloart laughed, but he was to get increasingly used to the request, for as time went by and more and more companies became interested, fully half of the people wanted to be one of the crew. "All I want is a corner of your Shepherd's Bush works to make a table on which to make the balloon."

But Mr. Keil insisted on giving them the wood — five pieces of half-inch ply each five feet square — and he promised that when the time came they could have a locked-off area in which to make the craft.

Bushy roped Tim, his son, in on the table-making, and they carried the large pieces of wood one by one into the lift of the

Kensington flats. The porter made no comment as the first two came in, but when they appeared again with a third and then a fourth he couldn't contain his curiosity.

"Making a grand piano, sir?"

"No, just a battleship," Bushy said with a straight face. Nevertheless, he decided that perhaps it would be better if the rest of the equipment, particularly the six-foot trestles, came in after midnight when the porter had gone to bed, for if it got back to the landlords that he had practically turned his 'luxury flat' into a light-engineering factory there would be trouble.

Sylvia had written to say that she would need a special tram-line heat-sealing iron and also a patching iron. Bristol University made them the first out of an ordinary domestic iron fitted with two ridges underneath.

The patching iron was to be made out of an electric soldering-iron adapted from a drawing of Sylvia's and this, a rheostat control, and a thermometer were made by Tim Eiloart in his spare time. Tim was not, at this time, a member of the crew, but was working full time at Cambridge for a degree in chemical engineering. Every time Bushy saw him he asked him for either practical or theoretical help.

Colin finished the drawings for the balloon and got on with a model of the craft, everything was ready for Sylvia, and it all seemed to be going well when they ran up against an 'insurmountable obstacle'. They got used to insurmountable obstacles in the months that followed, and got to the point where, if everything seemed to be going well, they almost expected one to pop up. This time it was a letter from the propeller manufacturers telling them what thrust they could expect from propellers of differing sizes. The most efficient one was a four-foot propeller, which, if they could manage to turn it at ten times a second, would give them about ten pounds extra lift.

"Ten pounds!" Bushy said gloomily. "If we had one *each* it wouldn't be enough."

"Can't you just see all of us cranking away like mad and the balloon slowly sinking into the sea?" Colin asked.

"Then we should arrange it so that the same propellers make the boat go, too," Rosemary said, "like one of those Pedalo things on the beach." They laughed.

"It looks as though Tim was right," Bushy said, "and that we shall have to use leg power. It also looks as though we'll need four of us to get the necessary muscle power. According to these figures, four of us pedalling would produce twenty pounds of thrust, which is the minimum that will do us much good."

They discussed this for some time, and then they all agreed that the fourth place must be offered to Tim. Bushy wrote to him that night asking him if he would like to come along.

Tim, of course, had known about the flight since the beginning, but although he had been called in to help from time to time, he had looked at it as a very interested bystander. Now he was offered a place in the crew. It was a difficult decision.

I've known Tim all his life — the Eiloarts are not the kind of people who go in for honorary uncles, but if they were I should be Tim's. He has talked to me with quite remarkable honesty and candour about his role in The Small World.

Tim won a scholarship to Cambridge and, by the time the Trans-Atlantic balloon project started, was in his last year. The scholarship was from the Ministry of Supply, who required him to do practical work at the bench during the vacations, so that he had acquired considerable practical as well as theoretical knowledge. But, more important, he had learned how to think scientifically and how to tackle engineering problems. He had discovered that he liked mathematics, and mathematical problems were a form of relaxation for him.

He has a tremendous respect for his father's intelligence, and therefore listened carefully when told of the planned balloon crossing of the Atlantic. Then he went away, thought about it and made some investigations. As a result, he pronounced it impossible. He gave his reasons to me.

"In the first place, I don't think they can possibly depend on picking up a wind which will be guaranteed to carry them clear of the Canary Islands and into the region of the north-east trades.

Then I don't think that they've really considered the violent electrical storms in that area. I can't see how they'll avoid losing either gas or ballast from the moment of take-off," he told me. "Besides there's all the red tape — I can't think that they'll be allowed to take a balloon to the Canary Islands and launch themselves into the air without all kinds of licences, not the least of which is a balloon pilot's licence, and where is that coming from?"

All this was in the very early days of the project, and he didn't hide his misgivings from his father, but Bushy ignored Tim's objections just as he ignored every other person's. Nothing, he said, would ever have been done if people had listened to the objectors. If he couldn't think of an answer immediately he added the problem to the list of unsolved ones he already had, and carried on confident that he would find an answer in the end.

Tim thought that his father would probably spend all his money on the project, and quite naturally wished that he wouldn't. Nevertheless, whenever he was asked for technical assistance or any other kind of help he gave it most loyally.

As the months had progressed, he had been impressed with the way the difficulties were being overcome one by one, and most of his original objections disappeared. It seemed that the wind did blow off the Canary Islands from time to time in the right direction to carry them clear; he was satisfied that if they chose the right time of year the chances of an electrical storm were pretty remote. He still thought that it was going to be very difficult to get all the necessary permissions from the various authorities, but this was more likely to be solved. He gave them a much better chance, but he still did not think of going himself.

He spent most of one night trying to go over all the pro's and con's objectively. He knew that he could be of use apart from supplying the fourth pair of legs for the pedal apparatus. They knew nothing about radio and little of meteorology, and he was confident that he could learn much about both in the remaining year.

He was very conscious of the glittering prizes that would come if the flight was a success, such as fame at an unexpectedly early age.

There seemed to be little doubt that it would be very pleasant to be one of the crew of the first Trans-Atlantic balloon. Lastly, the whole thing naturally appealed to his spirit of adventure, although he tried to be scientifically objective and ignore that.

Chief of the con's was his still-present doubt about the success of the flight. He thought it likely that the balloon would have to come down in mid-Atlantic or, what would be much worse, fail ignominiously at take-off. Equally important, he was in his last year at Cambridge and didn't want to take on anything that would cause his degree work to suffer.

He realised that he didn't really feel happy about the material benefits of a successful flight, for somehow he felt there was something bogus about it — it almost seemed like cheating.

The pro's and con's seemed fairly evenly balanced until, quite suddenly and very clearly, he saw the simple factor which made up his mind. One of three things was going to happen: one, the balloon would make it; two, it would come down in the sea; three, it would never really get started. If it was successful he would kick himself for not being in it; if it came down at sea he would never forgive himself for not being there to help; if it failed hopelessly at the very beginning his place was there with the other three. He wrote and accepted.

The others were pleased, for not only would his special knowledge be valuable but he was also a good sailor, and they were always well aware that they might have to finish the trip by sailing a very small boat a long way.

CHAPTER THREE

Most of the furniture was taken out of Bushy's living-room, and it was fitted up as a balloon-making shop with a twenty-five-foot table in the middle, sealing iron, patching iron and huge rolls of polythene. Everything was ready for Sylvia, who had just become Mrs. King.

Bushy met the newly-weds at Paddington Station and took them to a friend's house where Sylvia was to stay. Her husband had to go back that evening. Bushy swallowed his impatience and let them have the day off for sight-seeing.

Promptly at 9 o'clock the next morning Sylvia was ready to start. They had Colin's drawings to work from, and it took all morning to cut out the centre sections. In the afternoon Bushy left her beginning to weld the seams.

The balloon was started at last!

Mr. L. A. Speed is the officer in charge of the Research and Development Establishment at Cardington, the official name for the Lighter-than-air section. John Davies from Bristol University had told him something of Bushy and Colin's scheme. L. A. Speed had reacted enthusiastically, asking how he could help and suggesting that Bushy telephone to him, as soon as the balloon-making was progressing. Bushy made an appointment for the following day.

Bushy left London at 8:30 the next morning, and two hours later drove up to the two enormous hangers put up to house the *R100* and *R101*, the largest airships ever built in Britain. At the gate he identified himself and, to make sure that he wasn't a spy, had to sign the visitor's book.

L. A. Speed had been most helpful on the phone: saying that he would be happy to show Bushy anything he wanted to see about balloons, their mechanism or material, and to help in any other way

44

that he could. He had suggested that Gerry Long, who also worked here, would be the best person to look after him. He had pointed out, though, that he couldn't lend him Government property, and Bushy had realised that that was only reasonable.

He found Gerry Long in his little office surrounded by photographs of balloons and balloonists. Looking fit and ten years under his age, he jumped up and greeted Bushy with a smile.

"Well, how are you getting on?"

"Fine — the envelope was started yesterday. I'm here to find out how to make a net, a load ring, a valve and a tester."

"Won't Mr. Speed lend you any of those?"

"They're Government property, aren't they?"

"Well . . . it's going to take you hundreds of man hours to make all those things. Let's see what we can do." He picked up the phone and asked for a Victoria, London number.

"What is the name of the subscriber?" asked the camp operator.

"I'm not allowed to know that," Gerry Long said, "and if I knew I still shouldn't be allowed to say."

"Oh," said the operator. Gerry winked at Bushy with the delight of a man who has long since mastered the intricacies of the military mind. He was soon connected.

"Hello, Bill," he said genially. "What's going to become of all that equipment of yours that was spoiled by the floods — can we write it off? We can? Good. We'll send you a detailed list so you can mark it off in the proper manner — nil returns *will* be made, eh?" He laughed. "There's one other thing; I've got a friend who's interested in doing some free ballooning. Would it be all right if I were to lend him one of your valves and load rings? Thanks, old man."

That was how they got their load ring and valve. The net was rather more difficult, though. L. A. Speed showed him one of theirs, and gave him a blue print describing how to make it from beginning to end. It was for a twenty-eight-thousand-cubic-foot balloon, whereas Colin and Bushy had decided theirs was to be forty thousand cubic feet. Mr. Speed sat down and showed Bushy how to extend the co-ordinates to the larger size.

45

The size of the balloon was determined, of course, by the lift they would need. At this time, they thought they would want about twenty-eight hundredweight, but later they increased this by something like a thousand pounds. This meant that in the end The Small World was fifty-three thousand cubic feet capacity.

A balloon is a thin bag filled with any gas that is lighter than air — even hot air, which is what the first balloons used, will do. A cube of air at sea-level measuring ten feet wide by ten feet deep by ten feet high weighs seventy-six pounds; the same volume of ordinary cooking-gas only weighs thirty-six pounds, so that a balloon of that size filled from the gasometer would lift forty pounds. Hydrogen is the lightest of all gases, and the same-sized balloon filled with pure hydrogen would raise about seventy pounds. It is not possible to use one hundred per cent pure hydrogen, though, and the usual figure of lift is sixty-eight pounds per thousand cubic feet. Therefore, their balloon of fifty-three thousand cubic feet capacity should theoretically lift thirty-six hundred pounds. This includes, of course, the weight of the balloon itself plus the net, load ring and everything else.

Another complication is that this is true only at sea-level. As the balloon rises into the thinner atmosphere the hydrogen expands. The neck has to be left open to let some of the gas out or the balloon would burst.

Therefore, a free balloon loses lift the higher it goes: it loses roughly one-thirtieth of its total lift every thousand feet it rises. Tethered balloons, like the barrage balloons of the last war, don't lose any gas because they fly at a fixed height and are not fully inflated on the ground.

In theory it sounds quite simple to control a balloon's height by either letting gas out of the valve or throwing off ballast, but in practice, as Bushy was to find out, it gets complicated.

Bushy asked Gerry Long if he knew anyone who could make their net for them, and fortunately Gerry did. Making a balloon net is a highly skilled business, and there are not many men left who know how. As well as a net-maker a covered place is needed where the hemp, of which all good nets are made, can be stretched.

Neville Holmes, to whom Bushy was sent, worked at a Ministry of Supply depot in Plymouth, and was given permission to make the net there in his spare time. Bushy found a specialist firm who made up the required quantity of best Italian hemp to the different specifications needed. The cord is of different thickness and, therefore, of different breaking load according to where it is on the net.

Starting at the top of the balloon around the valve were ninety-six meshes of sixteen-ounce cord, with a breaking strength of three hundred and seventy-five pounds each. The net consisted of ninety-six meshes continuing all the way down the balloon past its equator; the ones on the top were long shaped, the ones at the equator were stretched out. On the way down at a point called the 'first bridles' every two meshes are joined, and the number reduced to forty-eight. The weight and strength of the cord is increased accordingly. Then the forty-eight meshes carry on for a bit and the same thing happens again, and at the second bridles they are reduced to twenty-four of still heavier cord. Finally, each of the twenty-four meshes has a long line leading down to the load ring. These are called the 'leading lines' and are fixed round the load ring in twelve pairs. The breaking load of each leading line is eighteen hundred pounds, so that two or three of them could theoretically support the whole load.

But even this net was not as strong as the requirements laid down in the manuals. Bushy and Colin decided that the manual took into consideration the fact that the net would be used over a period of years, and allowed for loss of strength through ageing. As theirs would be used once only, they could start with a lighter one.

Bushy returned to London from his first visit to Cardington with his precious load ring, valve and the blue prints of a net. He felt pretty pleased with himself and was anxious to see how Sylvia was getting on with making the balloon.

She had been working steadily, but she was on her own, and Bushy's living-room was not exactly the balloon-making shop at Bristol University. She had been able to do only nine seams. At that rate it was going to take her a month instead of two weeks.

As the project progressed, so the jobs multiplied. Bushy found that he was having difficulty getting to sleep at night although he was dog-tired. His brain seemed to go on whirring away about balloon problems like an engine with a broken governor. One night he got up and wrote down his thoughts and this, in some way, helped. The night of the day the balloon was started he wrote:

> Sylvia is working on the envelope but there are so many other things to be done. The big job is the car, of course, and then the pedal propellers, but apart from those there are the load ring, the net, the valves, the ripper and the tester. None of these are big jobs in themselves, but they are all time-consumers and add up to several big jobs. I want to take no unnecessary chances — the necessary ones will be enough — and so every one of these things must be, in its own way, perfect. Every big and little thing we are to make has to be hunted down, analysed, improved if possible, then drawn and the specifications decided. We'll find some ready to buy; some we'll have to make, shape, drill, assemble — God knows what else. I suppose the sensible thing to do is to try and see the traditional things first. Get all the tips from experienced balloonists; Gerry Long, Lord Ventry and any others. Decide exactly what we want — then how to get it. The trouble is I'm too damned impatient. I want to see a thing at hand, just for the asking, as though I only had to rub Aladdin's lamp.

It was the next day that he went to Cardington and came back with a valve, a load ring and the blue print of a net — it was almost like having Aladdin's lamp, after all.

Now, he thought, was the time to approach the manufacturers of the polythene, as Rosemary had suggested, to see if they would knock something off the invoice in return for the publicity. The Press Relations Officer of The Metal Box Company, whom he telephoned to the next day, was interested and came round to see them.

They first swore him to secrecy — they were to swear many

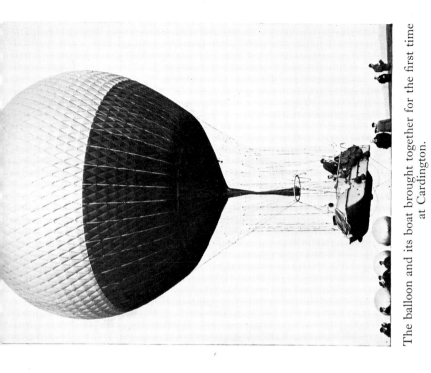

Test inflation of The Small World inside the airship sheds at Cardington.

The balloon and its boat brought together for the first time at Cardington.

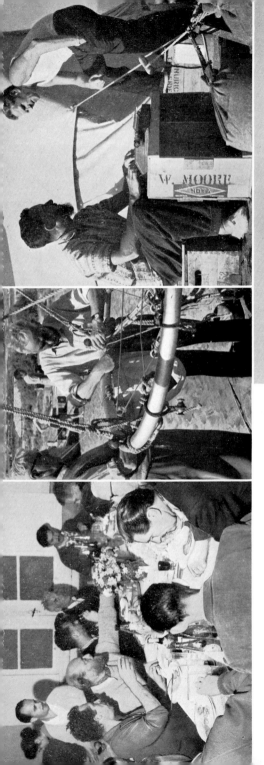

Last meal at Médano.

Gerry Long and Ralph Booth working on the quick release on Médano Beach.

Bushy Eiloart and Peter Elstob making notes for the book.

The balloon, half-inflated, pegged down against the wind on Médano Beach.

people to secrecy in the next year or so, and it says a lot for the standard of honour in British business that not one of them ever let them down and no word of the project ever leaked into the news-papers until they were ready to release the story — and then told him of their plans. He was enthusiastic and went away promising to speak to someone in Metal Box's Plastic Division about it. Bushy was doubtful, as he was used to people who were going to get in touch with someone else, but he agreed that they could only wait and see.

A day or two later a Mr. Conradi rang and introduced himself. He was the Sales Manager of the Plastic Division, and said that they were interested and would like to come along and see. Bushy asked him to come round, and in his mind there was no doubt that this was an important visit.

In fact, it was to be the turning-point in the enterprise because, before the day was to come when The Small World took off from the beach of Médano, more than forty companies, some of whom were among the largest in Britain, some the smallest, were to follow the lead of The Metal Box Company by giving them materials, labour, advice, technical assistance, carriage and just plain encouragement. The amount of money which all this was worth came to thirty or forty times the balloonists' first estimate.

But when Mr. Conradi called Bushy didn't know how his pro-posal that a big company give them something for nothing would be received, and he let him in showing more confidence than he felt.

A tall, dark man of about forty, relaxed, quiet, but with a suggestion of immense controlled energy, came in and was taken at once to the balloon-making room.

"What a beautiful big room — how extraordinarily lucky you are! I should think that you're the only man in London who wants to make a balloon in his flat, and one of the very few with a room large enough to do it." He picked up the polythene and inspected one of Sylvia's seams with approval.

Later, over spaghetti cooked by Bushy and served with Chianti, he heard about the Atlantic crossing attempt in detail. "Have you thought about the enormous publicity there'll be if you pull it off?" he asked. They hadn't, but it was obvious that there would be. "It means," Conradi went on, "that you should get the help of any wide-awake firm you approach, in return for letting them say later — when you've landed safely, that is — that you used their materials."

"You mean like the polythene in the other room?" Eiloart asked hopefully. "I've got the bill for that — it's sixty pounds. Do you think that your company might help us out on that?"

"I don't think there's any doubt about that, and I think that you'll find that all the other firms will co-operate, too. I don't say that you'll get absolutely all your equipment free, but you'll be wanting quite a lot of one-off jobs, and when a large firm undertakes one of those the real cost is enormous. I don't think that anyone will charge you the real cost for a moment, if they know about your plans."

This was, of course, tremendously encouraging. If some big companies were interested it would make everything much simpler. Bushy thanked him.

"As your needs crop up," Conradi went on, "let me know, and I'll do all I can to see that you get to the right man. For instance, have you thought about getting yourselves and your equipment shipped to Tenerife?"

"Good Heavens no — we thought we'd wait until we had something to ship before we bothered about that."

"Well, you can't start too soon, and when you do want to I will take you round to meet the Managing Director of Elders and Fyffes. He's a young chap, and I think this would appeal to him. I don't say that he'll ship you for nothing, but I'm sure that he'll help."

Bushy began to thank him again, for this was all so much more than he had hoped for, but Conradi went on:

"Then you'll need someone to handle the Tenerife end of things for you, and I think I know just the man. He's a Bradford chap who's been out there for years. Everybody likes him, and he knows the island and its people backwards. He comes to England twice a year, and I'll arrange for you to meet him on his next visit. But we can leave that until a bit later." He got up to go. "Now the first thing is for me to confirm that we'll supply the polythene to make the balloon free. I'll do that in the next day or two. Then as soon as you think I can help you in any way, let me know."

"Fine," Bushy said. "Perhaps I could come and see you at your office? I'll bring a list of the firms I'd like to get into and we could find out when it was possible to see the Managing Director of Elders and Fyffes. Would that be all right?"

All through the long months of preparation Bushy made it a rule never to leave the initiative for the next move to the other man if it was avoidable. This was not because he doubted his willingness, but because the Atlantic balloon would always be only one of his many interests. "Why should a man who is doing something for you out of the goodness of his heart think of it as a number one priority?" was the way he put it to me once.

Mr. Conradi was, perhaps, a little surprised by the way Bushy got the bit in his teeth, but he probably realised that it required that kind of temperament to pull off a new world's first at anything big.

"Come and see me in two days at 10:30 in the morning," he said.

Two days later Bushy went along, taking with him a long list of notes. "You've encouraged us immensely, Mr. Conradi, and I hope you won't mind if I get quite clear what we can expect from your company? We can then get down to planning the rest."

"Sensible idea — go ahead."

"Workshop space?"

"Almost impossible, I'm afraid."

"The use of your drawing office to design our man-powered propellers unit?"

"Terribly difficult, too, but I'll enquire about that one. I'm not very hopeful, though."

"If we could get someone high up in the Ministry of Transport and Civil Aviation interested, it would be a tremendous help."

"I'll do anything I can there — find out good contacts, write to them recommending you, use what influence we've got. In short, I'll do anything short of perjury to help you."

Nothing, Bushy thought, could be much stronger than that. He went on with his list checking off items, and at the end it was as though they had suddenly been joined by strong reinforcements. Already the task didn't seem quite so formidable.

There was a small packet of liquid shampoo on the desk, and as Bushy and I also manufacture cosmetics Bushy picked it up interestedly. It was made of a strong, pliant material that he recognised as P.V.C.

"This is a wonderful seal," he said, squeezing it hard. "It seems much stronger than polythene — perhaps we should use this instead?"

"That's quite a thought," Conradi replied. "It's no good for Professor Powell's met. balloons because it's too thick and consequently heavy, but your problems are not the same as his. Yes, it's very possible that P.V.C. might be the best material for your balloon. I'm afraid that we don't make it, though."

"Oh, well then . . ." Bushy put it down quickly.

"No, wait a minute. Why don't you go and see my friend, Dr. Herbert of Greenwich Leatherhide Co.? He can tell you everything you want to know about it."

"You've been so generous with all your offers of help. Don't you think that we should stick to polythene and stay under your wing?"

"Don't worry about that for a moment. Whether you use our polythene or someone else's P.V.C. our promise to help you in every way still holds. We like your project and we're keen to help, but the important thing is its success. If someone else's stuff gives you even a slightly better chance, then you *must* use theirs."

Bushy, like most of us, reacts strongly to unselfish offers of help, and when he told me about this interview he said at that point he felt like drawing his finger across his throat and saying, "Slit my throat and hope to die if I ever use anything but your polythene." Still, Conradi was obviously right and he would have to find out all about P.V.C.

He got in touch with Dr. Herbert the next day and asked him if he thought that P.V.C. could be used to make big balloons. It not only could, but had already been used most successfully. The thinnest suitable material would have to be six-thousandths of an inch. It would cost five and sixpence a pound though, which meant that the P.V.C. alone would be more than a hundred pounds. Another disadvantage was that the balloon would be almost twice as heavy as one made of polythene. Therefore, it would have to be bigger to get the same net lift, and if it was bigger it would, of course, be even heavier. Perhaps polythene would be better, after all.

Actually, in the end they had a second balloon of Terylene with Neoprene proofing made especially for them by I.C.I.'s Fibres Division. *Sylvia*, their home-made polythene balloon, was used by Bushy for his training and to qualify for a balloonist's licence and is still in existence, but the balloon that took off from Médano was the only one of its kind in the world. The long search for the right material was just one of the reasons they had so little spare time in the twenty-three months it took them.

But this was only the end of the ninth month, and although much had been accomplished, much, much more remained to be done. Bushy and Colin got down to making a list one night:

Pedal machinery to be made. (An arrangement of four seats facing each other in pairs, and eight pedals turning a crankshaft geared to two propellers had been designed in detail.)

Car to be made.

Quick Release to be designed and made.

Net to be made by hand.

Radio, aerials, batteries, lights.

Navigating instruments and charts.

Food. Means of cooking? Containers for food? Emergency supplies?

Hydrogen gas. Where from?

Tow rope and other lines.

Sleeping-bags.

Medicines and first-aid chest.

Sails, spars, rudder and lee-boards.

53

"They're the main things that have to be made," Bushy said. "Then there are the things we have to do." They made another list on a clean piece of paper:

Bushy to learn to fly a balloon and get a balloonist's licence.

Colin to make scale models of the car and to test them.

Tim to qualify as a radio operator and to learn meteorology.

Transportation to the Canary Islands to be arranged.

Launching crew — who else beside Gerry Long?

What licences and official permissions are necessary? Spanish authorities in Tenerife must be approached in plenty of time.

Colin to make the final craft and give it rigorous sea-trials.

"Can you think of anything else?" Bushy asked.

"Cameras and film for Rosemary," Colin said. Bushy added them to the list. "Special clothing to keep us warm and dry. Odd things such as binoculars, tools, sea-anchors, a grapnel and others that will occur to us as we go on."

"I can see we're going to be very, very busy," Bushy said. "How are you getting on with the design for the craft?"

"I've finished the first design and made a little scale model in cardboard. Wait a minute and I'll get it for you." He brought it back and put it on the table. "As it will have only a seven-foot-six-wide outside measurement and our pedalling apparatus will be plonk in the middle, we'll probably be a bit crowded. I've thought of a way around that, though, I think. We'll have an aluminium alloy tube above and around the car. It will be slightly broader so that all our clobber can hang clear from it. All the batteries, radio, ballast and so on."

"Wonderful idea," Bushy said. "But what will happen if we have to ditch?"

"We'll have thrown everything else over by then anyway, except our emergency food and water, and we'll stow those inboard. Of course, we'll have to make sure that we land bows forward and not broadside on, but our trail will take care of that. One good thing is that we shall be moving with the speed of, and in the same direction as, the wind when we cut loose, and so be going in the same direction as the waves, too, which will be a help."

"I've got an idea," Bushy said, grabbing a pencil and sketching rapidly. "Instead of taking our emergency food and water inboard why not hang them astern in long, strong, sausage-shaped bags? Their drag would slow us tremendously and help point us in the right direction. What do you think?"

Colin agreed. He had, of course, given a great deal of thought to the design of the car, which was full of unique problems and therefore an exciting challenge. It would have to be of the lightest practicable material, for every ounce of weight was important; but it would also have to be very strong, for if they had to abandon the balloon and take to the sea it might be in near-gale conditions. This meant that it would have to be able to survive hitting a rough sea at perhaps thirty miles an hour. If the quick-release hooks weren't quick enough the partially deflated balloon would drag them through the water, which would be a tremendous strain on the hull.

Then it would have to be large enough for four of them to be able to live in it for weeks as a boat; it would need shelter from the tropic sun; it should be self-righting or able to be righted easily by swimmers; it would have to be able to sail to windward as well as run before the wind.

Colin decided on a shape like a sea-sledge with a swept-up bow and the stern chopped off square. The mast would be raking and unsupported by stays so that it could give in a strong blow. The twin hulls meant that neither a keel nor a centre-board would be necessary, although, as the hull was so light, he provided for lee-boards to improve the sailing to windward, which might be necessary when they sighted an island.

He designed a sail which was a compromise between a Portuguese lateen and the *Lindström* double sail. When running before the wind twin sails are set, one each side of the mast. When a conventional mainsail is needed for reaching or tacking one sail is reset and overlaps the other.

He added two hollow buoyancy boxes to the top of the hull,

which raised the centre of gravity and made it easily rightable from the water.

They went into the pro's and con's of all kinds of material before deciding to be completely revolutionary and use foam plastic. This is a light, synthetic substance that looks like solidified froth. A cubic foot of it weighs only a pound or so, and as a cubic foot of sea-water weighs sixty-four pounds foam plastic can support many times its own weight afloat. Colin worked out that the bare hull would weigh not more than two hundredweight but could support two tons.

Foam plastic by itself would not, of course, be strong enough to make a boat, but Colin planned to cover it with a tight skin of Terylene, which would make it hard and capable of withstanding considerable stress.

As well as the first cardboard model, which was one-sixteenth scale, Colin made an eighth-size model out of balsa wood. Then Bushy spent most of three weeks making a quarter-size model incorporating new improvements, and as a result of testing this Colin made a half-size model out of foam plastic. Only after this one had been thoroughly tested did he set about making the final craft.

When Colin had finished the eighth-size model he showed it to Bushy, and they decided then and there to go and sail it on the Round Pond in Kensington Gardens.

It was a Sunday morning, and the many small children and their nurses looked curiously at the two full-grown men playing so seriously with the strange-looking boat. One six-year-old carefully aimed his clockwork-driven destroyer and knocked their precious model into the middle of the pond. Colin restrained Bushy.

"After all, it's their pond," he said and sat down, taking off his shoes and socks and rolling up his trousers. A crowd of children collected and watched fascinatedly as he waded out into the middle of the pond to recover his model. A policeman not far away began to move towards them.

"We don't want to attract too much attention at this stage," Colin said hurriedly. He clutched the dripping model and walked quickly away. Bushy followed behind, carrying his shoes and socks, while the park keeper watched them go with interest.

Bushy made the next model out of plywood, and it was big enough to help them plan the stowage and to test its ditching capabilities by dropping it from bridges into the Thames.

"Good O," said Colin. "Now we must get hold of some foam plastic, Terylene and glue and make a half-size model which will be large enough for us actually to sail it. Where will you get the materials from?"

"I.C.I., I think," Bushy said. He had been having quite a number of successes with large firms, both through the contacts Mr. Conradi had supplied him with and, in some cases, just by approaching them cold. He never ceased to marvel at how readily almost everybody they approached agreed to help them as soon as they realised that it was a serious attempt and a non-commercial one. It seemed to appeal to the imagination or perhaps the sporting instincts of the business-men they approached. Indeed, they got so used to being welcomed enthusiastically that they got quite annoyed when one company turned them down flat — or perhaps it was the touch of sarcasm in the refusal that rankled.

Bushy had written to a firm in the Midlands asking them if they would like to contribute some material to 'an all-British world record attempt involving a strong element of adventure'. He was intentionally vague in this first letter, because he always took great care that the story should not get into the newspapers, for he was afraid that someone else with more resources might try first. He offered, though, to give full details at an interview if the Managing Director was interested. He included particulars of some of the backing they had already got to show that it was being taken seriously elsewhere.

When it had become apparent that manufacturers were eager to help, Bushy had decided that it was only fair to give every one the chance to be in on it. He felt that any company supplying any material whatever might justifiably complain if they were not even given the opportunity to take part. Almost every company accepted, but this time they got a reply by return:

Dear Sir,

Your letter of 7th April addressed to the Chairman of this company has been passed to the undersigned for attention.

In view of the secrecy of your own arrangements, we find it rather surprising that you quote so readily the details of support already promised. In the circumstances we do not wish to take advantage of your kind offer.

Your faithfully,

(Manager)

After their first annoyance they had a good laugh about it. It was evident that the Midlands firm viewed the goings-on down south with dark suspicion.

However, in most cases, even with the biggest companies, they met with nothing but encouragement. It was always necessary, though, to establish their bona fides, and one of their most useful possessions was a letter from L. A. Speed of the Lighter-than-air section at Cardington.

Dear Mr. Eiloart,

You will be pleased to hear that short of spending the Department's money on your project, I have authority from Farnborough to help you in any way I can. An Atlantic Balloon Crossing is now, technically, 'on' and both Mr. Long and I think your plans will meet with success, so if there is any way we can help, short I must repeat of spending the Department's money, do let me know. The Americans are very active with their ballooning these days and we should both like to see you get in ahead of them.

Yours sincerely,

L. A. Speed

Officer in Charge

Research and Development

Cardington.

This letter was an open sesame to many doors. In his search for the best materials from which to make the balloon Bushy had been led to the vast Imperial Chemical Industries, who seemed to own most of the companies that made the materials.

He had approached them through their Public Relations Office and had been put in touch with an intelligent, shrewd, but, as he was soon to discover, exceedingly kind-hearted Scotsman named Gordon Long. Varied and weird are the schemes that are put up to the Public Relations Department of a big company, and a good P.R.O. has to have an instinct to separate them. Gordon Long is a good P.R.O., and so he moved quickly but cautiously examining the bona fides of the scheme. The letter from Cardington helped, but with Scottish thoroughness he approached one or two other people as well. When he was satisfied he told Bushy so and asked how he could help.

"Well, I've reached the point where I think the best material with which to make our balloon might be P.V.C., and I'd like to be put in touch with your Plastics Division."

Gordon Long agreed, but also suggested that I.C.I.'s Fibres Division might be approached and asked their opinion about the best material to make a balloon to drift across the Atlantic. Bushy, of course, agreed and thanked him.

None of this happened very quickly, although Bushy was always pushing as hard as he could — which is pretty hard! I.C.I.'s Plastic Division said that they would gladly supply P.V.C. to make a balloon, but I.C.I.'s Fibres Division said that the best possible substance was Terylene Fabric coated with Neoprene. Terylene comes under the Fabric Division of I.C.I. They listened to the story and said that they could supply a special Terylene suitable for the job, but that someone else would have to weave it, someone else proof it and then, of course, someone else make it into a balloon. As it was a one-off job it was going to be very expensive.

But they would not charge the cost of research if all the other companies involved in making the balloon would treat it as a special job and make it as nearly perfect as possible regardless of cost. It was a tall order, but that is what happened: I.C.I. actually gave the special Terylene thread and had it specially woven at great

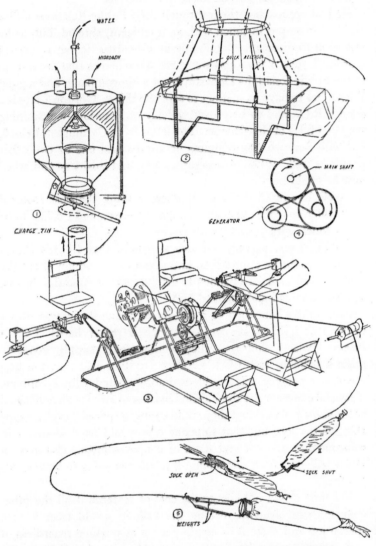

WATER

HYDROGEN

QUICK RELEASE

MAIN SHAFT

GENERATOR

CHARGE TIN

① ② ③ ④ ⑤

SOCK OPEN

SOCK SHUT

WEIGHTS

I   II

1. The Hydrogen Generator.
2. The system of suspension.
3. The Pedal Apparatus.

4. Chain drive to generator.
5. The final water-lifting bag —
    'The Weightless Wonder'.

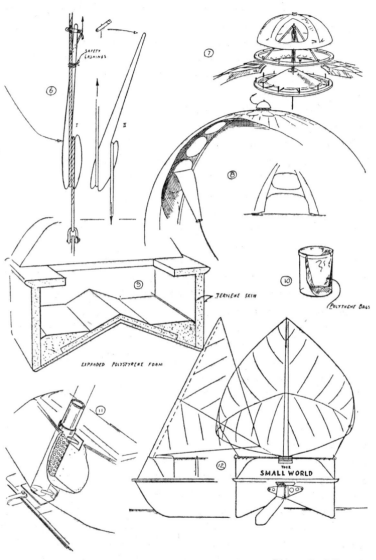

SAFETY LASHINGS

⑥

⑦

⑧

⑨

TERYLENE SKIN

EXPANDED POLYSTYRENE FOAM

⑩

(POLYTHENE BAGS)

⑪

⑫

THE
SMALL WORLD

Diagrams by Colin Mudie

6. Quick Release Hook — detail.
7. The Gas Valve.
8. The Ripping Panel.
9. Section through the hull.
10. The Poly-Lav.
11. The Mast Step.
12. The Twin Sails.

cost; then Messrs. Greengate and Irwell Coated the fabric and made it as near airtight as possible; finally R.F.D. Ltd., a firm that has been making balloons for years, made The Small World from Colin Mudie's detailed blue prints. All these firms worked at enormous loss because of their unselfish interest in the project. No time was lost, but it all took a full year, and the finished balloon was delivered to Cardington for its test inflation only a few weeks before they left.

While progress was being made in one direction after another, they could no longer ignore the prime problem of superheating. This is the sudden great lift that would come as soon as the morning sun shone on the balloon. Professor Powell had been the first to tell them of it, and to warn them that if they were to offset it by the conventional method of releasing gas they could not possibly stay in the air long enough to cross the Atlantic. They had thought that their man-powered horizontal propellers were the answer, but they knew now that they couldn't get enough thrust from them to overcome the added lift from the warmed gas, which might be one or two hundred pounds.

What was needed, Bushy decided, was a mysterious source from which they could borrow an extra hundredweight or so of ballast every morning and give it back every night. The obvious place was the sea, but how to take on water fairly quickly from a balloon moving at twenty miles an hour at three thousand feet?

One of Bushy's characteristics is the ability to give serious consideration to almost any idea or solution that is put to him, without preconceived prejudices. He does not regard any way of doing anything as final just because 'it has always been done that way'. He tried to think about the problem from first principles.

Any sailor knows that filling an ordinary bucket at the end of a very long line is impracticable. All right, many smaller containers then? Say a winch with an endless line of cups coming up and tipping into a trough like the irrigation wheels along the Nile. But the line wouldn't hang vertically because the balloon would be moving, and so most of the water would spill. Then perhaps glue sponges into the cups? How would they be squeezed out?

The final solution was evolved by examining all kinds of ideas, abandoning some, changing some and adopting some. The idea of using a winch was kept, for it would enable them to lift a heavy load of water and could be coupled to the pedal apparatus. The water picking-up device must offer the minimum drag and be quickly adjustable for small or large quantities. They decided on several ten-foot-long bags of three-ply Terylene. These were to be only eight inches in diameter narrowing to five inches at the mouth. The ends were clamped between rubber-coated iron bars, which could be fixed anywhere along the tube, so that it could hold from twenty pounds of water to two hundred and fifty. They looked like giant toothpaste tubes.

With these on the end of a line and operated by a winch they were ready for the problem of the early morning lift. The plan would really start the night before when the gas inside the balloon cooled at sunset and they lost lift. As they came down sea-water ballast would be discarded until their descent was halted at about one thousand feet.

During the night there would be little change in temperature or barometric pressure, and so it shouldn't be difficult for them to maintain height. Someone would have to keep looking at the altimeter ready to take instant action if they should start to rise or come down the last thousand feet.

Therefore two would sleep and two would stay on watch. It ought to be possible to make small height adjustments with the pedal-propellers, but if a big movement started all hands would be called either to man the propellers or to work the winch and take on more water ballast.

Just before dawn they would all get in their seats and start to winch up water as soon as the sun rose. They would keep taking it on as long as the superheating was increasing their lift. As the line would be three thousand feet long, they could even afford to let the balloon rise a bit.

Minor height adjustments during the day could be made with

the propellers. As soon as the hottest part of the day was over, they could start discarding water ballast until sunset, when the whole operation would begin all over again.

The final perfected form of water bags, winch, sea-water reservoir and other minor points were the result of discussions, advice from technicians and practical experiments. This was the way almost everything developed in The Small World.

CHAPTER FOUR

ONE of the first things Bushy had discovered was that he would not be able to learn to fly a balloon in England but would have to go to Holland if he wanted practical experience before they took off. He talked it over with the others in the early days, and they decided that, after all, practical ballooning experience wasn't really necessary if the launching was done by experts.

This looks like utter recklessness, but they decided that the main reason for having ballooning experience was to know how to manoeuvre the ballast and gas ratio to the best advantage. But in their case the man-powered propellers and the water-lifting bags made it unnecessary to dissipate either gas or ballast. So they were willing, if necessary, for their flight across the Atlantic to be their first.

But after Bushy had visited Cardington once or twice and talked with L. A. Speed and Gerry Long he realised that it wasn't quite so simple and he would have to have actual ballooning experience before risking his and his friends' lives. Then he found out that the Spanish authorities wouldn't let him take off without a valid balloonist's licence, anyway.

He spent a long time trying to get permission to fly in England and trying to borrow a balloon. He discovered that the balloons had been taken away from the Lighter-than-air section and been handed over to the Army, but the War Office were immovable. He doesn't give up easily, and he approached everyone he could think of who might be able to help him to get a balloon. Finally, when the most important man of all, the head of The Royal Aircraft Establishment at Farnborough, couldn't get them a practice balloon it looked as though they were stumped.

"There just isn't anyone else," Bushy said.

"What about the Duke of Edinburgh?" asked Tim. "I bet he'd help."

So Tim was permitted to write to Prince Philip explaining that they were trying to regain two world's records for Britain but were stymied because the War Office refused to lend them a balloon.

A few days later a long, white envelope with an 'OFFICIAL PAID' postmark and a small round purple royal seal arrived at Trinity College, Cambridge. It was from Prince Philip's secretary, who said that despite all his efforts at high levels he had been unable to get a balloon from the Army because they were all in use.

It was another disappointment, but it did at least show that the Duke of Edinburgh was interested and encouraged them later to ask for his Patronage.

Bushy reluctantly decided that he'd have to go to Holland to learn ballooning, so he wrote to the Hague Balloon Club and asked if he could have a flight with them. Jean Boesman, who had founded the club, replied that they usually came to England once or twice every summer, putting on balloon ascents at village fêtes, but that nothing was fixed for that year. He was welcome to come to Holland and fly with them when there was a vacancy. The cost was fifteen pounds per flight.

At the end of April Bushy flew to Holland and had his first balloon flight. He wrote to Tim as soon as he returned:

... Wednesday I went for my first balloon flight with the Hague Balloon Club of which I am now a member. The biggest impression I got is how simple our trip is going to be if we ever get our balloon into the middle of the trade winds and if we don't lose more gas — through porosity, leakage etc. — than we can make up for. Of course Holland is as flat as a table — no rocks, trees, valleys or mountains to start updraughts — and the conditions were ideal. Just about the same, I should think, as we'll get in the trade winds — it was sunny, warm and cloudless. It was all so simple that I should have no qualms taking a balloon up myself now on a similarly pleasant day.

I learned a lot of the little tricks of inflation and take-off that will be useful to us. The first 'musts' are that you've got to see that the line to the valve at the top of the balloon (for gassing, remember) and the line from the ripping panel are threaded inside from the top of the balloon to the bottom. When you've done that you fit the valve in and attach the net grommet and fit the filling tube into the neck of the balloon. Then you lay the whole thing out as flat as you can with the valve in the centre and the net and bag in a circle around it. Then you hook sandbags every yard right round the outside of the net allowing no slack cords anywhere. Now you are ready for the filling to start.

The cylinders are screwed up to the filling tube by the 30-odd converging pipes and when the gas is released out of several cylinders at a time it is surprising how quickly the bag begins to fill. But when the bag is nearly half full it seems to slow down and then when it is half full it seems as though it is never going to get any bigger. As it rises the sandbags are unhooked and lowered down one rung of the net's mesh. But a bit later, after the halfway mark, it starts finishing quickly and the job gets pretty tough for the gas bag moves up quicker and quicker and there are lots of sandbags to lift and lower. Then, because the lift is getting greater all the time, you have to use *more* sandbags. If you didn't have about twelve people running round lowering the sandbags you'd have to keep turning the gas off — which is probably what we'll have to do in the Canary Islands.

When the balloon is finally full there are several sandbags hanging from each of the twelve leading lines and several people holding on to each line too. The balloon is floating just above their heads and now the load ring is carried through the ring of helpers and put under the neck of the balloon and a bloke fishes around inside the neck with his hand feeling for the valve line. He waggles it to make sure that it is hanging free and not mixed up with the line from the rip panel. Then he and one other bloke put the load ring on to the leading lines (the helpers are holding the mesh end of the leading lines so that the loose ends are left free for him to button on to the toggles of the load ring). When the ring is on he tells the helpers to close in slowly, pushing their sandbags along the lines until finally they all end up at the load ring and are moved down on to the car, which by now has a dozen or so hands holding it down.

At this point I got in with Jean Boesman and we took a lot of sandbags off the ring and dropped them on the ground until we were left with just the right number. Then the launching captain said 'hands high' and everyone raised his hands to see how quickly the balloon came up to them. From this they judged whether it was too light or not. If it is, it is very dangerous, for it would rise so quickly that it wouldn't be possible for the gas to get out of the neck fast enough and the balloon would burst. (When this happens all you have to do is cut free the neck line and the lower half of the balloon folds up into the top half making a parachute — at least so I am assured!)

Now a bag or two was added until the balloon rose at the right rate, which one can judge only from experience. In our case, as I said, it all went beautifully and there was never a moment of anxiety.

Porosity loss in these tired old balloons seems big and it made me think that that might be our chief worry too. We started with nine sandbags and only had one left when we landed. We only used the valve to land too. We never went higher than two thousand feet so that the gas loss must all have been due to porosity. If only we can be sure that our proofing, seaming and the valve is O.K. I shall be pretty sanguine about the whole thing.

Bushy now knows that he was completely wrong about all this, for it was not porosity but the cooling of the gas as the sun went down that caused the loss of lift. The letter goes on:

It was a special flight because it was Queen Juliana's birthday and we dropped the orange banners and waved at the cheering crowds, all of which was fun. One thing that I've read in the old books which isn't true, though, is about the complete stillness aloft — I did feel one or two breaths of a breeze.

The Club call this a 'Balloon Fox Hunt' and the rest of the

members follow the balloon on the ground which is not as easy as you might think for the balloon is not very high and can easily get out of sight. Even if you can see it you can't always go in a straight line towards it and so the trick is to guess what it is going to do next, for while you are detouring to try and get to the place where it is, it isn't there any more!

When we found that we couldn't stay up any longer because we were down to our last sandbag we landed at a village called Kockengen. The landing was child's play for the rip worked beautifully and we just settled gently down. We packed away the balloon and then took a parchment scroll and a silver souvenir to the Mayor of the village. Of course he was pleased and so were the villagers and speeches were made all round. Then we drove back to the starting place and had a two-hour ceremony initiating the new members of which I was one. I had to make a speech and so I said that although it was the first time I had ever been up I wouldn't rest now until I had flown a balloon a long, long way — oh, over the Atlantic at least. This raised a laugh, as you can imagine.

From then on Bushy found that he had been bitten by the ballooning bug. Up until that first flight in Holland the actual ballooning had seemed almost incidental to overcoming the practical problems. After all, if they weren't solved there wouldn't be any ballooning, anyway. But once having been up, he couldn't wait for more. He wanted to solo, but before he could he would have to have a number of instructional flights under a licensed balloon pilot.

Jean Boesman told Bushy that the club had now been booked to put on tethered flights at the Midsummer Fair in Halstead, Essex. It would be an opportunity for the rest of the crew to watch a balloon being inflated, Eiloart realised, and he asked if he could supply them with a launching crew. Jean Boesman accepted readily.

Bushy flew back to England and told the others. He also got hold of Gerry Long and asked him if he could be there to act as instructor. It meant that Gerry would have to come back early from his annual holidays, but he agreed cheerfully.

I was lucky enough to be in England about this time too.

After I had withdrawn from the Trans-Atlantic balloon I had stayed on in Italy for a bit until my novel got going again and had then gone to Morocco, where it was cheap, sunny and beautiful and spent a year finishing it. All this time I heard from Bushy regularly and followed the steady progress of the Atlantic balloon. His letters were rather like an early film serial, usually ending with the heroes in an insoluble quandary and rescuing them the following week. Early in June 1957 I returned to London for a session with my publishers and, of course, lost no time in seeing how Bushy and the others were getting on with their balloon.

Even though I had heard much of it from Bushy's letters, I was amazed at the progress that had been made, particularly when I read the files and saw the enormous amount of help that had come from so many firms.

"Can I do anything to help at this late date?" I asked. "Anyway, can I be one of the launching crew?"

"Of course you can," Bushy said. "The Dutch Balloon Club are coming over to England in about a fortnight and laying on tethered flights for the Midsummer Fête at Halstead. I've told them that we'll help on the inflation, as it will give us practice that we badly need."

"Right. Anything else you need?"

"Yes — money. I'm about broke."

"So am I. Why don't you sell your story to the newspapers?"

"We can't sell it before we go, you mutt. After it's all over we'll write a book and perhaps get back some money, but who's interested now?"

"I'll bet the *Daily Mail* would be — after all, they've backed things like this before."

"I've backed it with everything I've got, and I can borrow the money to see us through these last few months."

"Well, you wouldn't say 'no' if the *Daily Mail* or some other newspaper offered you money for the story, would you?"

"I'm not awfully keen on making a song and dance about what we're going to do. I'd rather wait until we've done it, I think. Anyway, let's see what the others have to say."

I tried hard that evening to get the others to allow me to try to recover some money by selling their story, but they all agreed with Bushy.

"Bushy's about three thousand pounds out of pocket," I told them bluntly. "When you take off from Tenerife it's going to be in all the newspapers, anyway, so why not sell it to one first?"

"I see that it's easier for us to say 'no' than Bushy," Colin said. "But he's already turned it down — if he wanted to do it, I should agree, of course."

"I agree with Peter," Rosemary said unexpectedly. "The story is going to be told, anyway, and I'd like it told accurately."

"What about you, Tim?" I asked.

"Not my department," Tim said firmly. "I'll go along with the others. The only thing is that if it is going to be in all the papers I hope we can put it off as long as possible, because it will be hell up at Cambridge."

"That's a good idea," Bushy said. "None of us want what little private life we have left spoiled by publicity — imagine what a bore it would be if everyone you met asked you about 'The Balloon'. Let's leave it until the last possible moment — just before we go."

"The trouble with that," I said, "is that you can't really hope to keep it out of the newspapers that long. I'm amazed that nothing has appeared yet, with all these huge firms knowing about it. And if some paper gets hold of the story and prints it you won't have anything to sell."

But they were adamant that I wasn't to approach a newspaper until the last possible moment and, reluctantly, I gave in.

We drove from London to Halstead in Essex on a typical English June day — grey, cold and rainy. The fête was at the football ground, which, fortunately for the balloon, was next to the gasworks. When we arrived Jean Boesman, his wife and two other members of the Hague Balloon Club were already there, as was

Gerry Long, and inflation had just begun. We got down to work immediately, which consisted mostly of walking around the balloon as it slowly filled and lifting off sandbags and lowering them half a mesh when told to do so. The experienced members of the Dutch Club had brought their car to within a few feet of the balloon, and so were able to get out of the rain for a few minutes every now and then.

The gay fête was due to start in the afternoon, and by midday the field was studded with puddles; the flags, banners and streamers drooped disconsolately. The first of the volunteer tea-makers and stall-minders made their brave way through the mud to the marquees, whose roofs were already sagging under the rain.

"There'll always be an England," I said, as a stream of water ran off the balloon and down my neck. I was thinking of the sunny beach in Morocco I had recently left.

"If you don't like it here, why don't you go back where you came from?" Bushy said unoriginally.

"Don't worry — I will. I'm taking the first plane back, and you can wire me when you leave for Tenerife. I'll meet you there."

"Sunshine and swimming tomorrow," Bushy said brightly. "Mud and hard work today — get cracking on those sandbags."

Gerry Long, aged sixty-five, was working alongside of me and doing about twice as much, so I thought I'd better shut up.

Miraculously the rain stopped after lunch and that pale-yellow light we English call the sun appeared in the sky. Jean Boesman brightened up. "It is going to be all right," he said.

At the end of the inflation, as Bushy had warned us, everything went very quickly. We were all running about unhitching sand-bags like characters in an early film while the soothing tones of Halstead's Member of Parliament went through the speech-for-opening-village-fêtes.

"Very nice," said one of the Dutch girls when he had finished.

"It ought to be," I told her. "It has done good service for years."

The idea of the balloon was not only as a novel attraction to gather people from the farthest corners of Essex, but by charging five shillings a head for tethered flights to make some money too.

The M.P. declared the fête well and truly opened and the floats floated across the rain-soaked field to be judged for the prizes.

"I'll give anyone five to one the Young Conservatives win it," I offered, but they were all too wise to take the bet.

The balloon floated majestically up. We were ready for business.

The Mayor of Halstead was to be the first passenger, but Bushy thought that the pretty girl who had been crowned Miss Halstead of 1958 should share the honour and offered to pay for her. She came over to the car carrying her orb and sceptre carefully. It was obvious that she would have to be picked up and lifted into the car, and I moved quickly towards her, but not as quickly as Gerry Long — but then he had had thirty years' ballooning experience.

Miss Halstead, looking beautiful, and His Honour the Mayor, looking Mayoral, slowly rose into the sky acknowledging the cheers of the crowd. From then on it was practically continuous. Up would go the car with two passengers to four or five hundred feet and then we'd haul them down. By the end of the day we were quite exhausted, but had learned to respect the power of a free-flying balloon. It got out of control for a few moments once and bounced off the roof of the grandstand, but fortunately the passengers stayed put. We realised that a much larger balloon in a strong wind would be most difficult to handle.

The last item on the fête's programme was the free flight of the balloon from Halstead to 'an unknown destination', in traditional ballooning language. The balloon had lost a bit of lift with the cooling of the gas in the evening and had to be topped up from the gasworks again. Finally, at half-past seven, Bushy and one of the Dutch Balloon Club got in the basket and we gathered around and held it down. The order 'hands high' was given, and the basket allowed to rise to our hands; lift was adjusted and then we were ordered to stand clear. It rose almost straight up at first, and I stood beneath it gaping upwards like everyone else watching it shrinking as it got higher.

"It looks like a small world," I said to Rosemary.

"That's it, Peter," she said. "We've been trying to think of a name for weeks — we'll call it The Small World."

The balloon drifted over a low hill to the east of Halstead. "Come! come!" the remaining members of The Hague Balloon Club urged. "Now we have the balloon fox hunt — to see who is the first to reach the balloon when it comes down!"

Colin and Rosemary ran to their ancient Railton, Tim to his bubble car and I and my son for Bushy's car. "What about a small bet among ourselves?" I suggested.

"Five bob!" the Mudies shouted back as they jumped in and drove off.

We sighted the balloon as soon as we got up on the hill. It looked about tree-top height and I thought that it was going to come down almost at once, but as we converged on the spot they discarded ballast and she rose again. This happened several times, and each time the cluster of following vehicles had to back out of a narrow lane or country road, so that there was always a delay in taking up the chase.

Meanwhile, Bushy was enjoying his first flight over England tremendously. At a thousand feet or so he could hear the comments of the people below quite clearly, and could even carry on a short conversation with them. All that part of Essex is Gainsborough country, and seeing it from a low, slow-moving balloon is an unforgettable experience.

He watched his commander manipulating the balloon by careful use of ballast and noticed that sometimes he seemed to know that an upward or downward movement would be temporary only and did nothing, while at other times he took corrective steps immediately. They were moving at about ten miles an hour at under a thousand feet, although once they got into a thermal which carried them to three thousand and they had to valve out gas to stop rising.

Below we were all trying to follow them across the tangle of minor Essex roads, guessing from the wind speed and direction where they would be in the next five or ten minutes. I saw them just clear a small hill, but it took me some time to find a road to the top. Finally, I did, but when we got there the balloon was not to be seen. There was a small pub with a red-faced man standing at the door holding a large gin.

"Did you see a balloon go over?" I asked.

"Thank God you saw it too — I nearly swore off on the spot." He pointed to the way it had gone, and a few minutes later we came upon it settling comfortably down in a small valley. I jumped out of the car and ran towards it, followed by my son.

"We've won the bet, anyway," I said. "There's not another car in sight." The ground got softer and softer until we were half-way up to our knees in mud.

"What a horrible landing-place you've picked," I said to Bushy as I arrived just under the basket and reached up to pull it down.

"We're not landing," Bushy said. "Here have some sand — you look as though you need something dry." Half a bagful of sand came sailing through the air, and the balloon slowly rose and left us standing in the mud.

Several hours later, when it was dark, I found a main road — I didn't know which main road, but after floundering around rutted tracks and minor roads that ended at farm gates I didn't care. A few minutes later a car appeared coming the other way, and I jumped out and flagged it down.

"Have you seen a . . ."

"Yes," Colin said sweetly. "They went thataway. It's all over and the balloon is packed up and on its way back to Holland by now." He waited rather obviously, and I handed over the five shillings.

*   *   *   *   *

As soon as Bushy was sure that a bigger and better balloon was going to be made for them, which was when all the companies concerned agreed, he knew that he could use *Sylvia* for the practice flights necessary to get his licence. Up until then, of course, *Sylvia* had been kept in cotton-wool, for it is only too easy for a balloon to be damaged in use, and their schedule certainly didn't allow for another one to be made.

It was a good thing that they had *Sylvia*, for it had become essential for him to get a licence — the flight would not be permitted without one — and it was impossible for him to get in the necessary number of flights in Holland. Even at fifteen pounds a time they were fully booked for the season, and the most that he could hope for was two or three more.

The requirements for a Balloon Pilot's licence are six flights under an instructor, one with an instructor but in full control and three solo flights. Gerry Long was the obvious choice for an instructor, but unfortunately he had allowed his own licence to lapse. Bushy asked him to try to renew it, but it was apparently difficult — perhaps because there were no other licensed pilots to test him — and when the fine weather came and Bushy was eager to get on there was still no licensed balloon pilot in Great Britain to instruct him.

"How is it possible to get a licence under those conditions?" he asked a lawyer friend, who looked at the regulations for him.

"You can't," he said. "On the other hand, it was obviously not the intention of the drafters of the regulations that circumstances could ever occur whereby it was impossible for someone to get a licence. It is known as an 'intolerable position', and the solution for it is new legislation — you'd better write to your M.P. about it, old boy."

Bushy decided to hear what the licensing authorities had to say, and he phoned the correct department in the Ministry of Civil Aviation to ask for advice and help.

"Look," he said. "I've got a frightfully expensive balloon that I want to learn to fly. The position is that I can't fly in England at all legally. No one can, and it looks as though it's going to go to waste. Did you know that the only person who can fly a balloon in England is a foreigner?"

They asked him to explain why that was so.

"Well, I can't get a licence unless an instructor is present, and there is no licensed balloon pilot in England any more. There are foreign licensed balloonists, and they can come over here and fly, but no Englishman in this country. It's a sort of impasse — what do you think we can do about it?"

The official was obviously surprised but not unduly worried. He explained that it was very difficult, that the law was the law, that there was no one in that department with the authority to override it and that he would like time to think it over. He promised to phone back, but Bushy was not surprised when he didn't do so. Not for the first time the initiative lay with him.

He asked the advice of an old friend who had had more experience dealing with Government Departments than he.

"Ask your M.P. to help." It was the same advice that his lawyer friend had half-jokingly given him. "If the only way is to get the law changed and there is a good reason to change it — and it seems to me there is — the sooner you start the better. Get him to ask a question in the House about it?"

"But that will take ages," Bushy was dismayed.

"Perhaps not. I should get back to the Ministry if I were you and explain that obviously the law must be changed and that you are going to ask your M.P. to help you and would they just confirm that it's true that a British subject can't get a Balloonist's Licence in Britain any more — perhaps something can be done after all."

He was right. This time the official phoned back in ten minutes and made an appointment for Bushy to sit down with their lawyers and discuss the situation. Bushy also explained that he didn't want to fly a balloon purely for fun, but that it was for an international record attempt and he could sense their interest immediately.

There were four people waiting for him, two of whom were lawyers.

"The first thing to get into your head, Mr. Eiloart," one of them said, "is that we are not here as policemen to keep you out of a balloon: we're here to help you — to devise some way in which you can get in a balloon. If we start on that basis I think we'll get somewhere."

It was a nice surprise. They asked him about the Atlantic crossing and chatted about that for a few minutes and, once again, said that they wanted to help if they could.

They went word for word over the regulations.

"One can be 'under an instructor' without the instructor being in the aircraft," one of them pointed out. "You are still under an instructor when you go solo, for instance."

"Furthermore," said the other. "There's nothing here about a 'licensed' instructor. Obviously the instructor must be competent, experienced and have held a licence at one time, but if he's not going up in the balloon he needn't hold a current licence."

"Does that mean that I can go on those terms?" Bushy asked. "That Gerry Long instructs me from the ground?"

"I think that you had better interpret what we have said yourself," one of them answered gently. "I don't really think that anything more need be said." They shook his hand and wished him luck.

One day Gerry told him that he thought he was ready for his qualifying solo flights and that as soon as the Meteorological Office report of wind conditions was right he could start them.

Every morning for the next three weeks Bushy phoned Cardington, but the wind was always too strong. Then one day it was just right — an estimated eight-knot breeze (nearly nine miles an hour) at most. If he could get up there by half-past nine he could go, Gerry said, and he would lend him one of their nets. This was most welcome, for getting their new net made for them had been one of the small difficulties, and they didn't want to take any chances with it.

When Bushy got to Cardington *Sylvia* was laid out neatly on a groundsheet. The net was laid over her and the valve attached, which Bushy thought was the reverse order, but he didn't feel that he should make a comment. Gerry had to leave for a few minutes and the ground crew put the valve in but left out the cord. If it were inflated without the cord being in place they would have to let the gas go and start all over again. But Gerry was too old a hand to be caught like that, and noticed it immediately he returned.

By half-past eleven *Sylvia* was ready to fly and Bushy was in a welter of excitement. Gerry Long looked at his watch.

"The boys go to lunch from twelve to one," he said. "There's not enough time left — we'll get you away after lunch."

"But the wind might come up . . ." Bushy started to protest, but it was no use. They came back after lunch, and Bushy was glad to see that the wind was only a bit stronger. Gerry phoned Uxbridge for official clearance to make a free-balloon flight within twenty miles of Cardington. Bushy was like a boy waiting to get into the circus. Gerry Long looked at him and decided that he needed calming down.

"I'd better go with you for a bit," he said, ignoring the murderous look Bushy gave him. "I'll only come for half an hour or so, and then let you off on your own."

Off they went. It was unpleasant ballooning weather, for although there was hardly any wind, there were strong currents of rising air. Straw from the fields came floating up to them at seven hundred feet, and when they threw sand over it came up into their faces. After about half an hour of this Gerry gassed just enough to sink gently and expertly threw the grapple over a barb-wire fence. It held them until the launching crew, who had been following in a van, came and held them.

Gerry got out, carefully coiled the grappling-hook line and put it back in its proper place in the car.

"Right-O. You're on your own — good luck!"

Bushy's first feeling as *Sylvia* rose quickly was intense relief at being on his own at last. He watched the figures below getting smaller and smaller. The everyday noises of life on the ground could still be heard. At the same time everything seemed so quiet. It was an extraordinary detached feeling, as though he had stepped out of the world. The sight of the needle on the altimeter reminded him that he hadn't — it said sixteen hundred feet and still rising. He pulled the valve line and let out some gas, but the rise continued, and then he remembered that a balloon doesn't respond immediately like a car, for without friction it takes some time to overcome its momentum. Soon it stopped rising, and almost at once began to fall. He checked that by throwing over some sand and went on like that rising and falling and learning just how little gas or ballast he needed to lose to keep the movements at a minimum.

It seemed a very short time to him when there were shouts from below and he saw Gerry and the van. Gerry was giving him the signal to come down, and reluctantly he prepared to obey.

Gerry had indicated a field near the truck, which seemed to Bushy to be too close to two converging lines of high-tension electricity pylons. He decided to go beyond them over the next small hill. Then it occurred to him that perhaps Gerry had chosen that particular place as a test of his balloonmanship. He decided that he had better obey despite the hazard, for if Gerry gave him a bad report the Ministry might withdraw their support.

He valved and waited, but soon decided that he wasn't descending fast enough and valved again rather longer. This time *Sylvia* began to go down like a lift, but he still had plenty of ballast and knew that he could slow her up short of the ground. The vario-meter, which shows speed of ascent or descent, went from five feet a second, ten feet, twenty feet and then past the recording figures. He got three sandbags open ready to discard ballast at about three hundred feet and at one hundred threw out his trail rope. He jetti-soned sand until the descent was slowed right up and, a hundred and fifty yards from the high-tension wires, threw his grapnel over to the windward of a fine, strong hedge. He was pretty certain that it would hold, but just in case it didn't he got ready to throw two full sandbags over to leap-frog over the wires. The hook tangled in the hedge, he valved as fast as possible and the ground crew ran over and pulled him down. He had made his first solo.

There were, of course, many more solos to follow after that before he qualified for his licence, but there is never one just like the first. Some of them were quite uneventful; others were not, but there were no major mishaps, and *Sylvia* behaved like a heroine.

On one of his solos he was made aware of how uncertain balloon-ing can be and of the forces he was trying to control. The weather forecast had said that the winds might rise to moderate, which is too much for comfortable ballooning, but time was limited, and it looked as though he would never be able to get in all the necessary flights if he went only in light airs. He decided to take a chance.

When he got to Cardington the wind had freshened and he hesitated. Gerry Long was not there that day, and Bushy knew that if he had been there would have been no chance for a flight. But the man left in charge did not forbid it, and Bushy felt that he must get his qualifying flights in.

The ground crew manhandled *Sylvia* out of the hangar, but had to send for reinforcements, for six men couldn't hold her down. Now the man in charge of the launching began to doubt whether he should let Bushy go, particularly when he remembered that *Sylvia* had no ripping panel. This is the emergency panel to release all the gas at once and is most needed when landing in a high wind. But Bushy insisted, and after making sure that he was well clear of the hangars, they let *Sylvia* go.

She rose diagonally doing a full twelve knots, and as the speed of the wind usually increases with altitude was three miles away in eight minutes. Over twenty miles an hour in a free balloon is fast, and Bushy knew that he would have to come down fairly soon or be blown outside his permitted twenty-mile circle.

Once he dropped the knife, used to cut open the sandbags, on the floor of the basket. He got down and groped for it and when he straightened up again found that he was in the clouds at four thousand feet. He grabbed for the valve line and stopped the ascent. A few minutes later the balloon dropped silently out of the clouds.

The following lorry was nowhere to be seen, but from the way the trees were moving he could see that the wind was even stronger. He would have to go down.

With the wind at that speed he must land with the minimum amount of gas in the balloon, for the grapnel would never hold a full balloon in a strong wind. He had to let out the maximum amount of gas in the air, which meant also getting rid of most of the ballast to keep up while losing the gas. It was difficult to control the balance as he gassed and threw over sand and the balloon went up and down like a temperature chart. Sometimes he found himself falling through a cloud of his own sand going down more sedately.

When he was down to five bags of sand and *Sylvia* was much deflated he picked out a large field, gassed hard and dropped rapidly. At fifty feet he threw out his trail rope and a bagful of sand to slow his descent. Fifty yards or so before a hedge he threw out his grapnel to catch in it. When the basket went over the hedge at about twenty feet he opened the valve fully to let the remaining gas go as quickly as possible. The grapnel caught in the hedge and held fast, but the half-deflated balloon filled like a sail, and the basket was bounced viciously on the ground and then rose again and bounced again.

"I'll soon have you tamed!" thought Bushy, hanging on to the valve line to let all the gas go. Then, to his horror, he saw the grapnel pull through the hedge and in a matter of seconds he was being bounced and dragged over the ground at nearly twenty knots. The balloon cleared the next hedge; the basket did not. It bumped hard against it diagonally, seemed to try to climb over it but failed. It turned completely over once, then again and was then dragged along the hedge, spinning round and round.

As the car turned over the big knife slid out of its scabbard and started to float after Bushy like a sock chasing a shirt in a washing-machine. He had been hanging on to the valve line, but now he dropped it and tried to grab the knife. He thought better of it and used his hands to cover himself up. At the same time the sandbags, which he had opened in case he had to discard ballast quickly, emptied and the sand got into his mouth, eyes and nose until he was gasping for breath. Another hundred yards of spinning and bouncing, and the basket collided with a tree and was brought to a stop.

Bushy tied the basket to the tree with the trail rope and then tied the valve line down tight to the load ring to let the gas out as quickly as possible. There were no bones broken, but he was covered with bruises.

A few minutes later the owner of the farm turned up with some of his workers and helped him sort things out. He had been a wartime bomber pilot and still kept his own plane on the farm, but he had thought that he must be dreaming when he saw a balloon land in one of his fields. He took Bushy back to lunch and they phoned for the ground crew, who had lost the balloon completely.

These solo flights were the most important part of qualifying for a balloonist's licence, but there was plenty of other work Bushy had to do as well. He had to pass two written examinations — one in Aviation Law and the other a technical test about ballooning. Somehow he squeezed an extra hour out of his crowded days to bone up on these subjects.

Bushy and I used to fly in Tiger Moths at Brooklands Flying Club before the war, and he thought it shouldn't be hard to pick it up again. He found, though, that everything had become much more complicated and that to learn all the rules took more time than he had allowed. He cut down the number of hours he slept and all social activities. His friends who didn't know about the balloon thought that he was becoming a recluse. But he sat for his Aviation Law examination about a month before he was due to leave England and passed it with ninety-three per cent. Two weeks later he passed the other examination. Then he went for a medical examination and was able to apply for his licence. He got it on 7th October 1958, and became the only man in Great Britain with a valid licence to 'fly as a pilot of any type of free balloon other than a public transport or aerial work balloon'.

CHAPTER FIVE

MEANWHILE, the other members of the crew had been getting on with their jobs. Colin and Rosemary had made a half-size model of the car and tested it and then got down to the long job of making the actual craft; Tim had been fully occupied with the radio and the meteorology. Progress was being made in everything, yet daily the balloon and car seemed to get more complicated.

When The Small World took off from Médano Beach it was quite unlike any other balloon and car that had ever been built. The twin-hulled boat in place of the traditional basket; the pedal machinery; the helicopter-like propellers at each side; the winch and water-lifting bags; the water reservoir — looking like a miniature swimming-pool; the radio receiver and transmitter, the generator and batteries — each of these was unique in free ballooning. Each had evolved from an idea, a discussion, someone's suggestion or perhaps had just grown out of the use of something else. For instance, the pedalling machinery was installed to turn the propellers, then adapted to work the winch for pulling up the heavy bags of sea-water; finally, it was used to turn a generator, making it possible for them to have electricity for a radio transmitter, lights and instruments. So it was with most things in the car — a line of development ran back from them through some of the others like a genealogical tree.

Nothing seemed to come easily; nothing was thought of and then obtained without further ado. Every single thing seemed to have its own troubles at one time or another, and many of these troubles assumed great importance. Several of them looked like bringing the enterprise to a complete stop.

One of these was getting hydrogen gas available on the beach. For once it wasn't a question of money. There was no hydrogen on Tenerife or any of the other Canary Islands, and so they would have to take their gas with them. One of I.C.I.'s many divisions agreed to give them the hydrogen, but they couldn't spare any cylinders in which to transport it. They also pointed out the magnitude of the transport problem in a letter to Gordon Long of I.C.I.'s Public Relations Office. He had been of immense help, and Bushy had got to know and like him as a friend. He showed Bushy the letter:

> . . . you will recall that during the last war we supplied considerable quantities of hydrogen to the Royal Air Force and this was normally filled into cylinders at a pressure of 120 atmospheres and transported on special trailers each carrying 30 cylinders. If Mr. Eiloart is able to obtain from the R.A.F. cylinders of the same size and type as those used during the war he will find that each cylinder will hold 360 cubic feet of hydrogen. A little simple arithmetic will show you that approximately one hundred and fifty cylinders (or five trailer loads) will be required for one inflation.

The transport problem was going to be a tough one all right, but first he had to find the cylinders. The R.A.F. were unable to help them, and although Bushy was sure that there must be thousands of cylinders of hydrogen left over from the balloon barrage of the war he was never able to find one. British Oxygen own more cylinders than anyone else, but they were all in use constantly, and just couldn't be spared for that long. He tried everywhere else he could think of but without success.

One of Bushy's rules was that they should always carry on as though all problems were solvable, but when it came to July 1958, a few months before take-off with everything else on schedule except how to get the gas to Tenerife, even he began to falter.

But his efforts and enquiries did, as so often happened, lead to something else. A sympathetic Air Ministry official he had approached reported back that there were no wartime hydrogen cylinders left because it was dangerous to keep them for years.

"But why don't you set up a small hydrogen generator of your own in the Canary Islands?" he suggested. "There's a portable one on the market that makes hydrogen from magnesium–iron pellets and water."

"How much?" Bushy asked.

"About a thousand pounds."

That, of course, put it out of court immediately, but it started Bushy on the track of making their own hydrogen, and from a cloak-and-dagger man he met through one of the Service chiefs he learned about a method of generating hydrogen with a small generator made out of fabric.

"You just pop a couple of pounds of chemical in the container and fill it up with sea-water. The gas is formed immediately, and a pound of the chemical gives you a pound of lift. The whole thing costs only about a fiver."

Tim was detailed to find out all about it. He confirmed that hydrogen could be generated that way, but that it would be expensive — at least ten shillings a pound of lift or about eighteen hundred pounds to fill their balloon.

But, said Tim, if it wasn't practical to try to inflate the whole balloon that way why not carry a small hydrogen generator *in the balloon* and take this chemical instead of sand ballast? Then they would not only get the benefit of losing the weight of the ballast but could manufacture extra lift at the same time.

The suggestion was approved and passed unanimously by the committee — which consisted of the other three in the crew — and Tim was told to design and build a small hydrogen generator for them to take with them.

I think that it was about this time that it began to dawn on Tim that he had greatly underestimated the amount of time that he would have to give to the balloon project. Bushy had agreed in the beginning that his studies at Cambridge must take priority over everything else and that he wouldn't expect him to do any extensive work on the balloon. But inevitably he took on more and more jobs, and his University work began to suffer.

Anyway, he tackled the problem of a hydrogen generator to go with them, designing and building it himself. It and considerable quantities of the chemical, calcium hydride, were added to the always growing list of things that had to be carried to Tenerife.

A by-product of the production of hydrogen by this method is heat in the form of steam. This meant that the generator would have to be insulated from the hull and the gas cooled in a water-bag before being led to the balloon. This, in its turn, suggested a method of using this surplus heat: on the way to the water-bath for cooling, the hot gas was conducted through a sealed jacket round a saucepan. When they made gas they could also have some hot soup, coffee, cocoa, etc., which would be a great blessing.

Colin too was having problems with the craft, although all snags were shared, so that everyone could apply himself to solving them.

The testing of the half-size model had gone well. The Mudies had taken it on the roof of the old Railton to Kingston-on-Thames and thrown it off the bridge into the river, much to the amazement of the passers-by. It survived this simulated 'bounce landing' triumphantly.

Next they went down to the river-bank and squeezed themselves carefully into the tiny craft — it measured only five feet six inches by two feet six inches inside — put up their miniature sail and sailed it across the Thames several times. The members of the local yacht club racing their dinghies looked askance at the peculiarly shaped boat, but were too polite to comment. A group of Sea Scouts rowed by, and one shouted that they ought to take their bath back to the hotel immediately. A nautical-looking gentleman on the towpath gave an involved, ingenious and quite incorrect explanation to a pretty girl.

But Colin was well pleased with the way it had behaved and set about making the final version with little change in design. Freddy Keil, the Managing Director of City Display, kept his promise and walled off a corner of one of his huge workshops for them. Here, behind a locked door, Colin started to work. Anyone noticing the long lengths of incredibly light and seemingly fragile foam plastic disappearing into the secret room might have been excused if his guess about what was being made in there was wide of the mark.

By itself the foam plastic is too soft to be of practical use, for it is possible to push a pencil through it or break off a corner between finger and thumb. In order to give the craft strength and rigidity the foam plastic was covered with a skin of tough Terylene fabric stretched tightly over it and bonded to it with Araldite. But even this apparently simple operation had given them a great deal of trouble, for they had found, at first, that the resulting bond just wasn't strong enough — a good hard tug and it came away. This would not do, for, as Colin said, it would be positively embarrassing to start coming apart at the seams in mid-Atlantic.

Much time was spent experimenting with different fabrics and different glues, but none worked, and after many trials and nothing but error it looked as though they would have to give up the use of foam plastic. It would be a hard decision to take, for it meant that everything would be so much heavier that the balloon would have to be so much bigger.

They were rescued by I.C.I., who treated the Terylene with chemicals which had the effect of changing its surface texture so that it would take the adhesive. Then the Terylene stuck to the foam plastic like a coat of paint. The artificial skin enabled weight to be spread over a large area on the same principle as a rubber raft.

They had been able to start the half-sized model in March 1958, but it was not until October that the final craft was ready. All during the months of trying to solve that one little glueing problem, knowing full well that if they couldn't it might mean that the whole trip was off, they carried on at full pressure as though they knew that a solution would be found. If they had not always treated problems like this they would be waiting still.

Meanwhile, the jobs that Tim had taken on continued to multiply and become more complicated. The hydrogen generator took a lot of time; the radio receiver and transmitter had to be designed and built from scratch, for none of the available models was suitable for a balloon; he found that mastering morse and wireless theory took longer than he had allowed; the more he studied meteorology, the more he realised he ought to know if his knowledge was to be of any use in the actual flight. Studying wireless and meteorology were time-consuming but the sort of thing he knew how to tackle; getting things made and firms to do jobs in time was something that was quite new to him.

He had not, of course, had any experience along these lines and, at first, was apt to assume that progress was being made just because someone he had seen had promised that it would be. Bushy, used to the procrastinations of business, evolved a 'worrying schedule' which began with polite enquiries a week or more before a promised delivery date and progressed to full pressure three or four days after the promise wasn't kept. This was not difficult in ordinary business transactions, where he was the customer, but in the case of the balloon where most of the things were made at such a heavy loss to the makers, it took great tact to push for delivery. Tact or the ability to handle people smoothly are not qualities of Bushy's that would first spring to his friend's minds, but he trained himself, because it was the only possible way to get things done, to be tactful, polite and even gracious — it was a sight which caused his oldest friends to gape as though they'd seen an elephant on a tightrope. While he never learned to suffer fools gladly, he at least learned to treat them so they didn't know they were being suffered. Now he set about teaching Tim to overcome the difficulties of getting a job done.

The relationship between father and son is an exceptionally good one, which is remarkable in that they are very different types of men. Bushy gives the impression of being driven by an internal fire which he is afraid will consume him if he relaxes — he never takes a holiday in the sense of going somewhere and lying in the sun — and something of this drive is communicated to anyone with whom he works. He believes that almost anyone can do almost anything, but he hasn't much respect for 'How to do it' books and perhaps, in the early days of tackling something quite new, he wastes time in learning by trial and error what he could have discovered in a book. It is an attitude that often pays off, however, for his line of development can go off on an original track at any point, which can result in his discovering a better method.

He pushes himself — and anyone with whom he is working — mercilessly but not cruelly, for he is unaware when he has asked too much and will stop immediately it is brought to his attention. He is not a big man, but gives an impression of strength; there is no trace of truculence in his make-up, but he is not the kind of man who gets pushed. He is a pragmatist who has worked out his own social code and has no time for superstitions or the supernatural. He consequently has no time for formal religion either.

Tim Eiloart is tall, thin and, although physically tough, of a nervous and excitable temperament. He is shy and sensitive and although willing to drive himself beyond his physical powers hates the idea of driving anyone else. He has more than his share of youthful doubts about himself, yet will take on more than he can accomplish, get hopelessly behind and then, in a self-flogging period of concentration, somehow get it done. He has an alert, enquiring mind of good quality, the ability to concentrate and a sense of objectivity greater than is usually found in a young man of twenty-one. He is introspective and apt to examine his motives so closely as sometimes to make himself very unhappy. He is an idealist who believes that somewhere there is a philosophy of life which, if universally adopted, would bring happiness to everyone. There is therefore in the two natures all the elements of conflict but, fortunately, they avoid it by respecting each other's viewpoint.

It was not, at first, intended that Tim would have very much to do before the actual flight — that is, not very much by Bushy's standards, for he only asked Tim to qualify as a radio operator and learn about meteorology and the physics of ballooning. He was to do these things in his spare time while in his final year at Cambridge studying for his Chemical Engineering degree.

It soon became obvious that he could not do all this without help, and he set about finding other people up at Cambridge who would not only be willing to help but were better qualified than he. On meteorology he found help from the Air Ministry, from a fellow student who, although an amateur, was a very experienced meteorologist and, particularly towards the end, from The Imperial College of Science. To learn about the kind of lightweight wireless they would need he approached the Secretary of the Wireless Society at Cambridge and was led to other keen amateurs, and a set was designed.

A small, light transmitter with a two-thousand-mile range would need a power output of 50 watts. This usually means a source of power of at least 250 volts A.C. Normally this is taken from the mains or, in ships at sea, from large generators. To get it from ordinary car batteries might be difficult and would need a lot of experimental work in a well-fitted-out laboratory. Eventually, after one or two false starts, this set was taken on by a large company who said that they would make it without charge but also without responsibility, for they frankly didn't think there was enough time to make an efficient set for the job. In fact, there wasn't enough time, and the wireless was one of the things that was always behind schedule.

Tim decided that there wasn't much he could do about becoming a licensed wireless operator until the summer vacation. These months, because of the conditions of his grant from the Ministry of Supply, he was due to spend doing research work at a factory in Somerset. That meant that the only time for wireless was the evenings, and it was rather a lot to expect a healthy young man to work all day and spend the long summer evenings that way.

Nevertheless, with the best intentions he took wireless text-books, a file of technical magazines and a morse key when he moved to Somerset, and tried to absorb enough to pass the G.P.O. examination. Self-teaching can be deceptive, as he well knew, and when there was only a week left he decided to find an expert to coach him. He was horrified at how little he really knew. But he settled down to solid study — setting himself theoretical questions during the day and taking three hours coaching every night.

He took his examination in October, six weeks before they left England, feeling like a walking text-book, for he hadn't allowed himself to think of much else for days before. Not surprisingly, he passed the examination in Wireless Theory. But, as well as theory, he would have to be able to send and receive morse at a reasonable rate, and this is something that can't be done in a week or two of blitz studying. It takes hours and hours of practice. Tim fitted a buzzer in his car and practised in his spare moments, no doubt startling the other motorists waiting at traffic lights.

All this would have been more than enough for Tim to take on in addition to his regular work, but as well he tried to organise the building of the four-man pedalling machine which was to be such an important part of their equipment. He thought that there must be a lot of Engineering students at Cambridge who would be glad to take it on, and sure enough he quickly found one in his last year who accepted the job confidently. Greatly relieved, Tim dumped the project in his lap and forgot about it. It progressed with infuriating slowness, and when ready for its first test buckled under the load it would have been required to exert. Its builder confessed himself beaten and quietly dropped out.

This occurred during one of the black patches in the history of the project, for on the same day they had received the first delivery of foam plastic and found that it weighed nine pounds a cubic foot instead of just over one; Cardington had phoned to say they must have the valve back, one of the companies that had been going to build the wireless for them had backed out, there were still no hydrogen cylinders to be found anywhere and they had been told that to fly the balloon abroad meant that they would have to have it inspected by the Air Registration Board to fulfil the requirements for issuing a Certificate of Airworthiness.

A thoroughly gloomy meeting was held at which none of the problems were solved, but their determination that nothing was going to stop them was reaffirmed. That made them feel better.

"We'll go," Bushy promised. "Even if it means that we have to find an entirely new method of hauling up water, have no wireless, have to make our own valve, have to smuggle our balloon to a lonely beach on the west coast of Africa, make our own hydrogen and take off without telling anyone!"

In the end the problems were all overcome, sometimes unexpectedly, sometimes by tirelessly plugging away trying one source after another until they discovered the right one. They got a foam plastic that was light enough; another company took on the wireless, Cardington gave them back the valve in time; they carefully and conscientiously conformed with all the requirements and got their Certificate of Airworthiness. Of course, these problems were replaced by others.

The supply of cylinders for the hydrogen had become one of Bushy's worst nightmares, for it was getting very late, and if none could be found the attempt would have to be postponed. This he wanted to avoid at all costs and for many reasons, but one in particular — the fear that some other country might do it first. There were rumours that a trans-continental free balloon crossing was being planned in the United States and that an enormous balloon was being built in France — for an attempt on the altitude record, it was said, but Bushy was suspicious. Then someone sent him a newspaper clipping from Madrid:

INFORMACIONES. MADRID. April 30th 1958. Jose Maria Ansaldo, head of research of the Iberia Airlines, has produced a balloon capable of crossing the Atlantic to North America. Ansaldo is trying out an invention that will enable him to carry out a daring project, perhaps to cross the Atlantic, but in any case to remain aloft for a month.

Up until now no balloon, no matter how large, has been able to stay up longer than three days. Ansaldo has been able to add to the balloon a series of 'compensating balloons'. He will thus be able to rise or fall at will by injecting or extracting air from the compensating balloons which are to be made of nylon.

They had been confident that they were well ahead of everyone else, but now they were shaken. They could not waste a minute. They had to find some way of getting hydrogen to Tenerife.

"We've tried every possible source for those damned cylinders," Bushy said. "Now the only thing to do is to try them all again. The people who have them are British Oxygen — I just couldn't have been persuasive enough. I'll write to them again."

"Tell them we'll take jolly good care of them and see that they're returned unharmed," Colin suggested.

Bushy wrote a long letter to Brigadier G. B. Still, O.B.E., explaining how the balloon project had progressed in the six months since he had asked to borrow the cylinders and naming the other big companies who were helping. He pointed out that the cylinders would be wanted only for about six weeks or so, because Elders and Fyffes would undertake to return them; that he would see that they were insured comprehensively for their full worth (about nine thousand pounds) and he pointed out that the attempt could not be made without them and that he was afraid some other country might do it first. A few days later his phone rang and Brigadier Still told him that, subject to the undertakings he had given, British Oxygen would lend them enough cylinders for sixty thousand cubic feet of hydrogen — three hundred cylinders weighing fifteen tons.

In fact, at Bushy's request, this was later increased to six hundred and ninety cylinders weighing thirty-five tons or enough for two and a half inflations. Having decided to help, British Oxygen went the whole hog.

All these cylinders had to go from British Oxygen to Imperial Chemical Industries to be filled with hydrogen and then sent to Southampton docks to the boat. It would cost several hundred pounds just to move them twice. Bushy felt that he couldn't expect the companies to pay for that as well — it would have to come out of his pocket. But without his asking British Oxygen arranged to transport the cylinders as well.

In this way, with each development leading on to something else, the final shape of the balloon and car emerged: each adaptation brought up new problems: as each was solved the original conception was changed, until about all that remained of their early plans was the balloon, net and load ring, which, in form, were exactly the same as they had been fifty years before. Below the load ring everything was new.

New ideas kept occurring to them all the time until, near the end, it became obvious that they would have to stop changing things or they would never get off in time.

Often in the evenings all four of them, while working on the craft, would talk over their problems. Out of their talk came many of their innovations.

The building of the pedal-operated propeller unit took many months. It was one thing to decide that a modified form of bicycle frame, pedals, gears and a crankshaft ought to do the job, but quite another to design and build it so it worked. Colin did dozens of drawings, and at least two almost-completed versions were abandoned because of defects. It was one of the most difficult things to get just right, and the final model, which did all they required, was generously built for them by the British Cycle Corporation. It passed all its tests only a few weeks before they left England.

Painfully slowly, it seemed at times, they slogged on. There was a long, discouraging period when the whole adventure seemed to be bogged down. It lost its sparkle, and none of it was fun. There were days, even weeks, when it looked as though they had just taken on too big a job to pull off with their limited resources. If they had been sensible people they would have acknowledged defeat: if they had been sensible people they would never have tried to get a balloon across the Atlantic Ocean, anyway.

The mood of light-hearted adventure, perhaps even of reckless-ness, of the early days gave way to seriousness and careful prepara-tion as the project involved more and more people. As the difficulties mounted the jokes and teasing became rarer: the lark became a job of work — hard work.

Not everyone they approached encouraged them. Many said that it could not be done, and there were always the gloomy ones who told them that they were going to kill themselves.

And then one day, somehow, they seemed to be over the hill and everything began to fall in place. The balloon was nearly finished; the net had been made and delivered; they had a load ring and a valve; the craft was nearing completion; the pedal apparatus was made; the hydrogen generator worked; the gas cylinders were go-ing to be lent; supplies of calcium hydride had been found; the radio was being built by experts — it really looked as though they

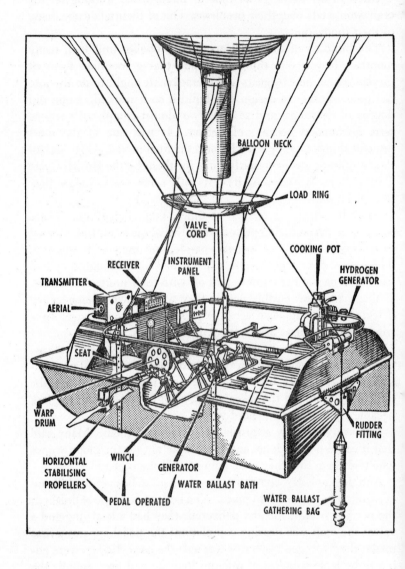

BALLOON NECK

LOAD RING

VALVE CORD

COOKING POT

HYDROGEN GENERATOR

RECEIVER

INSTRUMENT PANEL

TRANSMITTER

AERIAL

SEAT

WARP DRUM

RUDDER FITTING

HORIZONTAL STABILISING PROPELLERS

WINCH

GENERATOR

WATER BALLAST BATH

PEDAL OPERATED

WATER BALLAST GATHERING BAG

Rosemary and Colin Mudie.

Tim Eiloart.

Bushy Eiloart.

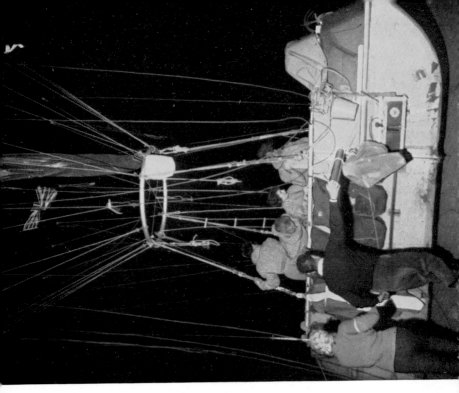

Take-off! The wind is banging the boat on the beach.

Bushy personally making sure there is no grit on the tarpaulin before laying out the balloon for inflation. The bare feet are for finding small cactus spines.

were going, after all, and something of the spirit of high adventure that had started them off began to come back.

"Now," said Bushy, "is the time for me to go to Tenerife and make sure that the launching site is all right. I'll write to Wilfred Moore."

The idea of trying to cross the sea in a balloon affected people in different ways: some thought it was pure lunacy; some thought it was a fine idea and ought to be encouraged. Most wanted to help; many did. Some gave odd hours; some gave up almost all their spare time for months. This is not the place to list their names, and that is not what they did it for, anyway — they helped because they wanted to share in the attempt. But there were some whose help was so important that it is difficult to see how any attempt at all could have been made without them. One of these is certainly Wilfred Moore.

One day in March 1958 some six months after their first meeting, Mr. Conradi, who had already been of inestimable help to them, phoned Bushy and told him that he had arranged for him to meet the Managing Director of Elders and Fyffes to talk about transporting them to Tenerife.

"Wilfred Moore, the Yorkshireman who lives there and who, if he chooses, can make all the difference to the way things go on Tenerife, will be there too," Conradi said. "I'm not guaranteeing anything, but they're both the sort of chaps I should think would want to help."

Conradi had known Jim Stockley, of the banana shipping line, for many years and he had met Wilfred Moore, who ran the company's estates on Tenerife, several times. He had spoken briefly to Stockley some months before, telling him that he had met a lunatic with a completely mad scheme but that he was sure he should be encouraged. One of the things which had impressed Mr. Conradi with the bona fides of the enterprise was that the order for the polythene from which *Sylvia* was to be made had been placed through the ordinary commercial channels first. "In other words," he has since said, "these people were asking for help, but they were obviously going ahead, anyway . . . they were getting on with the job, and that is something which is unusual enough to be refreshing.''

Bushy's first impression of the tall, handsome man behind the Managing Director's desk was of a film star rather improbably playing the part of a big business-man. Wilfred Moore, the other man in the room, looked like a prosperous, middle-aged Yorkshire farmer which, after all, wasn't far from the mark.

"Here's the madman I promised you," Conradi said. "He wants to take off in a balloon from Tenerife and float across the Atlantic Ocean."

"Why?" asked Jim Stockley.

"Because it's never been done," Bushy replied. "Columbus did it first by ship; Alcock and Brown did it first by aeroplane, but no one has ever done it in a balloon. If we pull it off we'll set up two new world's records for Britain as well as another first — first to cross in a free balloon."

"They're good enough reasons for me. It's just the sort of thing that ought to be encouraged in this dull world," Jim Stockley said. "We'll be glad to help you with the shipping and so on."

"That will be a tremendous help," Bushy said, "particularly as it's all so much bigger than we first thought — the equipment will run into tons, I'm afraid."

"Don't worry about that — our ships go out empty, anyway. How about you, Wilfred, will you handle things that end?"

"We'll be delighted to do everything we can. We've got a very nice plantation in the south of the island where we'll be able to put you all up."

"Wonderful!" said Bushy. "Do you think that you could organise someone to take a note of wind speed and direction daily for me on that farm as near the sea as possible? It would be very valuable if I could have some record of the wind at the actual launching site over a fairly long interval."

Mr. Moore agreed to this and put it in hand as soon as he returned to Tenerife, and every month thereafter until we left for the island ourselves the reports came.

These were correlated with any other information they could

get from other sources, for it was important that they find out as much as possible about the local winds. They knew that once they got clear of Tenerife the north-east trades would carry them in the right direction, but they also knew that the trades don't always blow from Tenerife. Yachts attempting the Atlantic crossing sometimes take several days tacking back and forth before making the region of the true trades, but The Small World, once aloft, could only go the way the wind was blowing. By studying all the information they hoped to find out how good were the chances of the right wind. The results were discouraging.

It looked as though the wind did not often blow from the right quarter in December or January. They might well get all ready and then have to wait two or three weeks. That would mean camping near the dump of hydrogen cylinders, for when the favourable wind came up they would have to start immediately because it would take four or five hours to inflate. The balloon could not be blown up in advance, for any strong wind would destroy it.

Bushy had accepted the recommended launching site in the early days when he knew little or nothing of the problems of inflating a balloon, but after having seen a few launchings in Holland and England he knew that the selection of a site was something he would have to do himself. It was one thing that he couldn't leave to anyone else.

Wilfred Moore had invited him to come and stay whenever he felt like it and now, when for once everything seemed to be going smoothly, he flew to Tenerife by way of Madrid.

All across the Atlantic on the last stretch from the mainland he could see from the condition of the sea that the wind was blowing at about the right speed but from exactly the wrong direction. If it blew like that after they had taken off they would find themselves over the Sahara desert, where their water-lifting bags would not be of much use to them.

Wilfred Moore met him at Santa Cruz airport, and they were driven down to the town to the best hotel, where Bushy was introduced to various people as 'The Balloon Man'. He spent an enjoyable evening with good food, company and relaxed conversation. It was most pleasant and brought home to him how unsocial had been the life he had been leading for the last year or so.

Bruce Norton, an Englishman who works for Wilfred Moore, had been given the job of taking care of the needs of the Trans-Atlantic Balloon Flight in Santa Cruz, and the next morning he took Bushy along to meet the British Consul, Eric Fox.

Mr. Fox has been British Consul on Tenerife for more than twenty-five years, and it was he and Wilfred Moore who had been patiently working on the local authorities for permission to bring a balloon, hundreds of cylinders of hydrogen gas and a large party to Tenerife to launch an Atlantic balloon from one of their beaches. It is always easier for an official to say 'no' to such requests, and the job took all the efforts and experience of the two of them. Fortunately they started well in advance, for it took eight months before everyone was satisfied and official permission granted.

Mr. Fox had also contacted the local meteorological officer for the island, Sr. Cañadas, on Bushy's behalf, and now he was taken along to find out about the winds outside the island and the chances of a favourable local wind.

No, Sr. Cañadas told them, it was by no means certain that they would get their ideal wind conditions at Tenerife in either December or January. He would, however, work closely with his opposite numbers at the weather-observation stations in Madeira, the Azores and the southernmost part of Spain.

"I think that we can possibly forecast three days of north-easterly winds for you, but if not there is a good probability of two such days, and we can absolutely guarantee to forecast a north-easter that will last at least a whole twenty-four hours."

This was a bit more encouraging, for three days would be ideal; two would get them into the true trades and even twenty-four hours, at ten to twelve knots, would carry them well on their way. They might then drift slowly south until picked up by the real north-east trade wind, but it was extremely unlikely that they could be blown back to Africa. As long as their height-stabilising devices worked satisfactorily they wouldn't mind drifting.

Early the next day Bushy was taken by Wildred Moore's chauffeur to the farm, Hoya Grande, where it was proposed they take off.

It took three hours to go from Santa Cruz to Buena Vista. It is about forty miles in a straight line, but they had to go around the peak of Teide, and the roads were not made for fast driving. Bushy had been noticing the wind from the time he landed, and was discouraged to see that it blew from the wrong direction the whole time. Now as he sat in the car and bumped over the pot-holed road he saw from the dust or the smoke from the bonfires of old tomato plants that it was still from the wrong quarter. It stayed that way even on the other side of the mountain.

Tenerife is an arid island of great volcanic rocks and broken lava fields, much of which looks like one's idea of a lunar landscape. It hardly seemed possible that the dry, dusty fields could grow tomatoes, but Bruce Norton assured him that they were passing some of the best growing land on the island. Nonetheless, he was as glad as any desert traveller to see the oasis of Hoya Grande ahead.

It was a large, white house set in a green and flower-filled garden. There was a fountain playing, and it promised to be a very pleasant spot for us all to wait for the right wind. The farm was on a fertile slope of the mountain a thousand feet above the sea and about two miles from the little jetty which had been chosen as the launching site. The wind was still blowing off the sea, and Tom Beasley, the farm's manager, said that it was almost always so, for north-east of them was the snow-covered peak of Teide, over eleven thousand feet high, which successfully stopped any north-east winds. It looked as though this attractive spot was not, after all, the ideal launching place. Still, Bushy decided to inspect the actual site before making up his mind.

He was driven to it early the next morning and saw immediately that it was not large enough. The Small World is forty-six feet in diameter: the jetty was forty-five feet wide. Also there was a sheer cliff immediately behind them which would produce dangerous eddies; there were jagged rocks all around and there was no harbour. He explored the whole area looking for a large, flat bit of ground, but there were cliffs and rocks everywhere.

On the horizon he could see another smaller island which looked far enough away to be out of the influence of the mountain. It was called Gomera, and the only Englishman on it was visiting Hoya Grande at the moment.

Yes, the winds blew from the north-east on Gomera quite often, Bushy was told, but there was no harbour at all. The task of putting ashore their tons of equipment and the precious gas cylinders was too much of an undertaking. But the winds blew just the same on the east coast of Tenerife the Englishman told him.

A large map of Tenerife was laid out on the ground, and Bushy was shown that to the south-east of the island — actually almost the southern tip — there was a large, sandy beach. The mountain of Teide would then be almost due north of them, and so would not stop the north-east wind they needed. Bushy ran his finger down the coast-line and stopped at the last little port — Médano.

"Right — let's go and have a look at it," he said. He had been standing on some rocks to get a look down the coast and now he jumped down, eager to get started. He landed on an irregular stone and his foot turned, badly twisting his ankle. He felt a searing pain and found that he couldn't put his foot to the ground.

He was taken back to Santa Cruz and hoped that a day or two's rest would at least heal it enough for him to walk, but he had torn a ligament and, to his chagrin, found himself helpless. He was determined to inspect Médano, and he borrowed some crutches and started out of the hotel. He was insisting that he was quite fit and able to get there when he suddenly collapsed. When he came round he found himself in his bed — it was nothing to do with his ankle but a tropical fever that had struck him down. By the time he was able to get out of bed it was impossible for him to go and inspect the site because there were things in England to which he had to get back.

There wasn't time for him to come to Tenerife again, even if he could afford it. He explained in detail to Wilfred Moore the requirements and entrusted him to choose the place. We should all have to arrive in Tenerife and hope that there wasn't some unforeseen reason why the selected site wasn't possible.

It was a depressing flight back to England, for he was still far from well and consequently unnaturally depressed. The wind was still blowing steadily from the wrong quarter, as though it would never change, and he had an awful picture of us all arriving in Tenerife and then just sitting, eating up our funds, while the wind blew towards Africa day after day. He felt so low that he was convinced that there would be some dire emergency awaiting him in England. He hobbled from the plane on his borrowed crutches to where Colin and I were waiting for him. He looked like a warrior home from the wars. But we had good news for him. The Duke of Edinburgh had granted The British Trans-Atlantic Balloon Flight his Royal Patronage.

"Just like Columbus," Bushy joked, but it was easy to see how proud he was.

CHAPTER SIX

B Y September 1958 The Trans-Atlantic Balloon Flight, which
had started so light-heartedly twenty-one months before, had
become a monster enslaving all four of them.

At the beginning Bushy had said that all work and no play
would probably be a bad thing for the success of the enterprise, and
had made quite a point of keeping up his week-end dinghy sailing.
He tried, during Saturday and Sunday, to put balloon problems
right out of his mind, and he succeeded for most of the first
summer. Then the increasing pressure made it impossible to take
week-ends off if they were to be ready by the end of 1958. He
surrendered, and from then on ate, slept and dreamt nothing but
The Small World.

Colin and Rosemary work differently from Bushy. They slave
day and night, weekdays and week-ends without a break for a bit,
and then have a day or two off. They had taken on the adventure
in a gay spirit, knowing that it would mean a great deal of extra
hard work. They didn't really think, though, that it would mean
their having no time for anything else, and they put up quite a
struggle, but in the end they, too, were doing nothing else but
working on the balloon.

It meant a complete change in their life, which they had had
carefully planned before starting on the balloon project. They
know what they want and what they don't want: Rosemary loves
her work and looks forward to a successful career; Colin is going
to become a successful boat designer. They don't want children
for a few years; they want to build their own boat, designed by
Colin, of course, and sail it around the world together, and this
was what they had been working for almost since they got married
— which was six weeks after they met.

They were hard up like most young couples, but it had seemed that by having Colin become completely freelance, which would mean his earning considerably more, they could start saving towards their boat. Then along came the chance to cross the ocean in a balloon.

They knew Bushy well enough by then to know that he was serious and that a balloon would undoubtedly get made and launched. They knew that it would mean lots of work for them and, perhaps, curtailed earnings for the time being. On the other hand, if the flight was a success there ought to be a chance to make some money by writing about it. Anyway, some things are more important than money, and this was certainly one of them.

They didn't foresee, though, as indeed did no one, that it would all become quite so complicated or involve so many people. I asked them once how they visualised it happening in the beginning.

"Well, I think we saw ourselves getting on a freighter with a couple of large crates holding the balloon and the car and going to the Canary Islands. Then getting our stuff taken to a likely beach . . ." Colin said.

"With no one knowing or caring what you were up to?" I asked.

"No, not at that point. After all, dozens of chaps turn up in the Canaries with small boats every season. I thought we might be looked on in much the same way. Anyway, then we'd blow up our balloon, climb into our car-cum-boat and have a shot at it. We'd either get there, coming down near one of the islands, or come down after a bit and sail the rest of the way."

"How about when you got to the other side? Surely you realised that there'd be a great deal of interest then, didn't you?"

Colin laughed. "As a matter of fact we were talking about that one night and I told Bushy that they are so used to small boats sailing across these days that if we came in in our little craft and told them we'd just crossed in a balloon they'd probably say 'so what?' "

The Mudies were prepared for the balloon to take up most of their spare time, but gradually it became obvious that it would need all their spare time and Colin's full time as well. Many of the things that had to be made were entirely new: every one of them had to be designed, drawn several times and then working blue prints got out to enable a manufacturer to make it. This meant that Colin was at his drawing-board until two or three in the morning for months.

Bushy, being the boss of his own business, could arrange things so that he spent a minimum of time at his other work, but even that minimum meant that he couldn't give all his time to the balloon. By April 1958 Colin had given up all paid work and was working five days out of seven on the balloon and, as even that wasn't enough to keep up, he gave up everything else from about June. This meant that Rosemary had to support them both, and it soon became apparent that something would have to be done about Colin's loss of earnings for some months.

This was before I had returned and suggested their selling their story to the *Daily Mail*, and no one could see where any money was to come from. They had had help with materials amounting to several thousand pounds, but they had not yet asked anyone for any money.

"I'm afraid there's no money in the kitty," Bushy said. "I'm going to have to borrow from the bank before we leave Tenerife as it is. What we need is a public-spirited millionaire ..." He paused. "Wait a minute — come to think of it I *know* a millionaire *and* he thinks we should be encouraged. All right — I'll ask him."

Bushy had become quite good at begging materials, Terylene, gas cylinders and many other things, but he had not yet begged for money, and if Douglas Collins hadn't been a friend of twenty years' standing he probably wouldn't have plucked up the courage to do it.

When Bushy and I started our small cosmetic firm in 1938 we met Douglas Collins, who was just starting a perfume-manufacturing business and, like us, was doing everything himself. Since then his perfume company, Goya, has become the largest in Britain, while ours, Yeast-pac, has remained one of the smallest, but we have tried hard not to be too envious of Douglas' success.

This is difficult, because he is one of those people to whom things come almost too easily, and he has a disturbing way of tackling something new and doing well at it. He had always been a small-boat sailor and had, in fact, when we first met him, been living aboard a ten-tonner named *Helen*. He had sailed her on several long ocean voyages and had knocked off an excellent book about his cruising almost in his spare time. During the years that he was becoming a rich and powerful business-man he found time to become a Master Mariner, write a dozen children's books, get himself made Chairman of British Lion Films for the Government, qualify in his holidays as a skiing instructor and take Bushy and some other friends as far as Tenerife in a Brixham trawler which the others sailed to the West Indies in 1954.

He was tremendously impressed with the balloon venture, and told me that he thought it was the bravest thing any of his friends had ever attempted. He had early offered to help in any way, but none of his companies manufactured anything that they needed. Now Bushy told him bluntly that he could help them by paying Colin's salary for the two months it would take him to make the craft. Douglas accepted immediately, delighted to be able to help in the first crossing of the Atlantic in a balloon.

Colin got down to a fourteen-hour day and a seven-day week, and whenever any of the others could spare an hour or so they turned up at City Display's workshops and were given a job. Even so, the craft was finished only a few days before the last possible date for its final testing.

To Tim Eiloart too the increasing demands on his time and energy now became critical. He had hoped to get a First both to justify his scholarship and to get a better job when qualified. But to do so would require complete dedication, and he had realised, shortly after agreeing to go on the balloon, that if he was going to contribute anything of value on the flight he would have to give up any ideas of a First. He thought, however, that by sheer hard work he could get his degree and do the necessary radio and meteorological studying to qualify for his membership of the balloon crew.

But the last year of Chemical Engineering is a full-time job, and it became apparent to him by the autumn of 1958 about three months before the scheduled time to leave England that he would have to make a choice between getting a decent degree or going in The Small World. If his withdrawing from the Flight would have affected only himself he would certainly have given it up, but with his meteorological and radio qualifications he had become pretty well indispensable and he hadn't the heart to let them down.

Rather than fail his degree, he tried to have it postponed for a year and to return to Cambridge after it was all over. Unfortunately it was not as easy as that. In the first place, his scholarship was a three-year one from his "employers", the Ministry of Supply. Secondly, the competition for places at Cambridge is desperately fierce, and the authorities would not agree to take him back into residence. If he went to London to work on the balloon he would be sent down and would have to make a formal application for re-entry next year. If the Chemical Engineering Department decided that he didn't deserve a place he would find himself without a degree.

All this was very worrying to Tim, but he decided that there was too much at stake to permit him to do anything else but devote all his time, energies and abilities to the Trans-Atlantic Balloon Flight.

He felt, too, that if he were to put this problem to his father it was very likely that Bushy would decide that he ought to stay at Cambridge and give up the flight. In that case Bushy and the Mudies would almost certainly still go, and if anything went wrong Tim would feel that it was his fault. Therefore, he decided that he wouldn't tell anyone else of his decision.

All this upset him considerably, and was the explanation for his being occasionally in a difficult mood in the last weeks of preparation. We all noticed it and commented on it, but none of us guessed that he had been sent down from Cambridge and that he felt that his future career was in jeopardy.

But he threw himself into the jobs of making sure the wireless would work, finding out as much as possible about the wind systems around the Canary Islands, the physics of ballooning, including the all-important effect of the sun's heat on the envelope, the safety ratio of various speeds of ascent or descent and trying to find out what information there really was about the behaviour of the air over the middle reaches of the Atlantic.

I asked Tim to tell me something about the meteorology.

I never liked the idea of a useless crossing in a balloon [he wrote to me]. I felt sure that we must be able to do something useful. Not quite two months before take-off I explained our project to the President of the Royal Meteorological Society, Professor Sheppard. "What a pity it isn't a met. expedition," was the first thing he said. "Almost any reading you can take would be useful." He arranged for special light-weight meteorological instruments to be prepared for us and prepared an extensive programme of observations.

These instruments were extraordinarily sensitive — for instance, the atmospheric pressure gauge showed the difference when I stood up on a chair and the temperature gauge was ten times as accurate as a clinical thermometer. On the other hand, some of them were extremely simple, like our calibrated rope to give us our exact height above the sea, a child's soap-bubble-making machine to test relative wind speeds and a small hydrogen-filled balloon at the end of three thousand yards of fishing line to test the direction of the wind above us. We planned to test the direction of the wind below us by dropping a roll of toilet paper.

The reason why we could take observations of value was that we would be the first weather station ever that would be stationary in relation to its own wind mass. That is, we would move with it and so be able to measure all the changes that occurred in it. . . . To do this we were to take readings of temperature, pressure and air dampness every thirty seconds for spells of half an hour from time to time as well as regular hourly observations. It promised to keep us pretty busy.

While Tim was at the Imperial College of Science he went

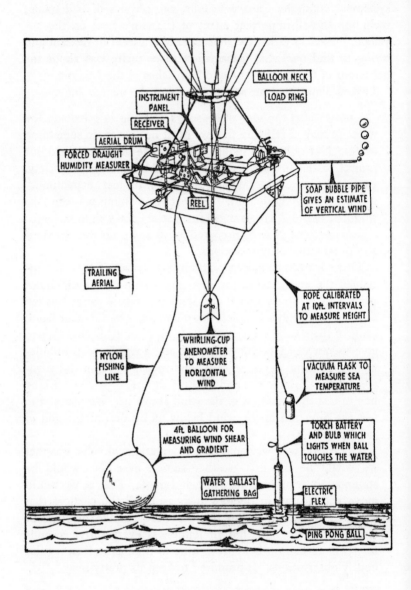

BALLOON NECK

LOAD RING

INSTRUMENT PANEL

RECEIVER

AERIAL DRUM

FORCED DRAUGHT HUMIDITY MEASURER

REEL

SOAP BUBBLE PIPE GIVES AN ESTIMATE OF VERTICAL WIND

TRAILING AERIAL

ROPE CALIBRATED AT 10ft. INTERVALS TO MEASURE HEIGHT

WHIRLING-CUP ANENOMETER TO MEASURE HORIZONTAL WIND

VACUUM FLASK TO MEASURE SEA TEMPERATURE

NYLON FISHING LINE

4ft. BALLOON FOR MEASURING WIND SHEAR AND GRADIENT

TORCH BATTERY AND BULB WHICH LIGHTS WHEN BALL TOUCHES THE WATER

WATER BALLAST GATHERING BAG

ELECTRIC FLEX

PING PONG BALL

pretty thoroughly into the whys and wherefores of the trade wind, which he explained to me like this:

"There is a belt of low pressure around the earth at the equator and if the earth wasn't spinning the air would rush in from either side — that is north and south — to fill it up. But the turning of the earth complicates things a bit.

"Let's take Tenerife. There's a wind mass tending to go towards the equator — that is south — but, remember, it is also moving from west to east because the earth is turning that way and so the air above it is too. But the interesting point is that the air over the equator is moving faster from west to east than the air at, say, twenty degrees north of the equator because it is the outside of a circle of greater radius. Therefore, this wind mass falls *behind* the air it encounters as it goes south and so moves southwest. That is the north-east trade wind — see?"

"Oh yes," I said.

"But the trade-wind belt moves during the year as it follows the sun. Obviously it must always be slightly south of the meridian of latitude the sun is directly above, mustn't it?"

"Certainly," I said.

"Now in December Tenerife is only just on the edge of the trade-wind belt, and half the time the north-east trade won't be blowing there then. But every hundred miles south-west we get away from Tenerife makes it a little more certain that we'll get the true trades.

"The other snag is that it's quite possible for the whole trade-wind system to be upset, and it's difficult to predict this ten days ahead, which is what we'll have to do."

"How do you mean upset?" I asked.

"Well there are things called 'Blocking Situations'. They're a little difficult to explain, but briefly it's when the Azores anti-cyclone that's normal is missing for certain obscure reasons. When that happens there's a zone of high pressure in forty-five to sixty degrees north over Europe and North America. Then, even though the wind might blow us to the west from Tenerife, it would turn abruptly over the Atlantic and start blowing us north, and our particular wind mass might just keep on going north."

"To where?"

"Oh, I don't know — Spitsbergen perhaps, but I expect we'd die of cold and exposure before that."

"Solution — don't take off in a Blocking Situation."

"Don't worry — we won't, but it's almost impossible to predict ten days ahead, which is the least we'll be in the air, so it's a chance we'll have to take. Fortunately Blocking Situations are rare in December and early January."

The instruments which the Imperial College of Science finally handed over to them weighed seventy pounds, and meant a considerable readjustment of ballast, but they were persuaded that they could make valuable observations and were glad of the opportunity to do so.

By October some of the red tape that had first worried Tim began to appear. Bushy had to have his Balloonist's Licence; Tim had to be licensed by the Post Office as a Wireless Operator; The Small World had to have a Certificate of Airworthiness; everything that was to be sent to Tenerife to do with the balloon and the craft had to be on an international Carnet, visas had to be in order, cameras and film had to be cleared with the Customs of both countries, and two or three times a week we found something else that had to be done officially. I went along to the Royal Aero Club to beg their help, and once again found instant willingness.

"You'll make it an official world record attempt, of course," said their Honorary Secretary, Colonel Preston. "We'll do the necessary liaising with the Federation Aeronautique Internationale in Paris and with the Spanish Aero Club — you'll have to take sealed instruments and get your take-off and landing properly witnessed. We'll get you a Carnet to cover the export of the aircraft and its import to any country in which you may land. Now what about a Certificate of Airworthiness? — you must have that, you know." I hadn't known, and Bushy, who had read up the regulations, thought that it didn't apply to The Small World because they weren't making a commercial flight, but it was explained that as it

Eddie Sampson, the *Daily Mail* photographer, taking wind-speed readings during his night watch.

01.07 a.m., Friday, 12th December 1958. The Small World bounces off the sea. The trail rope is already tangled, but was not seen by the crew.

Tim on 'trail watch' the last day aloft. Wet clothes drying.

Aloft and trailing on the last day in the air. Height about fifty feet; speed about twelve knots. The wake is caused by the trailing mast and water-lifting bag. The apparatus in

would be an international flight a Certificate of Airworthiness was essential. Colonel Preston promised to help with that too.

I had first approached Lord Brabazon of Tara when it became obvious that we should need the recognition of some official body to be able to take off from the Canaries. His was just about the only name that any of us knew, and although he had never heard of any of us he consented to see me, and as soon as he realised what it was all about agreed to help. He sent us to the Royal Aero Club, whose help was invaluable, and to the Royal Aeronautical Society with a recommendation that they give us their official blessing, but the Executive Council of that ancient society decided that encouraging the first crossing of the Atlantic in a free balloon was not for them.

Colin then approached the Institute of Navigation and explained their plans. Their Secretary, Mr. Michael Richey, immediately circulated the members of his Executive Council recommending that the Institute support the British Trans-Atlantic Balloon Flight. The Council did so unanimously.

Tim had been encouraged by getting a reply from Prince Philip about borrowing a balloon from the Army in their early days, and had suggested that they ask him to be their Patron. They had done so, and shortly after the Institute of Navigation consented to back them a letter came from Buckingham Palace telling them that the Duke of Edinburgh had granted them his Royal Patronage. It was this letter that Colin and I were able to take to London Airport to welcome Bushy back from Tenerife.

They were, of course, immensely proud of this and of the encouragement from the Institute of Navigation and the Royal Aero Club and the request of the Imperial College of Science for them to take meteorological observations. What had begun as an adventure had developed into something much more. At one time they had thought that if something went wrong with the launching and the balloon never left the ground, which was quite possible, it wouldn't have mattered to anyone but themselves, but now there were so many other people and firms involved that they dreaded an unlucky launching attempt.

"We can't possibly hope to keep this out of the newspapers any longer," Rosemary said on the evening of Bushy's return. "For one thing the Institute of Navigation will want to announce it."

"I'd better go along and ask the *Daily Mail* if they are interested," I said.

I phoned the Deputy Editor the same day and saw him the next morning. I hadn't told him what it was all about but had just said that I thought it was the kind of exciting story they liked. Nevertheless, my assurances had obviously not carried much weight, for Mr. Hardcastle, a large man with shrewd, twinkling eyes who looked at me across an enormous desk, was obviously used to people with 'wonderful and exciting stories' to sell.

"Well what's it all about?" he asked not unkindly.

There was a large map of the world just behind him, and I put my finger on the Canary Islands. "In about a month three men and a girl will ascend in a balloon from a beach on one of these islands and be blown by the trade winds' — I traced my finger slowly across the large area of the Atlantic Ocean and was gratified to see that he was interested — "to somewhere in this area." I indicated the West Indies. "On board they will have a short-wave wireless, and every day they'll send a situation report. When they land they will have an hour-by-hour log of the trip. If they succeed they will have broken the world's record for distance — at present held by Russia; the world's record for duration — at present held by Germany; and put up a new first for Britain — the first crossing of the Atlantic by a free balloon."

Bill Hardcastle, as I eventually got to know, had had a lifetime on Fleet Street and had heard many strange stories, but he recognised this one as quite out of the ordinary. I wouldn't go so far as to say that he was gaping when I finished, but he certainly was shaken a little.

"Would you like to buy their exclusive story?"

"I think you'd better come and have a word with Mr. Wareham," he said, and so I told the story again to Arthur Wareham, the Editor, and a day or two later was able to take a contract back to the others that meant that if they got off and well over the Atlantic they would get back most of the money they had spent. If they succeeded in flying all the way across the Atlantic they might have something to share out. They were as pleased as if they had won a football pool, and as the *Mail* was going to pay something immediately, it meant that there would be enough money available, without borrowing, to see them take off in Tenerife.

A few days later the *Daily Mail* carried the story all over its front page, and their friends and relatives learned about it for the first time. They were asked to appear on Radio and Television, other newspapers and magazines wanted stories and pictures and, as they had foreseen, their private lives came to an end. But as they were by this time working nearly twenty hours out of each day, it didn't make much difference.

Someone asked if there was going to be a film, and although we had always intended for Rosemary to have a camera along, we had not thought of making an actual film. But there had been so much interest in the story that they decided to find out if there was a company who would like to make one, and I was told to see about it. The best film of that kind that I've ever seen was the one about the Everest Expedition, and so I asked who had made it and went to see them.

The two directors of Countryman Films were immediately enthusiastic, and so it was arranged to hire a professional camera crew and start filming at the time of the first test inflation at Cardington and then go to Tenerife and film the take-off. If the flight succeeded they would try to film the arrival, although that, obviously, might be very difficult, as no one would know where the wind would blow them.

With the help of Countryman Films I was very lucky to be able to get an outstanding cameraman-director, Peter Hennessy, who had had years of experience all over the world. He recommended a second cameraman, Ron Bicker, who complemented him perfectly, and the two of them took over the job with a professional competence that was a great relief to us. It was decided that, if possible, Peter Hennessy would come on the boat to

Tenerife to film the voyage and that Ron Bicker would fly to the island ahead of us to film the arrival.

The *Daily Mail* had put one of its best reporters exclusively on the Trans-Atlantic Balloon assignment. This was John Starr, who had specialised in science and whose first reactions on hearing about the attempt was that it was either a crackpot scheme or a smart money-making idea from a couple of sharpsters who never intended to go. He was sent along before the *Mail* decided to buy the story to see just how valid it all was.

He arrived at Bushy's flat, and although he tried to hide his suspicions, they stuck out like tail fins, and up went Bushy's hackles. Bushy is probably the world's worst salesman. At the first sign of what is known as 'consumer resistance' he is apt to send the would-be buyer about his business.

I led the two of them into Bushy's living-room and started to mix drinks as they began to talk.

"Wait a minute," Starr said. "Don't the trade winds blow from west to east?" We found, incidentally, a surprisingly large number of people who thought this was so, and I think the reason is that most people know that aeroplanes flying from New York to London are helped by the west-to-east winds. But this is the jet stream at about twenty thousand feet over the North Atlantic — the same one that Wise was going to try to reach in his Trans-Atlantic attempt. The trade winds, much farther south, are at sea-level and blow approximately from the north-east to the south-west. Anyway, John Starr's mistake was a very common one and easy to understand, but his attitude had antagonised Bushy.

"My God!" he exploded. "Where did you go to school?"

John Starr had been a wartime navigator in the R.A.F., and he exploded right back. I stepped between them like a referee, and asked Bushy to get some tonic water from the refrigerator. He went off like an angry bear.

"Look," I said to John Starr, "I'm supposed to be the Public Relations expert on this scheme — Eiloart is a most unusual man, and he's going to have a shot at flying an unpowered balloon across the Atlantic come hell or high water. That's the only thing he's interested in — he doesn't give a damn about you, or the *Daily Mail*, or money or me for that matter. Now I know you have to find out whether this thing is bona fide or not, but neither he nor Colin Mudie will bother to defend themselves if you think it's not. I'll tell you everything I know about it and they'll answer any questions that don't sound as though you're suspicious."

"I'm not suspicious," John Starr protested. "I just want to find out how the hell they expect to float across the ocean in a balloon — that's reasonable, isn't it?"

"Very reasonable," I assured him. "And I think I can explain most of the plan to you." I got a sudden bright thought. "Eiloart is the Edmund Hillary type — you know, no time for anything but getting on with the job. I should imagine reporters found him difficult too, didn't they?"

"I'll say they did," John Starr chuckled, and told me one or two stories which quite restored his good humour, so that when Bushy came back the rest of the interview went well. We were all to get to know, respect and like Jack very much in the next month, and on Tenerife he worked as hard on the launching as any of us.

One day in October Colin announced quietly that the hull was ready for its sea trials and that he and Rosemary were going to take it down to Lymington and put it through its paces. With the help of the volunteers who had been coming in whenever they could spare an hour or an evening, we got it swung out of City Display on their crane and loaded on a boat trailer behind the Mudies' car.

It took them a long time to drive down, because it was really too wide for the trailer, and they had to drive slowly and gingerly, holding up a long stream of cars. They got to Colin's parents' house about one-thirty the next morning and took the craft down to the Lymington river about lunchtime to launch it properly.

Colin has many friends in Lymington, and he roped them all in to help carry it down on to the 'muddy hard' of the river at low tide and to where the water was just lapping her. Colin's mother had a bottle of champagne for the christening and she swung it at almost the only hard thing on the boat — the aluminium towing shackle. The bottle burst in the proper manner.

"I name this boat The Small World and may God bless her and all who sail . . ." At this point in the ancient and traditional form of christening Mrs. Mudie added — very quietly — ". . . or *fly* in her."

Then the boat was pushed out until she floated, which she did in about three inches of water, and then towed around to the Town Quay past the Yacht Club and many curious eyes. Colin and Rosemary sailed her down river in very light airs, but the lighter the wind the better she sailed relatively speaking because of her extreme lightness, and they had the enormous satisfaction of passing a catamaran, the fastest of all sailing-boats. She was moored for the night, and the next day, to their delight, the wind was blowing force six, which is quite strong. They were able to give her the thorough testing they had hoped for, and she performed remarkably well, sailing close to the wind, stiff and dry. The lee board was tested to breaking point deliberately and repaired, and the following day when the wind had moderated they sailed her up and down the river, beating, tacking and manoeuvring.

Finally, they tried to capsize her, but she was so stiff they couldn't do so. They sat out on one side, but all that happened was that she leaned slightly in that direction: they stood together right up in the bow; the stern lifted quite a long way, but she remained perfectly steady. They tied a line to her mast and with the help of the Harbour Master tried to pull her over, but without success. In the end they had to carry her ashore and turn her over and put her back in the water upside down. Because of her buoyancy boxes, she then rode high and was righted easily. They were well pleased with the four days' trials.

The craft, of course, caused a great deal of comment in Lymington, which is very interested in small boats anyway, and many and weird were the guesses about the use to which it was going to be put.

"I'd think it was a joke if it obviously hadn't cost so much money," one member of the Yacht Club said.

"It's a new type of Corporation dust cart," was someone else's opinion.

Colin and Rosemary brought her back to City Display for the final fitting out, which was expected to take a week or ten days, but which actually took nearly four weeks because of unforeseen difficulties with the radio and electrical installations. But by this time they expected difficulties to pop up suddenly, and if anything had gone without a hitch they would almost have worried.

November's days seemed to be disappearing like suds going down the drain, and it became obvious that the final assembly of all the parts and testing would have to be postponed to the last possible date in order to give us enough time to get everything done. We set ourselves a schedule allowing only the barest hours for eating and sleeping and as often as not cut out meals. This didn't bother Bushy, who never eats much anyway, but it affected all the rest of us, and we would suddenly find ourselves snapping at each other and then realise that our bad tempers were due only to hunger.

Colin and Rosemary practically lived at City Display's workshops, and there always seemed to be one or two volunteer helpers working away concentratedly. Now that it was known what the peculiar craft they were building was going to try to do, it became a focal point of interest in the works. Reporters and others also called to try to get a glimpse of it or an interview with one of the crew.

We still didn't know when the boat was sailing, for Elders and Fyffes had warned us that banana boats, unlike passenger liners, didn't run to strict schedules. Something had been said about 3rd or 4th December, but early in November Bushy decided to try to get a firm date. He also wanted to know how many passages we were getting, for if it was to be only the four members of the crew who went free, he would have to pay for the launching crew to go out and back. He telephoned to Jim Stockley, the young Managing Director of the line whose unhesitating offer to help them in the early days had so encouraged him.

"How many places do you want?" Jim Stockley asked.

"Well . . ." Bushy hesitated. "There's the four of us, of course, but there's also the launching crew . . ."

"Would ten passages be enough?"

"Absolutely marvellous!" Bushy exclaimed. "I don't know what we can do to repay you, though."

"Just pull it off, that's all." Jim Stockley told him "Your boat is the *Reventazon*, sailing from Southampton on 29th November."

Bushy hung up and turned to me. "Ten places, so we can almost all go on the boat," he said elatedly. "But it's three or four days earlier than I thought. God knows how we'll get everything done in time. Anyway, you let the others know the sailing date and I'll get on with laying on the test inflation at Cardington."

The launching crew consisted of Wing-Commander Booth, who would be in command, Jimmy Wildi, a young London business-man friend of Bushy's, who had volunteered to come a year before and had offered to pay his own way back, Gerry Long from Cardington, myself and two girls: Anne Boake, Bushy's twenty-year-old secretary, and Jenny Wybourne, a twenty-one-year-old zoologist and friend of Tim's, who had also volunteered to help. Anne Boake had been engaged as Bushy's secretary only in the last few weeks of the venture, when, as a result of the publicity and the pressure of the last days, his correspondence threatened to over-whelm him. She worked enthusiastically and didn't seem to mind either what jobs she was given or what hours she was asked to work. She also offered to pay her own fare back if she was allowed to be one of the launching crew, and Bushy was very glad to accept. Both the girls had been a little bored with their lives, when they suddenly found themselves in the Trans-Atlantic Balloon attempt, and they were enormously excited about the coming adventure.

The final test was arranged for 24th and 25th November at Cardington, after which everything would be packed up and sent to the docks at Southampton.

This tethered flight was, of course, very important, for it would confirm the amount of the lift, the set of the car, the practicability of the stowage arrangements, give the only opportunity for the wireless to be tested and, most important to my mind, confirm that the car-boat was strong enough to be swung from four points with everything in it. I had seen Colin picking up large slabs of what looked like solidified soap-suds and poking a hole through them with remarkably little effort, and although he assured me that his method of construction made it very strong, I really wouldn't have been terribly surprised to see the sides go up in the air, leaving the four of them sitting on the ground.

Wing-Commander Booth insisted that the balloon be inflated at Cardington for at least a week first so that they could measure its loss of lift through porosity. Only that way could they be sure that they weren't going to lose most of their lift through gas seeping out of the fabric. The balloon had been delivered to Cardington a week or so before, and Colin had gone up to supervise the air inflation.

He had crawled about inside when it was pumped full of air, and had been dismayed to see dozens of tiny holes. Most of the day had been spent in patching them up, and Colin felt reasonably sure that there were few if any left. He had been warned about pinpoint holes but hadn't realised there would be so many. It looked as though the fabric might be brittle and that any hard object pressed against it would make a hole. If this was so it would pose a considerable problem when it was laid out on the beach at Tenerife. Patching material and adhesive were added to the constantly growing list of things that had to be taken along.

Bushy agreed to Wing-Commander Booth's suggestion about a week's test inflation, and I went up to Cardington to try to film it myself, as our professional team had not yet begun.

It was, rather surprisingly, a beautiful clear autumn day, and although I had heard from all of them about the size of the hangars at Cardington, I wasn't really prepared for their immensity. The barrage balloons they now contained looked like child's soap bubbles lost in the dark corners of the enormous sheds.

The Small World was inflated with hydrogen for the first time, and it looked beautiful to us. Fully blown up, it took ninety sand-bags, each weighing forty pounds or so, to hold it down, and it tugged at them as though eager to start. The new Air Registration, G-APOB had been painted on and the name, THE SMALL WORLD. Colin and Rosemary looked at it affectionately — it had been almost their whole world for nearly two years, and here at last it was, tangible evidence that soon they really would be drifting across the Atlantic Ocean.

Two or three sandbags were taken off, and it was then light enough for us to pick it up and walk it. We carried it across the hangar and hitched it on to what looked like an oversize version of a housewife's kitchen scales.

"It doesn't matter what the lift is now for our purposes," said Wing-Commander Booth. "It is obviously the weight of the sandbags we took off, but we shall measure every morning after the gas has been cooled all night and before the sun warms it up, and we'll see what she loses."

Jimmy Wildi had been there for the test inflation in order to practise the sandbag-lifting routine, for he had not been able to go to Halstead when we all had our only other inflation. Now he was running with sweat. "I hope it's not too hot in Tenerife," he said and then grinned. "On second thoughts I don't mind how hot it is — just imagine a sunny beach in December!" We all looked forward more and more to the sea voyage and the sunshine of the Canary Islands during those last hectic November days of fog and rain.

The fog upset our filming plans, coming down as soon as the camera crew were engaged, the film bought, the cameras hired and everything made ready, and most of the final tests couldn't be filmed, after all. Rosemary had been practising with a film camera and had got some very good pictures whenever the light permitted, but England in November is not the best time for outdoor filming in colour. I had scrambled all over the hangars and shot fifty feet of film of the balloon inflation, but when it was developed it was obvious that we had been very wise to get professionals.

Meanwhile, most things were tested on the craft in London. The pedalling apparatus was given a long, hard work-out, and they discovered just how much work it took to turn the two propellers fast enough. It would obviously be practicable only for short periods. The electricity generator was coupled on to the pedals, and they were pleased that they would not have much difficulty in generating enough electricity for their wireless transmitter and receiver, plus an emergency supply for a powerful spotlight. This, Colin assured an enquiring reporter, was for picking out a clearing in the Brazilian jungle at night.

Tim assembled his hydrogen generator and produced some tins of calcium hydride.

"Who wants to see hydrogen made?" he asked. He was shooed outside to the concrete loading yard just in case something went wrong. It was one of the weirdest looking pieces of equipment they carried, and consisted of a metal box shaped like an inverted petrol filler with large corrugated rubber pipes leading off in every direction. One of these led around the double boiler saucepan, which, for effect, Tim filled with water, watched by some of City Display's staff.

He opened a small door in the bottom of his contraption and popped in an opened tin of calcium hydride. The door was then clamped shut and the whole thing propped against the wall. He surveyed the apparatus thoughtfully, and then almost as an afterthought added four tablespoons of cocoa to the saucepan.

Satisfied that everything was joined up correctly, he got a gallon tin of water and started dripping it slowly in the top down on to the calcium hydride. He had been warned that the action of calcium hydride and water was very violent, and he warned the onlookers to stand back. The water went on dripping for some time, but nothing happened. Tim looked puzzled.

"Perhaps it's one of the old models," Colin said unkindly.

"I don't think there's enough water to get the reaction going," Tim said. "Well — here goes!" He poured the rest of the water down the spout. Immediately there was a bubbling, hissing noise and some of the bolder spirits who had come forward moved smartly back again. The instrument gurgled, steam came out of one pipe and the four-foot meteorological balloon began to inflate. Tim looked pleased with himself.

Later he measured the amount of lift he had produced and was delighted to find that his theory was vindicated, for a pound of the chemical had produced a pound of lift. He announced that he could produce twenty-four pounds of extra lift an hour for as long as the calcium hydride lasted.

The cocoa was not exactly piping hot, but as it was perhaps the first ever made by this method, they drank it respectfully.

They got regular reports from Wing-Commander Booth at Cardington, and at the end of ten days knew that the balloon had only lost about thirty-five pounds of lift. Since they expected to take about seven hundred pounds of calcium hydride, loss of lift through porosity shouldn't bother them.

"Time enough to drift around the world," Colin said.

Whenever it was possible and practicable Bushy and Colin tested everything, leaving nothing to chance if it was avoidable. But they knew that there was no way to test most of their theories about controlling the height of the balloon until they were actually floating free over the ocean. If their water-lifting bags or propellers didn't work they'd have to ditch; if Colin's hull wasn't strong enough, ditching could be a disaster. The Small World would be proved over the Atlantic on its actual crossing attempt, but this was unavoidable, and they accepted it.

One thing that was agreed, though, was to get the ditching drill taped before they took off, and a meeting was called to discuss it.

"The first thing is to decide now under what conditions we're going to ditch," Bushy said.

"If we're blown the wrong way just after launching," Colin said, "so that we start going to Africa — well, I suppose when we see the shore we'd better come down. I don't fancy landing a hundred miles or so inside the Sahara."

"All right," Bushy agreed. "And then on the other side if we see that we're going to miss an island we'd better be prepared to come down and sail in — or if we hit the coast of South America."

"I can hardly believe it but all the balloonists say we'd have to come down before an electrical storm hit us, I'm afraid," Tim said. "Even a non-electrical storm could have so much inner turbulence that we'd have to come down or be broken up. It's conditions like that that I don't think we've thought about enough — I'm satisfied that we can come down nice and gently if the weather is fine and we've plenty of gas and it's broad daylight, but what about in a storm without much gas and at night?"

"That's being a bit pessimistic, isn't it?" Bushy asked. "All those conditions at once? Anyway, I suppose you're right and we have to be prepared to ditch in a storm with a rough sea. Now let's decide on the drill."

After some discussion on that night and at other times it was decided that the decision to cut the balloon loose would be entirely Bushy's responsibility, but taken if possible, after consultation with the others.

"Since the met. is going to be your pigeon," Bushy told Tim, "I shall have to be guided by you about whether it is too dangerous to stay aloft."

Tim didn't like this, but he had to accept it, for it was a responsibility he had taken on when he had agreed to be the meteorologist.

"We obviously get rid of all unnecessary weight first, because the lighter we are, the less cluttered up, when we hit the sea, the better. So we discard everything we won't need at sea. Then, to avoid this making us rise, we'll have to open the release valve enough to bring us down. Ideally we should come down slowly to a point just above the waves and then, just as the hull touches the water, pull the rip panel and the quick release at the same time, so that the balloon gets blown clear of us."

"The spar and our bags of emergency food will have gone into the sea before us," Colin said, making a sketch. "And they'll slow up our forward movement and keep us stern to wind and therefore into the waves instead of along them, which would be disastrous."

"Then we'll throw over our sea-anchors," Bushy added. "The first on a long stretch of line, the next shorter and the last only twenty feet away — no, we'll chuck those over *before* the hull is in the water to slow us up still more. Then when we're down we'll ride out the worst of the storm. When conditions permit it we'll get the mast and sail up, put in the rudder and leeboards and sail on."

"Supposing she capsizes?" Tim asked.

"We should all be lashed to the craft somehow," Colin said. "So that we don't get mislaid."

"Supposing it breaks in two or three pieces?" I asked.

"It has so much positive buoyancy," Colin said confidently, "that any large-sized chunk of it would support all four of us. Of course," he added almost as an afterthought, "it would be jolly uncomfortable."

It had been decided right at the beginning that if they were forced down command would pass to Colin, for he had had much more deep-water sailing experience. They were confident, though, that they were not going to ditch but continue all the way across by air.

"If you are forced down you should be able to fish, so don't forget fish-hooks," I suggested, "and lines, gaff hook and a net."

Bushy is a vegetarian, but the other three are not. Nevertheless, they turned down my suggestion.

"I don't really *like* fishing," Colin explained. "I hate seeing a fish with a hook in its mouth."

"I wonder how you'll all feel when you run out of food," I said gloomily.

"It's already been agreed that we eat Bushy first," Colin said. "As he's a vegetarian he couldn't eat any of us, so obviously he's the first one for the pot." He smacked his lips. "Just a pinch more salt in the Bushy stew."

On Tuesday, 25th November, everything came together for the first time: balloon, apparatus, the craft, the balloonists and the launching crew. Jack Starr from the *Daily Mail*, who was going to be with us right up to take-off, and a photographer were there. Most of the other newspapers and news services had also sent representatives. Cardington, being government property, could not allow only one newspaper to be represented.

As well as the Press two television companies had sent camera crews; B.B.C. sound radio were there; most of the companies who

had contributed materials had representatives there, and one of
them, I.C.I., had their own film unit. The newsreel cameras were
also there, and lastly our own camera team photographing not
only the trial ascent but all the activity too.

Until then the hangars at Cardington had seemed great empty
places, the crew had become friendly with the regular staff and
everything had been done quickly and quietly, but now, with
flash bulbs popping off and microphones being shoved in front of
them, there was an effect of frenzied preparation as though they
were to take off that afternoon.

In one corner, Tim, helped by volunteers from the Radio
Society of Great Britain, was trying to tune in the short-wave
transmitter, but the electric motors of the cameras caused static,
and as soon as he managed to stop one another one started.

"It's no use," he said to his helpers. "We'll just have to do
it aloft — which one of you wants to come up with us?"

Not surprisingly, neither of them did. After all, they had
probably never seen a passenger-carrying balloon before that
morning, and they don't look exactly safe. But it meant that Tim
had to try to get the set working himself in the air after changes
had been made to it by someone else — it was a considerable
handicap.

We carried all the necessary bits and pieces of equipment over
to the craft, fitted the hydrogen generator and made sure that the
pedals worked. We tried to think of everything, but we forgot the
shade flap that fitted round the balloon looking like a ballet
dancer's skirt. Except for this, the balloon was exactly as it would
be on take off.

The Small World looked very small indeed in the huge hangar,
but when we walked it outside it seemed to take on stature. A
rope from one of the special lorries was attached to the bottom
of the hull, sandbags were taken off until it began to rise and then
put back again to hold it. The four of them were inside wearing
their brand-new, bright-blue nylon suits. They could feel the
balloon tugging, and they wanted to get off.

The cameras were grinding away, and the B.B.C.'s interviewer,

Geoffrey Johnson-Smith, was trying to get a last-minute recorded interview, but there was so much noise it was practically impossible. Wing-Commander Booth and Gerry Long were in charge of the ascent, and L. A. Speed, who had helped so much from the earliest days, was there for the Air Ministry. There were several hundred other people and dozens of cameras, all photographing everything that anyone did. Peter Hennessy and Ron Bicker were there for our own film company, which Bushy had named Trade Wind Films, shooting not only the ascent but also the newsreel, and T.V. cameras filming us.

The rope from one of the Air Ministry's special lorries was attached to the bottom of the hull, and we took off sandbags until the craft began to rise, and then, on Wing-Commander Booth's orders, we put some back until the whole structure of balloon, net, load ring and car could be lifted easily.

"Ready?"

Bushy looked at the others, and they nodded. "Ready," he said.

"Two sandbags off each side and hold her down," Wing-Commander Booth ordered. I could feel her pressing gently against my hands.

"Hands off."

Slowly The Small World rose into the air for the first time, going up steadily and almost completely vertically until, at about three hundred feet, it was brought to a stop by the rope. Then it swayed slightly, but all they felt was a slight tug like a lift stopping. The cameras stopped grinding below, and after staring at the bottom of the hull overhead for a few moments the crowd drifted over to a mobile canteen.

Inside the car the four balloonists looked at each other. If it was not the end of the journey it was certainly the end of a long, hard approach road. They could hear the voices of the crowd below them; above them the balloon looked immense, very new and ready to fly.

"I wish they'd cut the damn rope and let us go," Colin said. But they had to get on with their testing. Tim tried very hard to get into touch with a radio amateur at Bishop's Stortford, only a few miles away, who was expecting his call, but he was unable to do so. The last few days before the Cardington test had seen Tim working day and night, helped by two members of the Radio Society of Great Britain, in an attempt to get the radio working well, but it had given them a lot of trouble. It was the latest in the series of mishaps that seemed an inevitable part of their adventure. As a result of this disappointing performance and because he decided that he needed more actual experience of using a short-wave set to talk with other sets at a distance, Tim volunteered to give up the sea voyage to Tenerife and put in an extra week concentrating on the radio. He would fly out to Tenerife to get there two or three days after the others, bringing, he hoped, a wireless set that would work.

It was difficult to tell just how much lift the propellers gave while the balloon was held by the rope, but they did satisfy themselves that they could work them in the air as well as charge the batteries. The winch was also tried and a water-lifting bag lowered over the side.

They went up several times, giving rides to many of the people who had helped them and taking up the B.B.C.'s Television interviewer, Geoffrey Johnson-Smith, who then and there decided to go to Tenerife as well.

They worked most of that night packing everything up, and the next day Colin accompanied the lorries to Southampton to make sure that nothing got lost. Three days later we all met on board the five-thousand-ton *Reventazon*.

CHAPTER SEVEN

Right up for'ard on both sides of the boat deck the six hundred and ninety hydrogen cylinders were lashed; also on the open deck were the boxes of calcium hydride; below in the empty holds were the craft, in the huge crate made by City Display, the various boxes and bags with the rest of the equipment, the food supplies, the tools, instruments and many other things.

In all it weighed forty-five tons, and the *Reventazon* was to make a special stop at Tenerife to unload it. At the other end we hoped that Wilfred Moore would be waiting with a fleet of lorries.

There were eleven passengers, ten of whom were The Small World party. The eleventh was a school teacher returning to the Cameroons, who was very interested in the balloon attempt and joined in all our activities.

The Chief Steward, an ex-R.N. petty officer, had invented a Small World cocktail to welcome us and the visiting Press aboard. When we were all mellow he promised us sunshine in two days. Three days later we were still being rolled about by twenty-foot seas and slowed down by a force-eight wind, but fortunately we all turned out to be good sailors and the *Reventazon* was a happy ship; her officers and crew could not have been more friendly.

Colin was afraid that his navigation might have become a bit rusty. He took sights every day and worked out our position. He was happy to report that the ship's navigating officer was right every time.

There had been some talk, beforehand, of exercises on board and a strict programme of work, but the balloonists were so exhausted that they spent most of the six days resting and recuperating. Wing-Commander Booth did rig up an arrangement of ropes to teach us how, at the last stage of the inflation, we should

lower bunches of sandbags by using a slip knot, and we all practised it faithfully. A day or so was spent sewing a complicated
series of coloured threads into the three-thousand-foot-long
Terylene cord to be used for hauling up the water ballast. These
were to be a code telling them immediately how much line had
been paid out and therefore how high they were, for, as they
wouldn't know the atmospheric pressure at sea-level, their altimeter wouldn't be accurate.

A daily conference was held at which any ideas or suggestions
were discussed and a detailed plan of action for Médano Beach was
worked out.

It had always been known that the inflation would be a fairly
complicated business, since they couldn't just go to the spot, blow
up the balloon and take off, because they would have to wait for
just the right wind conditions. But they had known that they
would have time on the ship, and there had been so many other
things to do that they had left the inflation plan to the end. Now,
when they got down to it, they found that, like so many other jobs,
it was a great deal more complicated than it had appeared.

The transporting of all the equipment to the spot had been
arranged with Wilfred Moore, but Bushy hadn't yet heard what
arrangements had been made to house and feed us all. There
were many other problems, such as the question of guarding the
equipment, gas cylinders and supplies. It might be two or three
weeks before we were able to launch them, which meant a good
deal of planning.

Now a lay-out was planned on paper, assuming a flat beach of
the minimum size. Positions were chosen for a main tent, the
supply of hydrogen cylinders, the craft and an area to lay out the
balloon when inflation was to begin.

John Starr, of the *Daily Mail*, was already at Tenerife finding
local radio amateurs who would act as listening posts when the
balloon had taken off. He had asked me to cable him daily with
news of what we were doing, and to one cable we added some
instructions which were to keep him very busy. He was asked to
approach the authorities and try to borrow a hundred soldiers for

guard duties, a tent or tents, arrange for ample lighting on the site and a few other little things such as official arm bands for people allowed within the barrier, no smoking signs, etc.

One of the most important jobs completed aboard the *Reventazon* was the final designing and, unexpectedly, the manufacture of the triggers for the quick release. This was one of those things that had early been thought of, designed and made and then found to be faulty. The first ones which had been guaranteed to have a breaking point far above anything they would ever need had been tested at the National Physical Laboratory and had snapped at about a quarter of the weight they were expected to support.

As new ones had then to be made, Bushy tried to improve on the design, for he had been impressed, by Gerry Long's stories, with the importance of being able to get rid of the balloon in a hurry if necessary. However, Colin and he had not been able to agree on how the trigger was to be operated and they went aboard the *Reventazon* with the problem still unsolved.

The Chief Engineer was interested in The Small World and had offered to help in any way he could. He was shown the problem, and as a result of discussion among Bushy, Colin and him a final design was agreed and the four most important pieces of equipment made in his workshop.

On the fourth day the waves were twenty feet from crest to trough, and the wind, blowing very strongly from the north-west, was whipping the tops of them off and blowing a solid sheet of spray from one wave to the next. I pictured, in my mind's eye, the fragile boat of The Small World coming down in conditions like that and I shuddered. I turned to Bushy standing next to me.

"How would you like a wind like this in the balloon?"

"I was just thinking the same thing that you were," he said gleefully. "A wind like this would carry us straight to New York in about four or five days. Wouldn't that be something!"

I agreed that it would, indeed. The First Officer joined us and told us that a hundred or so miles to the north-west the wind was force ten, which is hurricane strength, and that it was possible that we might run into it. In fact, the storm blew itself out during the night.

A day or two before Tenerife the promised sun came out and dried the decks, and we all lay on the hatches and sopped it up. But Bushy was now fully rested and probably felt that we had been having things a bit too slack, and so put us all twice through a dummy run of our duties during inflation. Jimmy Wildi and I were to be on the hydrogen cylinders, and Ralph Booth (he had told Jimmy quietly one day that we were to stop calling him 'Sir' or 'Commander' and from then on he was Ralph to all of us) showed us how to attach the ten-way valves, which looked like oversize milking machines, to the taps on the cylinders. He warned us about bashing reluctant ones with spanners, which might cause a spark and an explosion. Jenny and Anne were shown how to search the balloon fabric for pinhole leaks as it went up and also how to inspect every knot of the net to detect the faulty ones that might run under strain. The actual laying out of the balloon, putting in of the gas valve, its line and the one to the ripping panel, would be done by Bushy, Ralph and Gerry Long. At the end of these practice sessions we felt sure that, given time, we could get the balloon inflated properly.

Peter Hennessy had been filming all this activity in colour and, as we were due in in the morning, intended to get the approach to Tenerife, while the reception there was covered by Ron Bicker. But bad luck seemed to dog our efforts to make a film, for just as there had been days of thick fog during the final testing in England, so now the gales and rough seas had so slowed us down that we didn't get into Santa Cruz until after dark.

Tenerife is really the top of a mountain, the last twelve thousand feet of which rise abruptly out of the sea. As we approached, a series of headlands jutted out in front of us like a staircase laid on its side. In the dusk the nearest was a silver grey, the next a slightly darker shade, until the last, which was jet black against a dark-blue sky. Between the headlands we could see white spray against the rocks and the lights of cottages. It was a dramatic entrance to a strange adventure and, as voyagers have always done, we lined the rails and peered at the land ahead.

The sheer black rock of the island was majestic and, to me at least, a little frightening. It seemed to epitomise the enormous size and strength of the forces The Small World was going to challenge.

Jenny and Anne were standing next to me exclaiming at the beauty of it all; I saw Rosemary and Colin up in the bow watching silently. I made my way to them and, as we rounded the last headland and the lights of Santa Cruz suddenly appeared, I saw their faces looking forward eagerly.

"Childe Roland to the dark tower came," I said.

Colin turned. "What did you say?"

"A penny for your thoughts," I replied. "If I'm going to write a book about all this I ought to know what you're thinking about at this historic moment."

"I was just thinking how little the chaps on enormous boats like this have to do with the sea," Colin said. "Even at the height of the storm it was rather like watching it on the pictures. . . ."

"Except that the cinema doesn't stand up on end," I said.

"There is that, of course, but I mean we're so far away from everything. In a small boat in a sea like we've just come through you'd jolly well know it."

"I *did* know it."

"Oh, you know what I mean . . . take coming into Santa Cruz like this — it's fine, of course, but I remember when Pat and I made Las Palmas in *Sopranino* — that was absolutely magnificent!"

"How about you, Rosemary, what were you thinking about?"

"What a shame it is that it's night-time and I can't film all this," she laughed. "Sorry, Peter, no great thoughts for you."

I found Bushy inside talking with the Chief Steward, but there was no need to ask him his thoughts, for he was arranging the details of the formal dinner that the Captain had laid on for the officials of Tenerife. He was worried, for he has never had much time for social formalities, but I persuaded him to leave it all in the capable hands of the Chief Steward and come up on deck.

As soon as the gangplank was down an excited crowd surged aboard, camera flash bulbs popped off and the three balloonists were soon being passed around the crowd, having their hands shaken enthusiastically and, in Rosemary's case, being kissed soundly. It was difficult to sort the officials out, but everyone was so obviously overjoyed that protocol went by the board.

The drinks which had been laid out disappeared in a few moments, and the dinner guests flowed down to the little dining-saloon of the ship.

The dinner, over which the steward's department had worked so hard, was very good and there was plenty of wine and champagne to help. By the time the coffee and brandy came everyone was feeling almost embarrassingly fond of everyone else.

The way we were handled by the Customs and Immigration authorities was an illustration of how easy things can be when officialdom is wholeheartedly on your side. The Spanish Immigration authorities, who, I have heard, sometimes take rather a long time, found me and asked almost apologetically if I would collect all the passports. I did so and received them back in about fifteen minutes with all the proper stamps. Spanish Customs can also be very thorough, but in this case, immediately after dinner, we left the ship, climbed into a fleet of waiting taxis, which carried the ten of us and a hundred pieces of baggage straight into town. The leading taxi slowed down at the Customs gate and the driver shouted, "El Globo!" importantly. The officials saluted and smilingly waved the convoy on, and that was our Customs inspection.

We had hoped that we would have some help from the authorities in Tenerife, but it had never occurred to us that almost every person would be eager to do anything we wanted. The guards were already at the beach, the Mayor of Médano had made the long drive over twisting roads to greet us on board and had started back immediately to see that everything went right his end. Almost the first person to greet us was the President of the Aero Club of

Tenerife, who announced that they would lay on a daily passenger service from Santa Cruz to Médano Beach. Bushy thanked him and made a tentative offer at least to pay for the petrol, but this was brushed aside immediately. The Aero Club would be proud to do anything to help the Trans-Atlantic Balloon Flight.

It was to make things very much easier, and Bushy, Colin and Ralph took off at eight o'clock in the morning of Friday, 5th December from the seventeen-hundred-foot-high aerodrome at Santa Cruz, which is often, at this time of year, blanketed by low cloud. The President of the Aero Club flew them down the coast to Médano on the extreme south-east tip of the island in about twenty minutes, putting his plane down on a small landing-strip that had been prepared.

Behind them, as they looked over the sea towards the island of Las Palmas, was the mountain peak of Teide, now covered with snow and looking like post-cards of Fujiyama. To their left was the little fishing port of Médano, with its rectangular, clean white houses shining in the sun; to their right there was a dark, cone-shaped hill about three hundred feet high right at the water's edge. It was obvious that they must start from the other side of that and they got into a waiting jeep. In a few minutes they passed through fields of tomatoes and came down to a large, flat beach of black volcanic sand, south-west of which lay three thousand miles of the Atlantic. There was a gentle breeze, and it looked like the perfect place to launch The Small World.

They walked across the sand towards the water and selected a flat spot about a hundred yards square and drove a white stake into the centre. On the way back towards the village they stopped at the top of the hill. The little white stake was the first sign of the activity that was soon to take place on this lonely beach, where probably never before had there been as many as a dozen people at once.

The eight lorries, with all the materials from the *Reventazon*, had driven through the night and were waiting in the village for instructions. The Mayor had come back with them and had had no sleep, but was now waiting to instruct the police, the guards and the local workers who were going to unload the supplies and help with the work.

The lorries were already moving off towards the selected spot as Bushy and Colin flew back, and when Jimmy Wildi arrived a few hours later on the next aeroplane the hydrogen cylinders were already stacked five high in a long line, the large crate with the craft in it put down carefully on top of the white stake and all the rest of the gear was moving slowly over the lava.

There was one hotel in the little village, but it wasn't quite large enough for all of us. A local tomato grower, whose father had come from England, married a Tenerife girl and stayed there, offered us his house as well.

By noon the next day we had all arrived except Mrs. Booth, who, having come for a holiday, decided to stay in Santa Cruz. The Aero Club had flown Ralph and the three girls down; Peter Hennessy, Ron Bicker and I had hired a taxi and loaded the cameras and equipment in it and driven along a road which twists and turns so much it nearly doubles the actual distance.

Gerry Long had arrived by air, and Bushy had brought him in a small van with the rest of the equipment; Tim was expected the next day: so far everything seemed to be going according to plan.

When our taxi arrived at the Fonda Israel, Médano's only hotel, we found that all the rooms had been taken and that we had been relegated to the house. We felt a little hard done by until we arrived at the Casa Davidson and found that it was not only in a most beautiful position on a cliff about sixty feet above the beach but was also a very comfortable and charming house. Mr. Davidson's sister had come from Santa Cruz with her maid and opened it for us.

"This will do very nicely," said Peter Hennessy. "Very nicely indeed."

"We mustn't let the others find out how good it is," I said. "Or we'll lose it."

Peter Hennessy had made one round trip on the second aeroplane in order to film the site before all the gear had been delivered.

Now he took Ron and me along the beach and over the cone-shaped hill to see it.

My first impression was of its unusual beauty. The beach is held between low hills which move slowly up into the mountains and lead the eye to the beautiful white peak of Teide twelve thousand feet above. All around are fields of tomatoes, green against the dark hills; the sea is unbelievably blue, and the sun glints on the crystals in the black sand. No wonder Colin had replied, when I asked him what it was like, in one word, 'heaven!'

We walked towards the site. The hydrogen cylinders made a long wall, four feet high, and beyond them the packing-cases seemed to be strewn about the beach as though from a shipwreck. The Guardia Civil, who had been on watch through the night, had made a lean-to shelter out of the big packing-case — it looked very much like a shipwrecked sailor's snuggery.

The rest of them arrived shortly afterwards, and by the end of the day the higgledy-piggledy mess had been sorted out, the craft was rigged and the most important instruction of the Air Inspection Board had been carried out — the NO SMOKING sign, without which their Certificate of Airworthiness was not valid, had been carefully lettered by Colin.

The wind, I had immediately noticed, was blowing steadily from exactly the wrong direction — off the sea and towards the peak of Teide. I remarked on this brightly to Bushy and had my head bitten off.

"I can see that." He glared at me as though I had moved the wind around when he wasn't looking. "As a matter of fact, Colin and I are very *glad* that it's blowing the wrong way." I looked puzzled. "Because we can't go anyway for at least three days, and if it was blowing the right way it would be heart-breaking." I never commented on the wind's direction again.

The next day local helpers made a tower out of pieces of Dexion, and Bushy hoisted to its peak our Terylene wind sock. The wind was still blowing from exactly the wrong place, and the sock pointed unerringly to the mountain. We filmed it blowing the wrong way, so that later, just before take off, we'd be able to show it coming round dramatically like the wind vane in Shaw's *St. Joan*.

Bushy had arranged for the hotel to send food down to the site so that no time would be lost, and we had a picnic lunch made palatable by plenty of the very good local wine.

As it was Sunday we had the first of the crowds who were to collect every day thereafter. There was no fence to keep them away, and I was a bit worried, but I needn't have been, for the Guardia Civil had erected a circle of posts at about twenty-foot intervals around the camp and indicated that this was the barrier. It was evidently all that was necessary, for the crowd always stayed obediently behind the invisible line.

We worked steadily and hard, knowing that if, suddenly, the wind direction and speed was right we'd have to get them away with the least possible delay, for the combination of favourable circumstances could happen only rarely.

This was, in fact, one of Bushy's deepest worries, for he had begun to suspect that a not-too-strong off-shore breeze combined with the correct wind system fifty or so miles away was so rare that it was possible for it not to occur at all during December, and a postponement until January would be most unwelcome. He had nightmares about their staying on until all their money ran out and then having to return ignominiously to England. At one time such a prospect would have been disheartening but not disastrous, but by now there were thousands of pounds of contributions represented by the material on Médano Beach; the *Daily Mail* had spent a lot of money and had their reporter and a cameraman at Médano and even a portable wireless photo transmitter set up in Santa Cruz. There were representatives of other newspapers there, and the B.B.C. had flown the 'Tonight' team out as well. The authorities in Tenerife had spent time and money on them; the Royal Aero Club had taken a great deal of trouble to get the attempt officially recognised and lastly, but certainly one of the most serious considerations, was the patronage of the Duke of Edinburgh. If they made a good try but failed it would be unfortunate; if they never got off — no matter how good the reason — the whole affair would seem a farce. And yet, if the wind didn't blow from the right quarter, they couldn't take off.

Colin, Bushy and Ralph Booth had agreed on the right conditions at Médano. One of the most important things, Ralph explained, was the speed of the wind.

"It shouldn't be stronger than eight knots gusting to ten," he told us. "For when she's nearly inflated the pull will be tremendous against the guy ropes, and if the wind is much stronger she could do herself damage or even tear herself to pieces. Once away when she's no longer held, then, of course, it doesn't matter how strong the wind is, but for that critical half-hour or so when she's nearly inflated we can't risk a strong wind."

"We've got enough hydrogen for two and a half inflations," Bushy said. "As soon as the wind is right we'll start inflating and try to get off as quickly as possible. If the wind does get too strong we'll just have to let the gas go and try again."

"About wind direction," Colin said, pointing to a chart of the Canaries. "Over here to the south-west is the island of Hierro with a five-thousand-foot peak. It's only forty miles away, so we don't dare take off if the wind is from the north-east. We can't take off if it is from any farther west than due north, for that will eventually take us to the African coast, so it looks as though it must be from somewhere between due north and north-north-east."

"So we've got to have a wind coming from one-sixteenth of the compass no stronger than eight knots," Bushy said. "And at the same time the wind over the ocean, which is completely independent of our local one, must also be a north-easterly."

"How will you know about the wind over the ocean?" I asked.

"The head of the Spanish Meteorological Bureau here is going to keep us informed," Bushy said. "Then the Commandant of the Air Force gets reports too, and he has promised to let us know. But all that is Tim's pigeon, and as soon as he arrives I'm going to have him get together with them. Meanwhile, let's get on with things in case the wind comes round." He glanced towards the wind sock, which was still pointing at the mountain behind us.

In the afternoon a small plane appeared and landed, not on the landing-strip, but right next to the site. Several pretty girls came out first, followed by the tall, thin figure of Tim in a long black overcoat. Bushy had told him not to worry about bringing any clothes, as he would take them on the *Reventazon*, and Tim had therefore come dressed as he was in London. The temperature was in the seventies; we were all in shorts or bathing-suits, and poor Tim, with a beautiful girl clutching each arm, looked uncomfortably warm.

"Here comes my city slicker son," Bushy said.

Tim shed his overcoat, jacket and the señoritas and asked for his shorts. Bushy looked dismayed. "I forgot them," he confessed.

Then one of the incredibly generous Tenerifians flew back to Santa Cruz, got a shop opened and brought some back. It was typical of how eager they all were to help even in the smallest things.

Tim had brought the wireless and two thirty-five-millimetre cameras for Rosemary and a number of other items of equipment, and had had the same easy time with the Spanish Customs. Also accompanying Tim was an expert on short-wave wireless who had been sent by the *Daily Mail* to help with the final testing and installation of the set on the craft. He, Tim and three radio amateurs from Santa Cruz got to work on the set immediately.

We inflated a four-foot meteorological balloon with hydrogen and used it to carry the aerial aloft so that it would be in the same position as when the balloon was flying. Then they tried to get into contact with another amateur in Santa Cruz.

By Sunday evening almost everything essential had been done. Just about dusk the off-sea breeze dropped, and a half an hour or so later the wind started to blow very feebly from exactly the right direction.

"If everything goes right we might get off tomorrow," Bushy said excitedly.

But by nightfall they still had not been able to get the radio working. An emergency conference was held, and it was decided to send it back to Santa Cruz, where they could find out what was wrong.

As there was a possibility of a take-off the next day, we stayed on, working in the dark getting everything ready, and by the time we got back to the hotel for our evening meal everyone was very tired.

Médano had been slowly filling up, for the next day was a national holiday, and many of the islanders were expected to come and have a look at El Pequeño Mundo. The Mayor had had signs erected pointing to the site, and some enterprising peddlars were busy setting up stands to sell drinks and sweets.

A few feet outside our ring of stakes a tent had been pitched by four young Finns, members of an under-water marine biological expedition spending a few months in the island gathering specimens and making an under-water film. They were gay and friendly, and had invited us all to a party at the village's only bar, but as it shut at seven o'clock their plans had to be quickly changed. I don't know how it was done, but we finished up in someone's house dancing to the music of an accordion and a guitar. Our fatigue somehow had mysteriously disappeared.

At dawn the next day I hurried out to see what the wind was doing. It had swung round again, and was once more blowing off the sea.

"Never mind," Bushy said later. "We're not really ready anyway, and we've seen that it *can* change. If we put in a full day today we'll be ready to go at short notice from tomorrow."

The Meteorological Officer arrived later in the day and told us that just beyond the island the wind was blowing steadily from the north-north-east, and that he was sure that the local wind on our beach was only at ground level. He thought that at about five hundred feet up the wind was blowing from the north-north-east.

"We'll soon see," said Tim and inflated and sent up one of the expeditions met. balloons. It went off at about forty-five degrees back towards Santa Cruz north of us until it disappeared. Tim and the Met. Officer then went off in one of the aeroplanes of the Aero Club with a number of balloons, which they released at various altitudes and places, they also dropped dye-markers in the sea, but everywhere within a few miles of our beach the wind was in the wrong direction.

Meanwhile, it was thought that the most important job was to test the new quick-release pieces made on board the *Reventazon*. A gallows was erected and the load ring suspended from it just as it would be from the balloon. The ropes leading to the craft, by way of the quick release, were weighted down and the quick release pulled. It worked perfectly every time.

Tim, impatiently waiting for the radio to come back from Santa Cruz, got out all his meteorological instruments and installed them in the craft. Rosemary got her cameras rigged up, including the beautiful Vinten movie camera with the three lenses powered from the batteries. This was fixed to the load ring and would be able with the electric motor to take pictures of all four of them through its wide-angle lens.

The radio experts phoned from Santa Cruz to say that the radio was still not right, but that they would work on it all night and bring it back the following day, Tuesday.

"As long as the wind is in this quarter it isn't urgent," Bushy said. "But if the wind comes round we'll go, even without the wireless."

All day people had been arriving from all over the island, some coming on foot, some by bicycle and some in cars. There had never been a road to our beach, but the Mayor of Médano had had a rough one made in a few days by filling in gullies with stones and removing the largest rocks. By mid-afternoon on Monday many cars had found their way there, filled with families who had brought their own food and drink and were determined to wait for the take-off, which, it had been widely rumoured, was to be that afternoon. They were disappointed at not seeing anything of the balloon, which was still packed in its bag, but they wandered around outside the magic Guardia Civil circle and pointed at things and guessed at their use. Whenever one of the balloon party went outside he was grabbed for a photograph or asked to sign an autograph book.

Rosemary and the other two girls were the objects of much admiration, and Anne and Jenny, being single, were particularly pursued, always having two or three young men around them. Brown-haired Jenny had been christened 'Blondie' and was judged to be a typical English beauty; Anne, on the other hand, is small and dark and was called 'Gypsy' and claimed for a true Canary Islander. The newspaper reporters, who are rather more poetical than we are used to, had painted so glowing a picture of the beauty of the three girls that young men from all over the island were beating a path to our beach. All this, of course, did the girls no harm at all, and certainly during working hours they were most conscientious. After work, Colin and Rosemary disappeared together; Anne and Jenny, being younger than the rest of us, were able to dance half the night and still work hard all day.

On Tuesday morning I got up for my early swim as usual and immediately noticed that the wind was just right — coming from the north-north-east steadily but not too strongly. I started to run towards the Fonda Israel with the news, but, of course, it had been noticed by everyone, and I met the car full of the launching party on their way to the site.

Peter Hennessy, Ron Bicker and I went over to get a film of the balloonists leaving the hotel 'for the last time'. Bushy had already left, but we photographed Colin, Rosemary and Tim as they came out laden with supplies and got into the car. I travelled with them to the site.

"How do you feel?" I asked.

"Excited," Rosemary said. "Butterflies in my stomach." We passed one of the Mayor's signs. "Damn, I never did get a picture of that," she complained.

"What about the wireless, Tim?"

"It'll take a few hours to get us off. There's a chance that it'll get here in time. If not we'll have to go without it."

At the site there was an air of tremendous urgency. The wind sock pointed straight out to sea in just the direction they wanted to go. It was the right strength too.

Ralph Booth and Gerry Long were connecting the three

The balloon riding up on a thermal. The white sunshade skirt lifts with the force of the updraught. The balloon has lost some gas by now and the bottom is sucked in. This thermal took the balloon up to 3,400 feet.

The first morning after coming down in the sea. Bushy is slowly getting the mast in, which had been left towing astern during the night.

Bushy, Tim and Rosemary struggle to get the mast up.

ten-way fillers to the triple end of the inflation pipe; Jimmy Wildi was getting the valves on to the hydrogen cylinders. This was my job too and, knowing that Peter Hennessy and Ron Bicker were well able to carry on filming, I took my place at the hydrogen cylinders. Gerry Long produced a long spanner, which was a great improvement on the wooden hammers we had been going to use, to tighten and loosen the valves. It was made of aluminium alloy, and the valves were brass, so there was no chance of a spark.

The local helpers were laying out a fifty-foot-diameter circle of sandbags around the area where the balloon was to be inflated.

Everyone was working quickly but well. We had rehearsed this, and each of us knew his job.

"We must find out what the wind conditions are over the ocean," Tim said. "There's no use taking off from here if the wind fifty miles away is wrong."

This was obviously sensible, and Bushy sent Tim back to phone Santa Cruz for a met. report. Because I speak Spanish and the local telephone could be a little difficult, I went with him. We got on to the Met. Office without much difficulty. Tim spoke and I could see by the look of disappointment that the news was bad.

"There's a depression from Gibraltar to the Canaries," he told me. "That means a north-west wind which would take us to Africa. I'll try to get on to the aerodrome for confirmation, but you'd better go back and stop the inflation."

On the way back the taxi-driver asked me what had happened. I told him that the wind over the sea was wrong.

"If you want to know what the wind at sea is going to do you should ask one of the old fishermen," he said. I told him to stop the next one we passed, and a minute or two later he stopped the car and called an incredibly old man over to him with a face almost concealed by wrinkles, blackened by sun and wind. "What will the wind do today?" he asked.

The old fisherman turned and pointed to the mountain. "When the clouds cover old Teide's head the wind is from the north: if this is so at sunrise the wind will come round to the east," he said confidently.

I reported this bit of local lore to the others.

"These old fishermen," I said, "know better than anyone."

"We'll see," said Bushy. "The wind's due north now."

At sunset it was still due north and stayed that way all the following day, despite the clouds around old Teide's head at sunrise.

"I don't believe he was an old fisherman at all," Colin said. "I bet the B.B.C. T.V. boys brought him along for local colour."

The air of urgency had disappeared, and as we had not made any arrangements for lunch to be sent down, we all went back to the Fonda for a leisurely meal and in the afternoon had a swim in water warmer than it ever gets in England.

Ralph Booth sent me off to get a five-gallon tin of water to earth the hydrogen cylinders. I climbed up into the fields of tomatoes on one of the nearby hills and found a Canary Islander working quietly away. I explained that I was from El Globo and that we needed some water. He got it for me.

"Tell me, señor, is it true what they say that three men and one lady are to float off in the sky in that little boat?"

"It is true."

"Are they, perhaps, all one family?"

"No — there is a father and a son and a man and his wife."

"Then no doubt the father and the husband are *very* old friends?"

"Very old friends," I assured him.

Late in the afternoon we released another four-foot balloon, but we weighted this one to keep it low so that we could watch it longer. When it was about a thousand yards away and perhaps two hundred feet high it suddenly changed direction and started travelling almost due east.

"It's the effect of the mountain," Tim explained. "The wind blows around it, you see. I think the only thing is for me to go to Santa Cruz to the airport, where I can get hourly met. reports and to keep in touch with you here on the site by wireless." The wireless had come back that afternoon and they had made contact with Santa Cruz. "Then as soon as I get a report about a favourable wind at sea I can find out from you what the local wind is like; similarly, if it is just right here, you can get on to me and I'll see if it is at all possible for us to go."

Tim left after supper for the long drive back to Santa Cruz. He had not had the six days' rest the others had enjoyed on the *Reventazon*, but had continued to go without enough sleep in England while doing the last-minute work on the wireless. He had arrived at Médano in time to do his share of the work, and consequently by Tuesday evening he was nearly at the point of exhaustion. He spent the next day between the met. office and the airport as well as going to Tom, a Tenerife radio amateur, and trying to get into touch with the radio operator left behind at Médano to find out what the wind was doing with us. He got through once or twice instead of every hour as was planned and then had to depend on the telephone, which does not run straight to Médano, but has to be linked by operators in the villages on the way. The wind direction over the ocean was just right, and if it was at all possible to get off the beach at Médano he thought that they should go.

Meanwhile at the site we sat inside the tent while the wind blew from exactly the right quarter but at about eighteen knots. Ralph said that it would be madness to try to inflate, for the balloon would be sure either to tear out of its moorings or damage itself, and there wouldn't be enough men to hold it when it was fully inflated.

There are few things more nerve-wracking than sitting in the sand with a hot, dry wind blowing and this, combined with the effect of waiting and wondering if they would ever get off, made us all irritable. Most of the work had been done, so that there was very little activity, and the crowd who had waited day after day began to get impatient. It was said that we never really intended to take off but that it was all a publicity stunt. Some of us swam, but the wind took the edge off that too.

We had an instrument for measuring the speed of the wind, and every now and then Bushy or Colin would go out and stand on the gas cylinders and take a reading. It never dropped below sixteen knots, and often gusted over twenty.

I found a corner of the tent and made myself a desk out of boxes and made some notes for this book. I tried to get each of the balloonists talking in turn, but they didn't feel like conversation. Earlier Bushy had told me a lot about his struggles during the year when I was in Morocco, but there were still some things I was puzzled about.

"Can you give me about twenty minutes, Bushy?" I asked.

"No," he said.

All that could be heard was the wind whining outside and the sound of sand blowing against the tent. Bushy had a worried frown that seemed permanent; Colin and Rosemary looked haggard. A few minutes later they began to argue about the ratio of food to water they would take and which food to leave behind. They became quite short with one another, and the rest of us quietly left them alone in the tent.

"I wish that it was possible to get them off," Ralph said to me. "But this wind is much too much. I know it must be nerve-wracking for them to sit and wait when they're all ready and the wind over the sea is all right, but there's nothing to be done except to wait for a lull."

One of the radio hams came running. Tim had got through from Santa Cruz and wanted to talk to Bushy.

"The wind is still perfect out at sea," Bushy told us a few minutes later. "It looks as though we'll have to chance a night take-off. If there's the slightest encouraging lull in the wind tonight we must go. What do you say, Colin?"

"I'm all for it," Colin replied.

"Right. What Tim suggests is for there to be a wireless broadcast announcing that we might take off tonight and that if we go we shall light a beacon fire on the top of our hill. This will be an invitation to all car owners to come and help with their headlights."

"Good idea," said Colin.

"Right — I'll go and tell Tim to lay it on his end, then."

No one else said anything, although a night take-off would mean that we couldn't get the most important part of our film; that Eddie Sampson, the *Daily Mail* photographer, couldn't get pictures of the inflation and take-off; that the B.B.C. T.V. team which had been waiting for several days to film the take-off would also miss it.

I went after Bushy.

"You *can't* go off at night," I blurted out.

Bushy turned to me. "I know it's going to spoil the film, Pete, but I've shown you the met. reports for the last few years, and you *know* how rare it is for all the circumstances to be just right. When they are we must go."

"But how the devil are we going to get the balloon unravelled and inflated in the dark?"

"We've practised it enough — we'll manage."

"But a night take-off will be dangerous."

"We can't help that — nothing is important but getting off. Now we'd better organise a wind-speed watch all through the night. You do that, Pete, and get everyone who is willing to have a go. I think the best place is on the end of the jetty with the instrument held at seven feet. When it falls to ten knots gusting to twelve for three successive readings taken at ten-minute intervals whoever is on watch is to come and wake me." He went off to arrange about the bonfire, and a couple of hours later we saw a long line of donkeys laden with brushwood toiling up the hill.

"It looks as though he means it," Peter Hennessy said gloomily. We had a talk and decided that the balloonists should not take a watch but try to get some sleep. John Starr and Eddie Sampson of the *Daily Mail* volunteered, as did Peter Hennessy and Ron Bicker, as well, of course, as the rest of the launching team. The watches were to be half-hourly, starting at eleven. Eddie Sampson drew the first one, starting in about an hour, and I walked out to the end of the jetty with him to show him how the instrument worked, for he had not used it before.

It was a moonless night with a clear, star-filled sky, as most of them had been. One of our ways of passing the evenings had been to try to identify the stars with one of Colin's charts, and we were getting quite good at it. There was a fresh breeze still blowing from a little to the right of the North Star.

I held the little funnel-shaped instrument up, and Eddie shone his light on it. The arrow showed ten knots, and as we watched it it flicked up to twelve and then back to between nine and ten.

"That's one, anyway," I said. "Let's stay and try again in ten minutes — perhaps this is it."

"I hope not," Eddie said fervently. "It will be terrible for us if we don't get any pictures. Ye gods, we've got Dai sitting in Santa Cruz with the transmitter, and the paper's just about going to bed now. It'll be awful if they go off tonight."

Ten minutes later we took another reading — this time the wind was blowing at twelve knots and gusting to fourteen or fifteen. Eddie and I walked back to the Casa Davidson. My watch was from two to half-past, and after me came Peter Hennessy, who had already gone to bed. I took off my shoes and loosened my clothes and lay on top of the bed. It seemed only a few minutes later that I was awakened by Jimmy Wildi shouting through my window.

"Come on, Pete, they're going! — we start inflating as soon as possible." I scrambled up, and in ten minutes or so we were on our way to the site.

There were a few cars belonging to determined people who were going to see the balloon take off no matter when it occurred, and at our approach they put their lights on. Nevertheless, there was very little light at first, but almost immediately the huge bonfire was lit. The flames leapt high and were seen for miles around. Within half an hour cars were descending on us with horns blowing madly. Jimmy Wildi and I took our places at the hydrogen cylinders.

"It happened on Eddie Sampson's watch," Jimmy told me. "Poor Eddie nearly wept when he got three successive ten-knot readings and he wanted to forget it, but he went back and told them."

Peter Hennessy came over. "There's no use my trying to film

anything in this light with only colour film," he said despondently. I gave him a ten-way set of valves and left him happily struggling with the hydrogen cylinders while I went to see what the others were doing.

Under Ralph and Gerry's orders the four large groundsheets were taken off the craft and the other things they had been covering and laid cornerwise to the centre mark of the inflation area. It was very important that there were no small sharp stones on them to make holes in the balloon, so each was carefully shaken and turned right over. When all four were in place Bushy walked over them barefooted and swept them clean. Then the balloon was got out of its bag and carried over to the dust sheets and carefully unfolded. This takes time, and as inflation obviously couldn't begin until the balloon was ready, I decided to make some notes. I discovered that I had left my notebooks and paper back at the house. I found a piece of expanded polystyrene and sat in front of one of the cars and wrote down the events of the night so far.

It takes an hour to get the balloon laid out properly — like a flower, with the top where the valve is to go, in the middle. Gerry Long disappeared inside the balloon to fix the valve and to bring down the lines from the valve and the ripping panel. I looked at my watch and saw that it was just before two o'clock. It seemed to me that the wind was rising, and I went to find Eddie Sampson and got the wind meter from him. It was up to twelve knots, gusting to fourteen. I decided to say nothing, but to leave it to Ralph Booth to notice when it got too strong.

Finally, the net was put on and then it was discovered that in the dark it had been put on inside out and it had to come off and be put on again.

At last the triple inlet pipe was lashed to the neck of the balloon and we were told to start inflating. Peter Hennessy, Jimmy Wildi and I each had ten valves leading to one of the inlets and a section of forty cylinders to tackle. As they got turned on the noise, which started as a low puppy-like whine, built up until, when all thirty cylinders were emptying at once, there was a loud moaning which drowned out everything else. We worked as fast as possible, but some of the taps were stiff, and as the cylinders emptied they got cold and ice formed around the valves. Every now and then one of us spotted a cigarette in the crowd and shouted to get it put out, for we were very much aware of the dangerous hydrogen and air mixture all around us.

I don't know how long this went on, for I was too busy to notice, but after some time Gerry Long shouted "Stop inflating!" and Wildi, Hennessy and I got a chance to look. There was a large silver bubble on the sand reflecting the car's headlights. It looked as though it was quilted where the net pressed into the balloon. The helpers on the sandbags who had been lifting and lowering steadily took the opportunity to rest and flop on the sand. Bushy and Ralph were discussing the wind, which was occasionally gusting to sixteen knots, and it was decided to hold the inflation with the balloon perhaps a third full to see if the wind would drop again. It was nearly four o'clock in the morning.

We were hungry and ate some of the tomatoes and bananas that had been given to us and passed the wine bottle around. The beacon fire had long since burned out, but cars were still coming from all over the island and had jammed the newly made road, been abandoned and their occupants had walked the rest of the way and taken their places in the crowd. I walked about to keep warm and to get a picture of how it all looked.

The site was ringed with cars, some of which had been pushed into place in the soft sand in order that the lights from their headlights could be directed where they were needed. In all of them there were cheerful people eating and drinking and enjoying the unusual experience. Someone offered me a bottle, and I took a long swig of Spanish brandy, which warmed me immediately. I handed it back with a 'gracias' and the driver replied in English. It was Tom Breasley, from whose farm it was originally intended to take off. He had driven around from the other side of the island like so many others.

"Start inflating!" Gerry shouted, and I ran back to the cylinders and in a few minutes the banshee-like moaning started again. In half an hour the order came to stop, for the lull in the wind had been only momentary, and now it began to blow again much harder.

The balloon was now inflated beyond its equator and the wind was getting underneath and pushing it up, bouncing the sandbags against the sides. It was straining at the guy ropes, and Ralph was afraid that it would be damaged and ordered some gas to be let out to get it down to a more manageable shape. But still it tugged and tugged at its moorings.

The launching crew and volunteers from the crowd were put all around the balloon to hold it by the net. We stood with our backs to the balloon and our arms interwoven through the net. Some sat on the sandbags to hold them still while others hung on to the guy ropes. It was about half-past four, the wind was cold and dawn seemed a long way off.

Tim had arrived from Santa Cruz at about three and had been told to try to get some sleep, for he had obviously had very little and looked extremely tired. The rest of the balloonists were also trying to get some sleep, for if the wind dropped we could get them off in another hour and a half, and they obviously shouldn't start completely exhausted.

The car lights were put out and everyone who could slept. Some wrapped themselves up in the remains of an auxiliary balloon that had been brought along but was now not going to be used. Ralph Booth walked about for the rest of the night inspecting the lines, the net and watching the half-inflated balloon trying to escape.

Like many others, I hung in the net of the balloon and cursed the wind, which was obviously getting stronger, for now the sand was stinging our faces. A few yards away Anne and Jenny sat on sandbags for added weight, looking dead beat. I realised that the exertions of the last few days had begun to affect everyone. The two hours before the sky began to lighten seemed like ten.

When at last Thursday dawned and the red sun came up, bringing a little warmth, we ran up and down the beach to get the blood circulating again. The cocoons of pink polythene of the auxiliary balloon unrolled and bodies crawled out into the sun.

Although the wind was blowing hard, it was thought possible that it might drop just after dawn, and so we all stood by to carry on inflating.

"How about some breakfast?" I asked hopefully. We searched in the tent among the supplies that it had been decided to leave behind and had an unusual breakfast of sardines, mint cake, tomatoes and Guinness.

The day before, when everyone had been feeling at his most irritable, a newcomer had joined us. He had introduced himself as Ed St. John, an American news cameraman from Madrid, and had been told that he couldn't take any close-ups or get any interviews.

"Well, what can I do to help?" he had asked, and when given a job had put his cameras aside and got on with it. This, of course, had completely won the balloonists over, and he had become one of the party without further ado. He had been going to serve his turn on the watch the night before, and he had worked hard all night, alternating between helping with the launching and trying to get some shots in the light of the car's headlamps. Now, as we stood and looked gloomily at the balloon struggling and tugging in the wind, he came up with a suggestion.

"Why don't we make a wind-break out of packing-cases?" he said. "It would take the worst of the wind off the balloon, wouldn't it?"

"O.K.," said Bushy. "You've got yourself a job." Ed St. John collared four of our local labour force and explained what he wanted them to do, and three hours later had erected a useful screen, which immediately took the strain off the balloon. We were all very impressed with this example of American ability to get on with the job.

By nine o'clock it was decided that the wind wasn't likely to drop suddenly and we were put on one hour's notice. Most of us had had no sleep, but as the sun got warmer and we went for a swim we felt better.

"Early to bed tonight," I told Peter Hennessy.

"Too true," he said. "I'm sorry in one way that they didn't

go, but I think that it would have been a bit of a shambles in the dark, and I think they must have decided that too. Perhaps they'll go tomorrow, and we'll get our pictures, after all."

The wind blew hard all day, sometimes gusting up to twenty-five knots, and we thought more than once that we would have to deflate the balloon, but it was well pegged down, and Ed St. John's wind-break helped enormously. Still the sand was being blown against it with considerable force, and everyone was afraid that the fabric might be damaged. In the afternoon I found the four balloonists sitting in the tent. They all looked tired and obviously in need of a good night's sleep, for although they had tried to sleep, the tension of waiting to take off hadn't permitted it.

"It doesn't look as though this wind is going to die down," I said. "The local fishermen say that when it blows like this it goes on for seven days . . ." Bushy made a rude remark about the local fishermen which I ignored. "Why don't you go back to the hotel and have a wash and a rest and turn in?"

"We took too damn long last night," Bushy said. "We never practised laying out the balloon, inserting the valve and getting the net on in the dark — we should have, that was a slip."

"We never thought a night take-off was a possibility," Colin protested. "Anyway, we couldn't have practised doing anything with the balloon without running the risk of damaging it."

"It's getting damaged now all right," Bushy said gloomily.

We opened the tent flap and looked at the half-sphere of the balloon held down by a hundred sandbags but heaving and lurching as though it was alive. Every time a rope went taut against the fabric or the balloon scraped on the sand Bushy looked as though his own skin were being grazed.

"Perhaps if the balloon is going to leak like a sieve you'd better call it off. . . ." I began and was squashed by both of them, who told me that short of it ripping in two they were determined to go.

"I think we should plan to go tonight," Tim said. "It seems to me that the wind will probably drop about ten or half-past, as it did last night. It might stay down for two or three hours, which is plenty of time for us to get away."

I didn't dare express my disapproval of this, and was dismayed to see that the others all agreed with Tim. I could see our film disappearing again.

"As a matter of interest, what will you do if it turns out that the balloon *is* leaking like a sieve?" I asked.

"Well, we've got the means for making more hydrogen, five hundredweight of calcium hydride ballast, and then we can start chucking everything else overboard," Bushy said.

"And then?"

"Then we'll be there — or nearly there. What you seem to forget, Pete, is that we've got a perfectly sea-worthy boat . . ."

"You never have understood the principle on which that hull is built," Colin said accusingly. This was because at one time I had thought that it was built around a nice strong aluminium frame — an idea that had horrified Colin. "It's a damn sight stronger than half the boats that make the crossing from here every year."

"Look, Pete," said Bushy, in his patient, explaining-things-to-an-idiot voice. "Every year a couple of dozen people start from these islands to sail the Atlantic. Some of them have next to no experience, a smattering of navigation and rotten old boats. They all — or nearly all — make it. Now we've got a well-tested, sea-worthy boat, we've both done the crossing under sail before, and Colin is a fine navigator. We've got bags of emergency food and sea-water stills. We could take three months over the voyage and still be all right."

"If you come down in one piece."

"Why shouldn't we? There's no possible way that we could drop like a stone. Even if the balloon bursts, the lower half just folds up into the upper and makes a parachute. Anyway, the odds against the balloon bursting are a thousand to one. We might be forced down for a number of reasons, and if we are we'll sail on."

"Until you're picked up?"

"No, certainly not. We should refuse to be picked up. We're

perfectly capable of sailing that craft from this beach to the West Indies."

"If you're missing there's bound to be an air-sea search laid on . . ."

"Then you must stop it. It will be quite unnecessary, and we don't want it," Colin said firmly.

"Get this into your head," Bushy said. "We spent two years preparing for this flight, and we've tried to think of everything to make it as safe as possible. We hope that we've succeeded and that it's a great deal safer than most people believe. We're pretty sure that we're going to make it, but there's always the chance that we may have to ditch. If we do we've got a craft that will run before the wind and even sail fairly close if necessary. Therefore if you don't hear from us or get a message saying that we're coming down, it only means that the aerial part of the voyage is finished and the sailing part — which we know more about, anyway — has begun. We don't want any ships diverted to look for us; we don't want any ruddy air-sea rescue operations."

"Remember that, please, Peter," Colin said. "No panic stations. We'll come sailing smartly into the West Indies if we have to come down."

"We shouldn't have asked the Duke of Edinburgh to be our patron if we had had any intention of requesting an air-sea rescue," Tim said.

"You don't have to request it," I said. "It's automatic if they have reason to think that you are in distress."

"We're not going to be in distress," Bushy said firmly. "Or if we are it will be too late for an air-sea search to do any good. We shall either come down in one piece and sail on quite happily or in many pieces, in which case rescue operations will be a waste of time."

"Personally, I think we're safer than many people who tackle the Atlantic every year," Colin said.

It was a conversation I was to remember many times in the next few weeks.

Outside the tent I ran into John Starr.

"Any news?"

"Yes — if the wind drops they're going tonight."

"Oh, Lord," he groaned. "Too late for most editions. I bet they take off tomorrow night just too late to make Saturday's paper, and as we don't publish Sunday, that will be that."

Hennessy and Bicker were also as put out as I was, but we all realised by this time that they would have to get off whenever they could, all other considerations notwithstanding.

Jenny and Rosemary were struggling with tins of sea-water, with which they kept filling the solar still, which had been under test on and off for two or three days.

"How much fresh water have you made?" I asked.

"Not a drop," Jenny said. "I can't understand it — it just doesn't seem to work."

"It must work," I said. "I expect you're doing something wrong." Needless to say, I practically got a full solar still in my lap for that remark. Eventually they decided that moving the still after it had been filled had prevented it working properly.

I walked back to Médano past dozens of cars, crowds of people picnicking and past the air-strip, which seemed as busy as a small airport, past sellers of soft drinks, food and knick-knacks, past a contingent of the relieving guard marching to the site, policemen on duty everywhere, signs every hundred yards or so and all the activity that had come to this little place in a few days.

Médano, of course, had been completely unprepared for the earthquake that hit it, and the second day saw the village turned upside down. The little post office was sold right out of stamps, and its entire stock of post-cards — eleven dating from the efforts of a local entrepreneur in 1931 to popularise Médano — had been sold to the first customer. The postmistress, faced with continuous demands for stamps of any denomination and a mounting pile of unstamped letters and money, finally burst into tears and locked up. The two or three provision shops were cleaned out of butter, tea, coffee and tinned foods; there were no cigarettes to be had anywhere; the bar on the beach had its entire stock drunk up the first evening; there was no room at the inn. The only thing that never ran out was the red wine.

I went to the Fonda Israel, ordered a bottle of wine and wrote some letters to give to George our interpreter, guide, counsellor and man of all work, who somehow managed to go back and forth to Santa Cruz every day on his Vespa and ran errands for all of us.

The wind was still blowing much too hard, and I felt sure that they wouldn't be able to get off that night. About an hour later, just at dusk, they all came wearily back to the hotel, and Bushy produced a bottle of whisky and a bottle of gin and we had a party. We were joined by the Finnish boys, a German photographer, two Dutch women journalists and many local people.

Bushy had been slipping out from time to time to take a wind reading, and about 10 o'clock he decided that the wind was abating and that if we got down to the site we could start inflating at the first possible moment.

There hadn't been enough liquor for anyone to be drunk, but most of us had had little or no sleep for about forty hours and had passed through sleepiness to a state of excitement that was itself a kind of intoxication. We rocketed down to the site through the dark, car horns blowing madly to let everyone know we were going and needed help.

Many of the visitors had waited for two days, but had then given up and either gone home or found somewhere in the village to sleep, but there were some of the stubborn ones still there with their cars, and we woke them up and asked them to put on their headlights. Other cars appeared as the night before, and soon there was a crowd of several hundred. By 10:30 the wind had dropped to ten knots and we began inflating again, but within half an hour it had increased to fourteen knots and we had to stop.

The balloon was now three-quarters inflated, which was a very dangerous shape for a strong wind. It seemed to be throwing itself against the guy ropes like a bird trying to get out of a cage.

"I don't like this at all," Ralph Booth said. "It must be doing quite a bit of damage to the fabric. I'm afraid that if the wind doesn't drop we'll have to deflate, or we'll lose her."

A meeting was held inside the tent.

"If we have to deflate," said Bushy, "we'll move everything right over to the lee of the hill where we'll be out of the direct wind. It will be a hell of a job. I went over there this afternoon and had a look at it. The sand is too soft for vehicles, so we'll have to manhandle all the cylinders and everything else, and it'll take a full day or perhaps two. Then we'll wait for the wind conditions to be right — that might not happen again for two or three weeks — and then have one more go."

"Have you got enough gas?" I asked.

"Yes, we've got enough for another complete filling if we have to let this one go. But that's all, and if we go over there and the wind comes up on the next attempt we'll carry on, anyway. In the lee of the hill I think we'll stand a good chance in almost any wind."

"Don't give up hope for a launching tonight," Gerry Long said. "If the wind drops we can get you away in less than an hour now."

"Why don't you get some sleep?" I asked. "Even a couple of hours might make a difference." Tim and Bushy agreed and went over to the craft some fifty yards or so from the balloon and out of the glare of the headlights. They crawled inside to their sleeping-places and wrapped themselves up in pink polythene. I went around to the cars thanking the drivers and telling them that they could turn their lights out and shut off their motors, as we had to wait for the wind to drop. Many of them were disappointed, but all were sympathetic.

Ralph and Gerry seemed to be able to do without sleep, for whenever I looked they were walking around checking the guy ropes or inspecting the net. Gerry had found two or three of the meshes broken by the force of the balloon pulling against the wind and had patched them.

"Do you think the balloon is badly damaged, Gerry?" I asked him.

"No, I don't think so," he replied. "It's brand new, after all. The thing that worries me is that we don't have enough men to

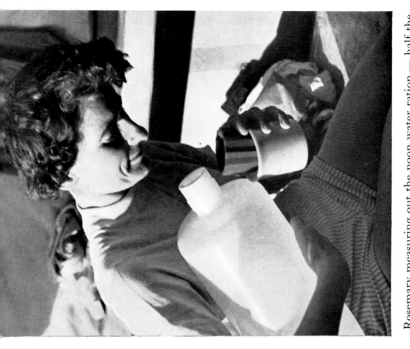

Rosemary measuring out the noon water ration — half the container each.

Pulling for Barbados — 1,500 miles to go!

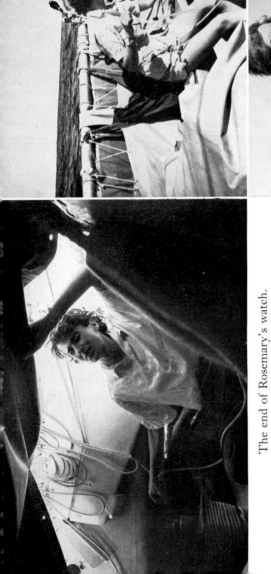

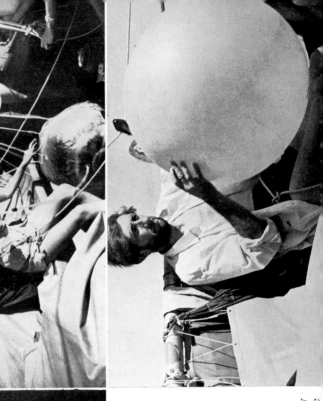

The end of Rosemary's watch.

Getting a solar still ready.

Colin blows up a balloon with a message inside which they hoped would get to the West Indies before them — none have

hold her down. I think that we'll need about sixty on each guy rope."

Ralph Booth, in command of the inflation, had a very difficult decision to make. He knew that they were eager to go and willing to take a chance in a high wind, but he also knew how quickly disaster could come if the balloon got out of control. It was now blowing fourteen knots gusting to eighteen, and he had originally thought that eight knots with occasional gusts to ten was about the safe maximum. He had been persuaded to raise that two knots, but he felt that any more would be almost impossible.

Just before midnight when everything was quiet the wind dropped noticeably. By this time we were pretty familiar with the pattern: it dropped quite suddenly and usually stayed down for about an hour and then rose again and blew very hard for twenty minutes or so.

"We'll try it," Ralph said, although he thought that two knots more would be disastrous. I ran over to the craft and called the crew, and in a few minutes the pipes were turned on and the gas was moaning and groaning again. Now the inflation went very quickly and the workers on the sandbags hadn't a moment's rest. At last the balloon lifted clear of the ground, enabling Gerry Long and some helpers to get underneath and fix the load ring.

As the gas inflation part was now finished, Jimmy Wildi and I were able to go over and help with the last part, which was the moving of the sandbags down to the lines from the bottom of the net, each line holding about five sandbags weighing approximately forty pounds each.

The B.B.C. T.V. team had not been able to wait any longer, and had returned to England that same evening. Peter Hennessy had had the bright idea of borrowing some fast black-and-white film from them, with which he hoped to get some shots of the night take-off by using the light from the cars and running the camera at about one-third the speed. He and Ed St. John, the news cameraman from Madrid, were now filming.

The load ring was fixed and the sandbags moved down, allowing the balloon to go up until the neck and load ring were off the ground. Then we walked it over to the craft, where the four balloonists were waiting to attach it to the quick-release lines.

It took many people to hold it down, for the wind was blowing hard, and with every gust the balloon tried to lift. It was held by a long Terylene rope attached to a heavy lorry intended to get it to rise as quickly as possible. There was a great deal of excited shouting and yelling of orders in English and Spanish and some confusion. The last stages were necessarily complicated, and it was difficult to explain to the Spanish-speaking helpers exactly what to do.

"Interpreters!" Tim shouted. "We need interpreters!"

Bruce Norton went up to him at once and began relaying orders from the craft to the crowd, but by this time there were not only voluntary helpers but many sightseers who just wanted to get up as near the balloon as possible.

Meanwhile Gerry Long, worried that too many sandbags might be dropped too soon and the balloon be whipped away with the craft half on, went around the circle of the net tying each group of sandbags with a new, and to the rest of us, a complicated knot. I don't think it occurred to Gerry at that moment that he didn't have any of his trained Cardington ground crew but only a crowd of amateurs to whom anything more than a square knot or the simple slip knot we had been taught to manipulate on board the *Reventazon* was a mystery.

When the time came to release these knots and lower the bags to allow the balloon to take the weight of the craft most of us pulled at the wrong end of rope and tightened them. Some, however, were loosened and the balloon began to rise and, in the stronger wind, lift clusters of sandbags eight to ten feet in the air.

I was struggling to untie one group when it was lifted high out of my hand, but a willing Spanish helper leapt up and held on to the bags. He was carried up with them. He immediately whipped out a knife from somewhere and slashed the rope holding the sandbags. He fell with them on to the crowd below. Miraculously no one was hurt. As the sandbags came off everywhere the balloon, bucking in the wind, jerked the helpers about.

Everyone seemed to be shouting at once, and there was a feeling of a disorganised rabble, among which a few people like Gerry Long, Ralph Booth and one or two others were working quietly and quickly. They were not enough to do everything that was necessary though, and many of the volunteers, although willing, were working to cross purposes.

Bushy stood up in the craft with a look of sick anger. He shouted in Spanish for the crowd to get back. The authority in his voice penetrated the babble, and the excited mob quietened momentarily.

"Who's in command of this launching?" Bushy roared.

"I am." Wing-Commander Booth raised his voice. "Let go the guys! LET GO THE GUYS!"

We quickly got the remaining sandbags off and all guy ropes were released. Now was the time for the final adjustment of ballast to enable the balloon to lift off slowly, but a gust of wind caught her and tipped the boat on to its side. It banged down on the ground. They had to get rid of ballast quickly!

It hadn't been possible for them to know exactly what the lift would be under the particular conditions at Médano, and they had taken on excess tins of calcium hydride at the last moment to make sure that they wouldn't be underweight. These were the first to go, but as they continued to lighten the balloon so the wind was able to lift them and bang the boat on the ground.

We knew that we had to get them off, and I and the rest of the ground crew feverishly dumped the tins of calcium hydride out of the bags that had been hung outside the boat. Now they were so near to being airborne the wind was able to drag them across the sand. I heard the hull hit the ground with a crack — Colin's theory about its strength was being proved, for it was certainly never designed to be banged about like that. I fully expected to see it split down the middle.

"Still not light enough!" Bushy shouted. "Get the big bag off for'ard."

I ran to untie the bag of calcium hydride tins, but pulled my hand away as a large sheath knife came flashing down. It was wielded by Bushy, who looked a bit like a pirate boarding a ship.

Finally, with a great heave, the craft lifted clear of the ground and the crowd cheered and clapped and car horns started to blow. Rosemary had tied a Union Jack and the flag of Tenerife to the rigging and they blew out bravely, illuminated by the cars' spotlights. I thought that they were airborne at last, but they came down once more, and then more tins were thrown over and a great yellow, sausage-shaped bag of provisions. I thought that this was part of their emergency rations and picked it up and ran to the boat with it, but Bushy shouted for me to leave it. The craft rose, pulling against the long rope from the lorry, Bushy stood up, cut through it and the balloon flew across the beach, bounced once or twice and hit the water with a splash. We all ran after it and into the water. We could hear them shouting to each other as the wind pulled the boat over the water and then, as they got rid of much more ballast The Small World suddenly lifted clear of the water. A tremendous cheer went up from the crowd.

We stood knee deep in the sea shouting our good-byes. I heard my own voice as though it was someone else's shouting urgently, "Let go your ballast!" over and over. It was, of course, quite meaningless, but in the excitement I hadn't known what I was saying.

For perhaps a long minute we could make out the shape of the balloon against the dark sky as it rose rapidly. Then all that could be seen was their navigation light like a new star. It was suddenly shut out as they rose into a low cloud and the crowd gasped as one person, and then it appeared brighter than ever in the clear air above the cloud. We kept our eyes glued to the little light like children watching a toy balloon disappear; it became faint, glimmered and then disappeared for good.

We stood in the water for a minute or two longer, our eyes straining in the darkness, but they had gone. The crowd went quiet, as all of us thought of them a mile or so away and a few hundred feet over the waves struggling to control their balloon at last flying free.

CHAPTER EIGHT

I WAS suddenly aware that the water was cold and that I was very, very tired. I looked around for the others: Jenny, who had run into the sea up to her waist, was now standing, dripping wet and crying softly. She was being comforted by Anne. Jimmy Wildi and Gerry Long were already picking up the discarded ballast; Ralph Booth stood at the water's edge staring at the place they had last been seen.

"What do you think?" I asked him.

"I'm afraid they went too high through that cloud — it looked like a couple of thousand feet to me, which will mean that they've lost gas already."

We moved to help pick up the tins of calcium hydride and other things spread all over the beach.

"Look at this!" John Starr held up a yellow canvas bag. "It looks like one of their emergency food bags — they only had two, didn't they?"

I couldn't remember how many bags of food they had intended to carry, but we opened it to see if we could tell from the contents. Tins of fruit, tomatoes, a bag of the local roasted wheat didn't look like emergency rations, but then we saw a packet of Permutit chemical for converting salt water into fresh. That was bad.

"It *is* one of the emergency packs," John Starr said. "It'll be short rations of food and water if they come down." He hurried off to write his story.

By 3 o'clock in the morning the last of the cars had been manhandled out of the soft sand and we had stacked everything inside the tent. Our hired car was waiting for us, and as we drove away from the site I looked back and wondered how soon it would be before there was no trace at all of our ever having been there.

We slept late and then went down to the site for the last time.

The feeling of anti-climax was very strong. With the balloon and the craft gone, the site looked like a stage being dismantled after the run of the play. It was difficult to work with any enthusiasm, and we argued listlessly about how much packing we should do.

Once again Wilfred Moore came to our rescue. I telephoned to him, and he told us that he and the Mayor of Médano would arrange for all that remained to be sent back to Santa Cruz and eventually shipped to England. We said our good-byes to Médano's willing helpers and drove back to Santa Cruz to a hot bath and a good dinner.

Gerry Long had had to leave immediately for England, and the next day Jimmy Wildi followed him. Anne and Jenny sorted out their many invitations and accepted a few, deciding to return in a week or so by another banana boat. Ralph Booth and Mrs. Booth decided to stay on in sunny Tenerife for a holiday.

I knew that I and the two cameramen ought to get back to London with our film as quickly as possible, but we waited for an extra day in case there was news of the balloon. I hadn't liked the way it had been knocked about on the beach and I half-expected to hear that they had been picked up at sea a couple of hundred miles off Tenerife.

Our first news came almost twenty-four hours after they had taken off. Tim got through to the Santa Cruz listening post.

WE ARE HAPPY BUT TIRED AND ARE HEADING FOR AMERICA, the message read. It was a tremendous load off all our minds, and each of us now admitted how worried he had been.

To me it meant that they were still aloft after a day in the air and that therefore everything must be working all right. It meant that they had a good chance of making it. We caught the next plane to London, but were delayed in Madrid for the whole of the next day. None of the Spanish papers had any further news, but we found a copy of the *Continental Daily Mail* with a front-page story:

THEY'RE QUARTER WAY ACROSS!

The story said that wireless operators in Britain had picked up

Tim, identified his call sign but got nothing else but a string of 'V-for-Victory' signals. They had then worked out the probable position of the balloon from average wind speeds.

"It looks as though they'll be in the West Indies before we get back to England," said Peter Hennessy, who was thoroughly fed up with sitting all day in Madrid's airport.

I wanted to believe it, but it seemed strange that only a call sign and a string of V's had been picked up. Tim and I had worked out the code together, and he was able to convey a great deal of information with just a group of five letters.

We landed in England late Monday night. I phoned the *Daily Mail* immediately for news. Yes — the balloon had been sighted by a German ship, the *Bertha Entz* at 10:45 on Sunday night nine hundred miles from Tenerife. They had then been aloft nearly three days, and if they continued at that rate they would make the West Indies in six or seven more.

"Any more wireless messages?" I asked.

"We're not sure that we've identified them. We've picked up some signals, but they were so weak we couldn't read them over all the other traffic."

The *Daily Mail* had set up a Balloon Operations Room as soon as The Small World took off and kept it manned twenty-four hours a day.

"If they're still up they broke the world's record for duration at about 6 o'clock this evening," I told them. The world's record for free balloons was eighty-seven hours, and it had been set up by a German exactly forty-five years before their flight. But his balloon had been very much larger than The Small World, and the world's record for balloons of their size was only sixty-nine hours. This had been accomplished by two Russians in 1941.

The next night the wireless listening posts in Britain picked up a snatch of a message which when decoded said, 'ROSEMARY IS WELL.' But there was nothing else — no position which, Tim had agreed, would always be the first thing he would try to transmit. I knew that the message 'Rosemary is Well' could have been conveyed by two letters only such as ML or WP, providing they were in their proper position in a larger group. If that had been the case I couldn't understand why they hadn't had the information that the other letters gave. It was all very confusing, and I decided to speak to John Starr as soon as he got back from Tenerife.

The *Daily Mail* had sent another reporter to Barbados, the nearest West Indian island from Tenerife, and arranged for him to move quickly to wherever they were spotted. They had had a series of scoops, and they didn't want any other newspaper getting to the balloonists first on the other side. The *Mail* had also generously offered to fly me to the West Indies when they were sighted. I spent the next day, Wednesday, getting my visas and making all arrangements to leave at a moment's notice.

By now we were all optimistic; we phoned the Balloon Operations Room frequently; we listened to every B.B.C. news. Colin and Rosemary's parents, Tim's mother and I daily expected the exciting news that The Small World had been sighted off the West Indies.

But the message about Rosemary was the last. Slowly the days dragged by without any sign from them. Radio operators on ships anywhere in the South Atlantic were told Tim's frequency and the intended transmission times and asked to listen, but none reported anything.

On Christmas Eve we heard that a Liberian tanker that had docked at Tenerife had reported severe rain storms in the probable route of the balloon. By then I was fairly certain that they were down, and I hoped that they were sailing. I reasoned that if they were not, then they had been drifting on the wind for twelve days. If so, they could not have covered less than three thousand miles, with something like thirty-six hundred miles the more likely figure. In either case it seemed to me that they must have been sighted.

I told the Editor of the *Daily Mail* this. He said that if that was so, perhaps we should ask for a search to be made, for they might need help badly.

"No, not yet," I said, remembering my last conversation with them.

"All right, we'll talk about it again after Christmas," he said. "That will have given them two full weeks."

On Christmas Day I went to see Tim's mother and his twin sister and told them that I thought The Small World was down but sailing on. They both have great faith in Bushy's ability to do extraordinary things and thought the balloon was still aloft and would be sighted any day.

There was no news that day and none on Boxing Day. We listened to every wireless news bulletin and we telephoned the Balloon Operations Room in Fleet Street, where the duty men waited for a report from any of the wireless listening posts in Great Britain, Tenerife or the West Indies which were being manned right round the clock, but none of them had heard anything.

These amateurs — hams as they proudly call themselves — had all volunteered to listen for Tim's signals, and they did so conscientiously day after day, night after night. The first message had been picked up in Great Britain and Barbados, as well as in Tenerife. The next day at the scheduled times they had all listened, confident that if Tim had got through once he could do so again. But as the days passed without his ever coming up again they became discouraged. Nevertheless, most of them carried on to the end trying to receive him.

When a lot of hams are listening for a long period and don't know exactly what they expect to hear it is inevitable that somebody will think that he has heard something. This was the reason for a number of false reports, but as only the *Daily Mail* and Tim had copies of the code, most of the supposed messages were easily seen to be impossible. There were a few attempts by practical jokers to pass themselves off as Tim, but none of them fooled the hams who had worked with Tim and knew his style of sending morse. A ham's 'fist' is as distinctive as his voice.

Although they continued to keep watch conscientiously, the British group of hams had just about decided by Christmas that no messages were being transmitted by The Small World at all. This could mean that the wireless had been jettisoned or that they were down with a damaged set or water-soaked batteries.

There was always in my mind a horrible feeling that they had come down in a storm and a heavy sea and that the boat had either been broken up or overwhelmed. I kept remembering the sound of the hull crunching on the beach at Médano and of how small it had looked in the water with all four of them in it. A feeling of disaster grew on me, and I found it difficult to sleep. I was jumpy and bad-tempered, and Christmas was not very pleasant for my own family.

The telephone rang on Boxing Day night. I jumped for it. It was the *Daily Mail*.

"We've just had a flash that they're down in Venezuela!" an excited voice told me. "Near the mouth of a river just opposite Trinidad."

Three hours later I was in an aeroplane flying to New York. I phoned the *Mail* office there from Idlewild Airport.

"No confirmation of the report yet," they told me. "But the Venezuelan Government have got planes searching and are sending soldiers in — it's apparently a pretty wild bit of jungle."

I imagined them spotting land after all that time, coming down, letting the balloon go and sailing into the beach — or perhaps they had been over the jungle before they realised it. I had been told to go to the Venezuelan Consulate and meet Geoffrey Blythe, the famous *Daily Mail* foreign correspondent. We were to get our visas and catch the afternoon plane to Caracas.

"But we gave you a visa yesterday," the Venezuelan Consul said with some surprise. "Here — a visa for an English newspaper-man — the *Daily Express*, no?" We learned that the *Daily Express* office in New York had got a man away on the aeroplane that left the night before.

"He'll be there by now," Geoffrey groaned. "Probably getting a lovely story — I'll be shot at dawn."

"Don't worry — they'll only give their story to you," I assured him.

As our aeroplane didn't leave for several hours, I walked about New York City. I spent my childhood there, and it is always magic for me to return. In Times Square the news was travelling around the *New York Times* building in electric lights just as it always has and I joined the crowd staring up at it.

SMALL WORLD BALLOONISTS DOWN IN VENEZUELA, the lights twinkled out, ALL FOUR BRUISED BUT SAFE. I waited for something more concrete, but that was all. Still, it was the confirmation we had been waiting for, and I thought of how overjoyed Colin and Rosemary's parents must be and of Tim's mother's relief. I went to the *Daily Mail* office at Rockefeller Centre in case they had later news there.

"It's a hoax," they told me.

"A hoax?" I couldn't believe it. I couldn't believe that anyone could be so cruel.

"Yes — some chap in Tenerife sent a message to Trinidad saying he'd heard from them, but there's not a word of truth in it."

In the next few days we heard the rest of the story. Hoax was not the right word, for the man who started the false report believed it himself. He was a spiritualist who believed that he received messages from the spirit world. He had become convinced that The Small World had come down in the Venezuelan jungle. He felt that it was his duty to get a search started, and so he sent an anonymous cable to the Harbour Master at Port of Spain, Trinidad, who, not surprisingly, assumed that a wireless message had been picked up at Tenerife.

The air search was called off, but not before thousands of dollars had been spent and men and equipment risked. There was a good deal of anger and bitter disappointment among the balloonists' friends and relations. We screwed ourselves up again to the daily waiting for news.

The *Daily Mail* man in Barbados reported that a local wireless ham had picked up a message from the balloon placing them about eight hundred miles due east of the island and still aloft. I could hardly believe this, for it seemed incredible that the balloon could have made only nineteen hundred miles in sixteen days or, if the wireless was still working, that none of the other stations had heard anything.

The days passed and I sat in the New York office of the *Mail* and watched the machines of the Press Associations that type out the news almost as it happens. The days passed with nothing about The Small World, and all my former fears returned.

On 1st January an aeroplane pilot reported something in the sea about fifty miles from Barbados that might have been the boat of The Small World. A search was made but nothing found. It began to look very serious.

The responsibility for asking for an air-sea search had been placed on me, and, although I remembered how vehemently they had all been against it, I couldn't help wondering whether one or more of them might have been injured on ditching. Or the boat itself might have been damaged or lost its mast and be unable to sail. If it was drifting with any of them in need of a doctor, the sooner a search was asked for the better.

I tried to be cool and calm and work out the possibilities. I took a piece of yellow ruled paper and roughed out a map from Tenerife to Trinidad. The distance was twenty-seven hundred miles, and if they had drifted between two hundred and fifty and three hundred miles a day they would have made at least a thousand miles before running into the storms the Liberian tanker had reported encountering. If they had still been aloft on 22nd December they would have covered at least twenty-five hundred miles, and even if they had then come down they would certainly have been seen by someone by now.

Therefore, I reasoned, they came down sometime between 17th and 22nd December. "My guess," I wrote on January 2nd, "is that they are no nearer than 300 nor further than 1000 miles from the West Indies."

I took the farthest figure and reckoned that at the slowest speed, which I calculated was three knots, the latest arrival date was 14th January, after which they could be assumed not sailing. I decided that if nothing had been heard from them by then I would ask for an all-out search to be made. "Earliest arrival is about January 5th", I wrote.

Having made up my mind, I stuck to it, although there was

considerable pressure from all sides. I knew that if, as a result of my stubbornness, the search was delayed and they were later found, perhaps dead from exposure, that I should come in for a lot of criticism. But I could not ignore their explicit instructions to me, and I knew that if it had been I in the balloon and had told Bushy what to do he would not have let anyone else change his mind.

When I got to the *Daily Mail* office on Monday, 5th January there was, as usual, no news at all. My brother, Winston, had come to New York from California to spend two or three days with me. We planned to go out for an hour or two from time to time during the day, but there was a message for me — Bill Hardcastle, the News Editor in London, would be telephoning at 1 o'clock and was anxious to talk to me.

"I know what he wants," I told Winston. "He wants me to reconsider my decision not to ask for an air-sea rescue operation."

I sympathised very much with the *Daily Mail*, for they, too, would come in for a great deal of criticism if The Small World adventure ended in a tragedy, and they naturally didn't want it to be said that they hadn't done everything possible.

The call came through exactly at one o'clock.

"Have you thought any more about asking for a search, Peter?" he asked. "Everyone here is pretty worried — don't you think January fourteenth is leaving it a bit late?"

Before I could reply my brother, who had wandered over to the ticker-tape machine, shouted and ripped the sheet off. He pushed it into my hand:

BRIDGETOWN BARBADOS JAN 5 OFFICIALS HERE ANNOUNCED THE GONDOLA OF THE BRITISH BALLOON SMALL WORLD ARRIVED TODAY AT THE CRANE HOTEL BEACH ON THE SOUTHEAST CORNER OF THIS ISLAND. THERE WERE NO IMMEDIATE DETAILS.

"Wait a minute — listen to this!" I read it over the telephone. He got a reporter on another line and had me read it again. A minute or two later the tape machine in the London office spelled out the same news. In our case it had come from the office beneath us in the same building: for mechanical reasons it took a few minutes more to reach London.

I have spoken to Bill Hardcastle about this since, and he told me that what happened next was among the most exciting nights in his newspaper experience. It was 6 o'clock in London, and the front page had to be completely made over as the details came slowly in from Barbados.

I got out to Idlewild and on the first aeroplane and reached Barbados by 11 o'clock the next morning.

I only had to say 'Small World' to the smiling taxi-driver and he drove straight to the small, but beautiful hotel where they were resting, and I was taken upstairs to see them.

I wouldn't have believed that twenty-four days could have made so much difference — they looked as though they had just been released from a concentration camp. Particularly Tim, who was thin at the start and had lost a further thirty-three pounds. His face was skull-like, his eyes lost in bony sockets, and his ribs almost seemed outside his body. But he smiled cheerfully and joined in the general welcoming. Bushy and Colin had grown magnificent beards — Tim had a silky mandarin type — and had not lost as much weight, but both looked gaunt and tired. Rosemary had also lost about eighteen pounds, but except for this looked the fittest of them all. They were not as sunburned as I had expected, and I wanted to know why. I wanted to know everything that had happened to them since we had seen their balloon disappear into the darkness over the Atlantic Ocean.

BUSHY'S STORY

CHAPTER ONE

WE flew to Médano from Santa Cruz in twenty minutes and I was vastly relieved not to have to spend a precious six hours driving there and back on that first day when there was still so much to do. I glimpsed Médano itself as we came down. It was a typical little Spanish port with a jetty, a harbour and white buildings. It looked a pleasant enough place.

The pilot put us down on the airstrip and I was disappointed to see that they had unloaded the hydrogen cylinders there on the assumption that it was to be our launching place. There was a big hill between the airstrip and the sea, so, of course, it was an impossible site. I told them to start loading the cylinders back on to the lorries while Ralph, Colin and I went in a jeep to find a spot where the hill would not obstruct our take-off.

I had decided quite early on that I wanted to launch as near the sea as possible and was pleased that beside this hill there was a long, flat beach, very suitable indeed. The hill, which was about five-hundred feet high, might have been the end of a lava stream, I don't know, but it could have made a good screen. If the wind had been blowing any harder than five knots then or had done so during the week that I had spent in the island, I should probably have chosen a spot nearer to the hill, and therefore more out of the wind. But I had no reason to think that too strong winds would be a problem, and therefore I chose a site that was easily accessible from a sort of farm track that ran along the back of the beach. Colin and Ralph agreed that seeking the lee of the hill at the cost of manhandling everything another two or three hundred yards wasn't worth while. We walked over towards the sea and chose an

175

exceptionally flat area of sand. Then we got out a compass and the ground plan we'd made on the *Reventazon* and marked with stones where everything was to go — the crate with the car well to lee-ward; the balloon to windward, because we planned in the end to walk the balloon to the car, and not vice versa. A spot for the tent and so on. Ralph was left behind to tell them where to put every-thing and Colin and I flew back to pay our formal calls on the Captain General and other officials. The next time I saw the site was the following afternoon when everything was going splendidly.

The wind blew from the wrong quarter for the first two days, but I thought of how awful we should have felt if the wind had been right and we couldn't have taken advantage of it. I was thankful that we were spared that. I was delighted with the way the launching crew worked, considering that they were all volunteers, untrained and doing their jobs for the first time. It all got done quite quickly, and I think we enjoyed ourselves too. I know I did, and I felt that the others liked the picnic lunches, the chance for an occasional swim and the informality.

I won't pretend that everything was ideal, though. One of the things that I won't say irritated me, but rather that I wished had been different, was a feeling that Colin and Rosemary were a team within a team. I suppose that as Tim is my son, perhaps they felt it necessary, but I don't think it was, for Tim is very ob-jective, and I certainly didn't feel the need to protect him or any-thing of that sort. It wasn't very much, but only that I would rather have had three separate people to deal with instead of two who were always one. It made any discussion a bit difficult, for the Mudies never disagreed with one another — perhaps it was foolish of me to expect that they would — and although they had given me the authority to say 'do this' or 'do that', it is not my nature to handle people like that. I always want them to under-stand why and to agree that it should be done. This, sometimes, is hoping for too much.

Then Tim. He has a good mind, sees problems clearly and thinks out solutions. He's quite good at planning ahead too and at spotting something that hasn't been done that should have been.

It was useful to me to have someone as able as that checking on me, and many of his suggestions were very helpful. But dear me, the boy does love to argue! I got quite exhausted battling over almost every decision I took. He has a mathematical, logical mind, and I'm told that that is a fault I share with him. Well, he certainly got some of his own back on the beach at Médano, believe me. In the end I had to tell him that it was no good and that he'd just have to accept discipline like they do in the Army, at least on some things. I told him that a few wrong decisions were much better than the complete loss of peace and quiet that came with arguing about everything.

Anyway, I don't imagine that these small frictions would normally have bothered me at all if, say, we had inflated about the fourth day comfortably, as planned, and got away. But when the wind started to blow at twelve, fourteen and sometimes even twenty-two knots I began to worry about getting away at all. I had realised shortly after my visit to Tenerife that the ideal month, from the point of view of winds alone, was September. Of course, the chances of electrical storms are a bit worse then, but I think that the better winds are more important.

But by Wednesday night, when the wind had been blowing all day from exactly the right quarter but much too strongly, I began to get really worried, for I could see us sitting there for weeks waiting for exactly the right moment.

Wednesday was a long, hard day, and we got back to the Fonda Israel exceptionally late that night and completely bushed. Supper wasn't the usual pleasant meal of joking and laughter that night for we were all at that state of tiredness when nothing seems very important but to get some sleep. Tim had spoken to me on the phone from Santa Cruz, saying that he thought the wind might drop in the night, and I hadn't contradicted him, although I could hear it howling outside and thought that he probably didn't have any idea of how strongly it had been blowing all day at Médano. I agreed with his suggestion about keeping a watch going all night in case the wind did drop, but I didn't for a moment think that it would. I was glad when Pete insisted that the crew were not to go on watch, and I know Colin and Rosemary were too. I didn't take a lot of interest in the arrangements, for it just didn't seem possible to me that we could go that night. So I went to bed, shut my eyes and the next thing I knew was being awakened by Gerry Long.

"The wind's dropped to seven knots, Bushy," he said quietly.

My God, I thought, this is it. "Right-O, Gerry," I said, swinging out of bed, "I'll get the Mudies; you get the others."

I hated waking Colin and Rosemary. I hate waking them normally, for they sleep heavily and dislike very much being awakened, even in the mornings, and this time I knew that they had been dead tired, for neither had spared himself for a minute all day. I expect I sounded a bit hearty.

"Come on, Colin and Rosemary. All up, all up, all up. Wind's down to seven knots, and we're going. Come on, come on. The wind's down to seven knots. Wake up. Seven knots." Then I got out before I had something thrown at me, deciding to go back again in a few minutes, but then I heard them stirring, and knew that the excitement of going at last had got them too.

As soon as I had pulled on my trousers and shoes I went and woke up our taximan and told him to blow his horn and keep it blowing, for this was the signal to let the villagers know the balloon was going and we needed help. I also told him to send the boys to light Tim's signal fire on the hill-top, and by the time we were being driven to the site it was blazing away. It was a dramatic ride, going fast over the bumpy road, our horn blowing continuously. The signal fire had been answered quickly, for we could see the criss-cross of the headlights of the approaching cars coming in in droves.

Ralph, Gerry and I got the balloon out of its bag, laid it out and set about trying to thread the valve line through, but it was very difficult in the dark. I had wanted to leave the valve line in position, but Gerry had told me that it was never done that way, although I don't know why. Threading a rope from the valve at the top of the balloon to the neck at the bottom doesn't sound very difficult, but there are thousands of square yards of material, and the idea is to put your hand through the neck and then lift layer after layer of it over while you feel your way to the other man, whose hand is through the valve hole at the top. You soon feel his hand all right, but it is on the other side of dozens of layers of material and it's the devil's own job to fight your way around them and get to the hand itself.

I know now that this whole business of getting the balloon out of the bag and laid out and the lines threaded through, the valve in, the inflation pipe in place, the net on (we put it on inside out at first, and it had to be changed, for on the outside there were triangular wings for the guy ropes to be attached to) took three hours, but I didn't notice it at the time.

As soon as inflation had started and I had time to stand and look I noticed that the wind had got up again. I thought that Ralph would surely call a halt, and I was very surprised that he carried on for as long as he did. When I took off from Cardington once on one of my training flights in an almost too-strong wind it was very frightening to see how unpleasant things can become when the wind is too strong.

Some of the old hands told me what it's like when, as they say, the 'balloon takes control'. The men were tossed about like ants. But Ralph, who knew just how dangerous it was, carried on to the last possible minute. My heart was in my mouth when he decided to call a halt. We did try again in a lull, but it was obviously going to be impossible, and I was glad when he finally ordered us to let about ten thousand cubic feet go in order to reduce the balloon from three-fifths full to two-fifths.

That must have been about 4 o'clock, I suppose. We had to stand by and wait for another lull, of course, so I and most of the others rolled ourselves up in some pink polythene which was the remains of an auxiliary balloon and got some fitful sleep for a couple of hours. At dawn we ran up and down the beach a bit to get warm, and then Colin pointed out where folds of the balloon had been forced out by the night's wind and were being chafed against the beach or pinched by the sandbags, and we got them all under the balloon again, so as to reduce the damage to a bare minimum.

At about 11 o'clock that day, Thursday, Ed St. John offered to build us a wind-break, and I told him to go ahead, but never really thought that he'd get it done. By midday it seemed pretty certain that the wind wasn't going to drop, and I knew that we all ought to try to get some rest, so I divided the party up into two watches for the remainder of the day. One watch, consisting of Tim and myself, Anne, Gerry, Pete and the two cameramen, were to go off until 4 o'clock and then the others until 8 o'clock.

It had already been decided, on Tim's urging, that we would assume that the wind was going to drop again that night and try to finish the inflation and get off. Once again I didn't think it was likely, but by this time I was so depressed with the thought that the whole might end in a fiasco that I was willing to try anything. It was, of course, for Ralph and Gerry to decide, but I hoped very strongly that they would be more for audacity than caution.

The night before had been horrible, and more than once I had thought that we were going to lose the balloon. The thing was that, except for Ralph and Gerry, I knew more about how balloons could behave and was much more worried than anyone else. I cursed myself for not having put us in the lee of the hill, and I decided that if we missed on the next try I'd have the balloon deflated to the point where the available man-power could handle it and then have it walked across to the lee of the hill. All the cylinders would have to be manhandled over there, which would be a terrible job but not impossible. But I wasn't really sure that we had enough hydrogen for another complete inflation after this one, and I saw us sitting there waiting for the next boat from England with another batch of cylinders. A young chap had come up to me on the beach the day before and said that his father had plenty of hydrogen on the island which he would gladly give us and this did look like a lifeline, but I obviously couldn't bank on it.

Lack of sleep, disappointment and a feeling that it was all going to end disastrously — that is to say, that we'd not get off but lose the balloon — combined to make me depressed. Also Tim had been his most annoying that day, although not intentionally. He had queried almost every decision and had argued with me and with the Mudies constantly. As soon as we got back to the hotel and in our room I ticked him off soundly and, as he's always been taught to, he defended himself equally soundly. In the end I had to invoke army discipline, i.e., 'because I say so, that's why'. But it was an unhappy solution, and probably added to my depression.

So neither of us got any sleep in those four hours when we should have been restoring our strength, and my feeling of downright unhappiness was stronger than I can ever remember when we walked back to the site at four o'clock.

The first thing I saw was Ed St. John's wind-break, which gave me quite a lift. I didn't actually think that it would do much practical good, but I thought, "What a bloody hero!" It was not that everyone else hadn't also been doing his best but that this chap, floating in from nowhere had got down to a difficult job and accomplished it splendidly. Furthermore, his wind-break was really helping to keep our enormous quilted mushroom under control. The right man had often appeared from nowhere to help us: here was just one more instance.

If we were to get off that night there still remained a number of things to do, and I was eager to get at them. Pete came and asked me if I could give him twenty minutes. I was pretty sure that it was either about the film he was making or the book we were to write, and I decided at that point that I didn't give a damn if there wasn't any film or any book.

I suppose I must have a one-track mind, since everyone tells me so. I don't know, but one thing I do know is that I hate to be sidetracked into thinking about non-functional things when there is a job of work to be done. I was upset, of course, about the wireless not working, but my feeling about that was that it was really only necessary to send our daily messages to the *Mail*, and didn't have anything to do with the flight. Admittedly, if we didn't send our messages they wouldn't have to pay us what they had promised, and I like money as much as the next chap. But that was something we'd have to put up with.

I'm still surprised when people ask me why we tried to cross the ocean in The Small World. When Colin mentioned it to me I realised that this was exactly the kind of thing I had always wanted to do. It was a challenge that I couldn't say no to. After all, it's not yet five hundred years since it was crossed for the first time by ship, and forty years ago it was crossed for the first time in powered flight, but it had never been crossed in unpowered flight and surely that was a good enough reason to want to try to do it?

The others came back about 8 o'clock, and a bit later we started inflating again.

Tim had found out quite a lot about the wind in those parts, and he came up and spoke to Ralph Booth.

"I've found from local met. records that the wind hardly ever increases more than four knots at a time. So that must be your margin of safety. If three-quarters-inflated is safe at sixteen knots, then we'll inflate to three-quarters at twelve knots and so on." He explained. Ralph agreed in his quiet way, but a bit later when we had had to stop inflating, because the wind was up to sixteen knots again, Tim started to say it all over again and I had to stop him.

"You've said it once, Tim, and that's enough. Don't be a nagger and don't push Ralph into launching us if it's against his better judgement. The decision and the responsibility is his, and it's enough for him to fight the wind and the balloon without fighting you. Now, come on, we'll leave him alone — let's you and me get some rest." He saw my point immediately and let me lead him away. We climbed into the boat and wrapped ourselves in polythene to get some sleep.

I suppose that I hadn't had much more than two or three hours in the last forty-four, for I was too worried and depressed to be able to sleep. Now I tried to make myself comfortable while I listened to the wind howling and whistling outside. They'll never go tonight, I thought, and tomorrow we'll have to deflate and start moving all this stuff over under the hill. It was a disheartening thought.

Pete woke me by shouting something about starting to inflate again. I shook Tim, and we sat up. The wind was still whistling through the balloon's ropes.

"They'll never make it," I said aloud. I couldn't think that it was a good decision, and I was thankful that I hadn't made it. So far as launching decisions went Ralph was in charge. All I had to do now was to carry out my part and try my best to get the balloon off the ground.

Everyone worked at feverish speed to try to beat the rising wind, and I am convinced that it was a hair-breadth decision on Ralph's part and, in fact, he has told me since that another couple of knots at any time would probably have been too much. I kept pausing every now and then and trying to assess how near we were to the balloon taking control or destroying itself. The most dangerous moments were when we walked it over to the boat, for a gust of twenty knots or so could have lifted it several hundred feet in the air, shaking men off like ants on a bit of string.

I stayed with the balloon as we walked over and held on to the ripping-panel line. If it did get too much for us I was ready to pull out the ripping panel and let the gas go. We had brought a spare panel along, and with Gerry Long's help could probably have put it in.

But we got the balloon to the boat; I fixed on one of the four suspension ropes and saw that the rest of the crew were doing one each. For the first time the fantastic thought crossed my mind — we might make it yet!

Colin and I checked that the extra ballast had been piled in order of importance, with the least necessary on top. I had been badly shaken to find that the total lift of the full balloon at Cardington was only thirty-one hundredweight instead of the thirty-seven our calculations had told us. We checked our calculations again, but there was no mistake there, and there certainly was no mistake about the actual lift. I thought that perhaps the indentations made by the net had reduced the cubic capacity or that the weight pulled the balloon to a pear shape instead of a perfect sphere. I questioned Ralph about this, and he told me immediately, as though it was a well-known fact, that this difference in shape could mean a loss of nearly fifteen per cent from the theoretical lift. I had never found any reference to this in any of the text-books on ballooning, and it just goes to prove that there is no substitute for actual experience.

Anyway, this was a serious blow, for it meant that we couldn't take our safety margin of six hundredweight of ballast. I had a talk with the others about it, but it was November by then, and obviously we couldn't change our plans. We would just have to go and hope that our water-lifting device worked so well that we would never need that extra ballast.

I had hoped that Ralph was wrong and that there was some other mysterious explanation for the low lift at Cardington, and so we had piled on the ballast just in case we had thirty-seven hundredweight of lift. We had five hundredweight, mostly luxury food and extra calcium hydride, arranged so that we could get shot of it quickly.

Now I climbed in the boat while the ground crew and scads of willing but uninstructed Spanish helpers got the sandbags off. Gerry Long was patiently trying to show someone how to untie his knots, but I shouted to him that it was no good and he'd better use his knife, and soon the clusters of sandbags were dropping off and the balloon tugged and moved the boat a few inches. This was the most critical time, and I was feverishly impatient to get the last of the sandbags off, and I felt unreasonably that things were not going fast enough.

"For God's sake let's go!" I heard myself shouting. "Let's get out of here!" Then the last of the sandbags were cut loose, but we didn't move. Ralph had been proved right.

We started heaving off the top row of bags of calcium hydride tins, and after we'd got rid of quite a number a gust of wind lifted us and then slammed us down on the sand. As a safety precaution we were attached by a long line to a heavy lorry, and now I jumped up and cut through it. We were still unable to rise, but were light enough for the wind to be able to push us across the ground, which was, of course, very bad for the hull. We had to get up quickly, and we threw over calcium hydride and bags of extra food which we should have been glad to take but which weren't really necessary. They must have weighed about two hundredweight, which made quite a difference, for we rose and moved towards the sea, with the crowd chasing after us, led by Anne and Jenny, who, to my surprise, kissed me soundly while I was leaning over the transom adjusting the trail line.

The next moment we came down again in the water, but as we had been trailing our tow line, we landed bows first perfectly.

"Take it easy with the ballast now," I told the others. "We mustn't overdo it, or we'll be in trouble. Leave it to me." They did so, and I let go some more. We were being pulled through the water, and I heard someone shout, "Come back, Jenny, come back!" and saw staunch Jenny nearly waist deep in water.

We could hear the noise of car horns blowing, people clapping and the shouting. Every time we hit the water the tension wires under the hull hummed loudly.

"I've got an idea," said Colin. "Let's get rid of some of the water ballast." Of course that was the thing to do, for we shouldn't really have taken off with water ballast at all at night. It was intended for a day-time take-off, so that in the evening when the gas cooled we could compensate for the loss of lift by pouring over water. It was a slip all right. We should have gone at night with an empty water-ballast tank. If we had, we should have been able to carry more food and calcium hydride.

The bucket was tied on, but we soon unlashed it and began throwing water over. This did it, for we lifted out of the sea and began trailing our Terylene line and the two hundred feet of smooth high-pressure hose, which weighed seventy-five pounds and was to act as a brake on ascent and descent alike.

The feeling of serenity after all the noise and confusion was wonderful, and we looked at each other, hardly believing that we were actually on our way.

"I know what," Colin said. "I shall give them a reassuring blast on the bugle." The bugle was our fog-horn, and had been given to us by the local boy scouts. Colin blew an unhappy note on it.

"Not very good, Mr. Mudie," I said. "Have some water on your lips." He must have done something, for the next blast was long and loud, and we hoped that they heard it on the beach.

Without telling the rest of us, Tim had switched on our tiny E.M.I. portable wire recorder about half an hour before we took off, and it continued to run, forgotten by Tim too, its full length of nearly eighty minutes. From then on we were too busy ever to use it again, but we have that recording with us now, and I have just been playing it back. It recalled the scene on the beach and the first forty minutes of our flight to me vividly, and I was surprised at how many things I had forgotten.

After Colin had blown his 'reassuring blast' I suggested that one of our early jobs must be to untangle our trail rope, which was evidently shortened by tangles and was keeping us too near the water for comfort.

Tim had been envying Colin the trumpet, and now he got hold of it. "Let me just make a raucous noise," he said. He blew a most dreadful sound.

"Shut up, Tim," I said testily. "You're terrible!"

"Let me just try to blow a note," he said and made another horrible sound.

"Try it another time. You don't have to do it now — they'll think we're dying!" I told him.

"They *don't* think we're dying." Tim sounded quite annoyed. "I'll blow a beautiful note." We had to suffer while he blew a long, long blast. Then, thank goodness, he turned his attention to connecting up our sensitive electric altimeter. Everything seemed to be going beautifully and according to plan. We were bowling along just over the waves trailing our rope, rising and falling gently, sometimes fifteen feet high, sometimes a hundred and fifty, at the sort of pace few sailing-ships have ever done. Roughly, Colin and I reckoned that at a hundred feet over the open sea the wind was blowing at twenty knots, and we, slowed by our trail, were doing four or five knots less.

Colin was leaning over the stern looking at the waves as they occasionally reflected our navigation light.

"Look at the way we're leaving those waves behind! Lord knows they're moving fast themselves — it's incredible. We must be doing fourteen or fifteen knots, and here we are as steady as a house-boat. Think what this speed would be like on some enormous yacht — all the noise of wind and waves, sloping wet decks with no safe foothold and here we are sitting back laughing, no struggle at all. Fourteen knots — that's over three hundred miles a day. We'll get there in a week if we keep that up."

"And it's all so damned effortless," I said happily. "That's the miracle of it. I can't think why no one's ever tried it before."

Then suddenly I felt that the wind had disappeared. There could only be one reason for that — we were moving along in it at exactly the same speed, like a fly encased in amber. And that could happen only if our trail was out of the water and no longer slowing us down.

"I say, are we up, Colin?" I asked. "Are we free — no trail dragging?" Only a moment before, it seemed, we had been just above the water.

"The altimeter says five hundred feet," Colin told me.

"Five hundred feet?" I couldn't believe it.

"We're five hundred and sixty," he replied. I couldn't take it in, for it was only seven minutes, as we later learned from our wire recording, since we took off, and I couldn't think why we should suddenly be shooting up. Later on the voyage I decided that a ballast bag must have fallen off without our noticing, but today, after talking with some of the ground crew who were watching our sudden ascent from the beach, I think that it must have been caused by our first thermal. They tell me that they saw our navigation light disappear into the clouds and then two or three minutes later come out above them. Tim now says that he can remember the damp mist that must have been the cloud and thinking to himself how unpleasant it was but that he would obviously have to get used to it. Be that as it may, from a delicious feeling of serenity we were switched to a sense of emergency.

Colin spoke again. "Seven hundred feet."

" *Seven* hundred feet?"

"Seven hundred feet — going up!" he replied. We were shooting up.

"Shall we drop a water bag?" Yes, of course that was the thing to do. "Get the lashings off the pedals," I told Rosemary, for the pedals were still tied as they had been on take-off. She got working on them with her knife; Colin stayed at the altimeter, and Tim and I quickly got our carefully laid out coils of rope and the water-lifting bag ready to drop.

"Eight hundred feet coming up," Colin intoned.

The rope had been put in stops to prevent tangling and it took us a few seconds to cut them. "Now, what's the height, Colin?" I asked anxiously.

"Twelve hundred — still going up." Calculations raced through my head with dismay. That meant that already we'd lost a thirtieth of our gas through the open neck and we'd been launched less than half an hour. Tim and I leapt to get the stops off our water-lifting line — we had to take on water fast!

Our happy serenity had disappeared entirely: Rosemary was lashing away like mad to clear the pedals and get the seats in their 'action' positions; Colin had the altimeter in one hand and was trying to help Rosemary with the other; Tim and I were working feverishly to drop the water-lifting bag and fifteen hundred feet of line without it tangling.

Fifteen hundred feet is a very long line and, as I threw over those hundreds of coils, I felt far from confident that the bag would fall straight into the sea, even though the rope had been coiled to allow just that. But the whole lot dropped out of sight in the blackness that lay beneath us. The water-lifting bag should reach the sea, far below us, in a few seconds and start to slow up our climb.

"What's the height, Colin?"

"Nearly eighteen hundred."

"Hell! Quick — all hands to get another three or four hundred feet of line off the reel." We had only put fifteen hundred feet over which I had thought would be plenty, but we were rising fast.

The weight of the bag and the line hanging over the stern roller undid the reel so fast there was no need to increase it. The coloured silk threads, that told me how much line had been paid out, flashed by — yellow and blue, yellow and red, yellow and brown, yellow all the way. Yellow all the way? Damn, damn, damn — that was twenty-five hundred feet — much too much.

"Stop!" I yelled, "stop her."

In the bustle the colour code had slipped my memory and now we would all have an extra fifteen minutes, hard pedalling.

But we couldn't stop the reel, for the brake hadn't been rigged yet. Colin lifted his foot waist high and pushed the speeding line down on the floor with the thick rubber sole of his sailing-shoe and stood on it. The line kept running, and there was a smell of burning rubber. It was slowing down, but something more was needed. I twisted my arm, protected by several layers of warm clothing, around the line, and it slowed still more. It didn't seem to be burning my clothes and stupidly, desperately wanting to make good my error, I closed my fingers round the line. In an instant three of them were friction-burned to the flesh.

The running line slowed, halted and I cleated it astern. I found myself glaring at the others as though they were criminals until the unfairness of it hit me. Of course, the brake on the reel hadn't been rigged; nothing had been rigged. Why, damn it, we'd only just been launched, and how could they or anyone else have known that we'd be almost two thousand feet high within minutes of take-off?

Colin had gone back to the altimeter. I had made it very clear before we started that I must be told our height at all costs if I was too busy to see for myself.

"Still eighteen hundred," he said.

"Good — we must have picked up some water. Now for the nice long job of pulling ourselves down."

The others took their places at the pedals without talking, and I uncleated the line and took my place. We started the long, weary job, Colin holding the altimeter in his hand.

"Seventeen fifty . . . seventeen hundred and going down."

"Good!" The water-lifting bag was doing its job and the emergency was over. It was a great relief, but we must have lost almost two hundredweight of lift before we had been able to get it going.

"Going down to fourteen hundred," Colin said. We relaxed and went on pedalling for what seemed a long time, and then the pedals jammed. I got up to see what was wrong.

Looking down over the stern I found a warp of tangled line caught up in the rudder fittings and struggled to untangle it.

"What are we showing for height, Colin?"

"Nineteen hundred." I felt a heavy, sick feeling of dismay in my stomach.

"No — nine hundred," Tim corrected, and Colin agreed.

We were coming down and coming down nicely — we must have picked up a lot of water. I stayed aft and cleared the tangles; the others pedalled and more line came up and then more tangles. This happened several times until suddenly I found that the water-bag line was entangled with our trailing hose, which was supposed to be on a quite different line altogether.

Reaching down as far as I could, I grabbed the end of the hose, cleared it together with a great lump of tangled line from the rudder fitting and told the others to pedal slowly. Of course, I told myself, they couldn't pedal fast if they wanted to with the weight of the full water-bag added to the hose and both lines. Slowly I got one end of the hose inboard, and then the Mudies quickly and expertly started untangling it. This was clearly a number one priority so that we could get the trailing hose over and hanging in its place beneath us to stop us from hitting the water on the way down.

The main tangle, that of our long water-bag-lifting line, would be a much more difficult job. It looked as though it might be a full day's work, and meanwhile we should have to use our reserve, which was a bit shorter and lighter. But because of the great strength of Terylene I was confident that it would do the job.

Our altitude was still dropping, which was fine, and the Mudies worked away at the untangling, now and then asking Tim or me to hold a long bight freed from the main mass while they worked on the short ones. It was a job that needed experience and patience, and watching them working confidently was one of the best practical lessons I've ever had.

While I watched them I remembered a conversation with Ralph Booth about the problem of our lines tangling. I had heard that he was the most knowledgeable man in England on the handling of airships, and I asked him to call so that I could get his advice on certain points. One of the points was how we could best perfect a technique for dropping our water-bags into the sea without getting them tangled with our trail rope.

"If the only other line astern is your trail rope it shouldn't be too bad," he said, "but didn't you say that you were going to hang your emergency food and water astern as well?"

"Yes — on different lengths of line. The idea is that they'll act as a brake if we drop suddenly in a downdraught."

"I can see that, but it's not going to help the problem of tangling. The best way to solve that kind of a problem is in use, of course. Can't you get in some practice flights over the water using your practice gas-bag?"

"Not a hope — we don't have the time, and the following speed-boat, gas, transport and so on would cost five hundred quid a time."

"Then it looks as though you'll have to hope to find a solution early on in the actual flight, for I don't think it is the kind of pro-blem that can be solved sitting over a cup of tea. I doubt whether a team of bright people in a drawing-office could solve it without actual practice."

I was afraid that that was what he was going to say, for Colin and I had just about come to the same conclusion. It would mean that our record attempt would also have to be a proving flight, which was a pity but unavoidable. We made up our mind that we should go and try our damnedst.

Well, we had gone and here we were with the king of all tangles on our hands and no solution to the problem. Altitude was still falling nicely, but we had to get that hose line clear and hanging over the stern before we hit the water, because it would then pull us around and make sure that we were bows on to the waves when we hit. If we landed broadside to the sea it could be a disaster.

The Mudies finished untangling three hundred feet of the hose line and we lowered it gently astern and got down once more to pulling in the water-bag line. Once again, after what seemed an age of hard pedalling, the line stuck.

I got the spot-light and, leaning over the stern, aimed the beam down. There was a mass of tangled line caught in the rudder fittings and the water-bag — which was empty.

Empty! I couldn't believe my eyes. It *couldn't* be empty! Damn it, hadn't the weight of the water pulled us down? But it *was* empty, there wasn't a drop of water in it — it didn't make sense, but it was so.

My God, perhaps we hadn't gone down?

"How high?" I asked, "How high are we? Quick, Colin."

"Less than five hundred feet — we must be trailing again."

"We are trailing," Tim confirmed, "I can just feel the relative wind again."

"Yes, I can feel it too," Colin said. "And it's coming up astern, which means our trail has swung us stern to wind — exactly according to plan. Everything's working beautifully, Mr. Bush, our water-bag brought us down and our trail performed admirably — why so glum, Mr. Bush?"

"Because the damned water-bag is empty. It hasn't worked."

"Empty?" All three of them looked as puzzled as I felt.

"Perhaps it was full but got turned upside down by the tangles and emptied itself," Colin suggested.

The others pedalled it up until I could get hold of it and haul it inboard — it was bone dry. Obviously it had never reached the water, because the line had been too short with all the tangles.

Why, then, had we started to come down as soon as we pedalled? I couldn't think of the answer, and right at the moment that problem could wait.

We were trailing at about fourteen knots and rising and falling gently.

"There seems to be no great danger in the present situation," Tim said thoughtfully.

"We're very near the sea," Rosemary said, looking over the side.

They argued about how near for a moment or two, and then agreed that as long as we could hear the waves we were pretty close. Meanwhile, I was struggling with the knots and not feeling very happy. If we were unable to drop our water-lifting bags quickly into the sea we were going to be in a pretty bad way at dawn when the sun started heating up the gas and sent us soaring.

Gawd, I thought, fancy having a problem like this on our hands at this stage of the game. We were all very tired, for not only had we had little sleep for two days, but we had been working hard since take-off. Take-off, incidentally, had been only an hour before, as I now know from timing the wire recording. If any of us had been asked to guess I think we would have said at least three hours.

We finally dragged the knotted mess inside the boat, and I thought about why we had come down. The reason, of course, was elementary, but I was almost too tired to think. We had lost two hundredweight of lift by going up almost two thousand feet and had therefore been heavier than the air we were displacing and had started to fall. It had been pure coincidence that it had happened when we started pedalling. We should have continued to go right down to the sea if our trail hadn't relieved us of weight as planned. It was good that something was working, anyway.

"Would anyone like a cup of hot coffee?" Rosemary asked. Would we! It was delicious, and it was the last bit of warm food any of us were to have for a long while.

"How high are we?" I asked as I drank the warm coffee.

"Three hundred feet," Colin replied.

"Are we really three hundred?" I asked in surprise, for we had been down to one hundred only a few moments before. He looked at the altimeter again.

"We're twelve hundred and fifty!" he said.

I jumped up. "Twelve hundred and fifty!"

"No, sorry — two hundred and fifty." It was difficult to read the instrument, as our only light was the six-volt navigation light in the rigging above us.

"There's no *reason* for it," I said. "We're shooting up and down — are we still going up?"

"Yes — three hundred feet," Colin answered. It was our first hour of steady trailing, and somehow I had imagined that our height above the sea would be constant, but later we got used to oscillating between about fifty feet and two hundred and fifty. The rhythmical rise and fall was caused, of course, by the action of the waves on our trail. Once we were used to it, we didn't mind it, but this first experience was disturbing.

However, we saw after about an hour that nothing very dreadful was happening, and we settled down to wait for the dawn. We had a spare two thousand feet of line and an extra water-lifting bag and we decided, as soon as we felt the first of the sun's warmth, to lower it steadily and hope that we could keep ahead of the lift from superheat.

Tim got to work rigging up his transmitter. I took watch astern.

The job of getting the three-thousand-foot reel of tangled line off and the two-thousand-foot one on was done by the Mudies, and they also volunteered to tackle the unravelling of the knots. They were dubbed the 'Mudie knitting team', and they spent much of the next two days on the problem.

I had in mind to divide up every twelve hours into four watches of three hours each, but Colin pointed out that as I was the only one with practical ballooning experience, I should be on call at any time, and so the day was divided into watches of four hours each. The person on watch had to keep an eye on the altimeter and also keep looking over the stern to make sure that we weren't getting too close to the water.

I lay down to sleep for a couple of hours before dawn because I knew how busy we would be then. It was cold that first night, and because I flopped down on top of the sleeping-bag instead of getting in it I got thoroughly chilled. Tim woke me an hour before sunrise with some cheese and biscuits. As we were all munching them, someone saw a light.

One of the many worries on take-off had been our direction, for if we were much east of south we would finish up in Africa, whereas if we were as far west as west-south-west we might pile up on the mountain of Hierro. We had gone off a little west of south, which was fine and, as Tim had predicted, our course had been veering more and more westerly. Several times we had wondered about Hierro, and we were all looking out for it. If the mountain loomed up ahead of us it would be very serious, for if we had to go to six thousand feet to get over it we would lose a fifth of our lift, which might be decisive.

We identified the light as the Orchilla lighthouse on Hierro, and to our relief we saw that we were going to pass comfortably to the south of the island. A half an hour later it had disappeared, and no more land now lay between us and the West Indies.

It had given us a fix: we had done over seventy miles in six hours, and almost exactly in the right direction. At that rate we'd be on the other side of the Atlantic in eight or nine days.

Friday at dawn we got our first lucky break: the sky was overcast, and so there was no superheat. The Mudies kept up their 'knitting' between helping with other jobs such as unshipping the mast from inside the craft and adding it to our trail. Tim dried out his batteries and took them inboard; he had sent a message earlier in the night, but wasn't sure that everything was working correctly, for he had heard nothing on his receiving set, and he wanted to avoid the further damage the batteries would get by getting wet when we bounced on the water.

The sun came out briefly about the middle of the morning, and we had a chance to try again with our second water-bag. We let it fall into the water: it went straight down, filled up beautifully and we started to haul it up. It was pulled back behind us by the forward motion of the balloon and, as we were going slightly faster than the waves, was dragged along the surface of the sea, slowly over the crest and then slowly into the trough. To our dismay we saw, as it lay mouth down towards the trough, that it was emptying itself. When we got it back on board there wasn't more than five pounds of water in it. It was our second great disappointment.

We had to get up twenty or thirty such lots to take on enough water, which was very hard work indeed. I thought that the only thing to do was to make us almost too heavy as the sun came out. This would give us every opportunity of beating the effect of superheating. But being too heavy meant bouncing on the water. Someone suggested that we work the propellers to ease the bounces, and we tried this. It worked fine, even at times stopping us from hitting at all, but it was terribly hard work in our exhausted state.

At three in the afternoon the sun came out quite strongly and we pedalled like mad to scoop up enough water to keep down, but were unable to overcome the lift and up, up we went again. I hated to do it, but I valved out some gas on the way up. Even at that we went to eighteen hundred feet again. It was discouraging and when, at last, we got down to our oscillating heights of between fifty and a hundred and fifty feet for the second night I was quite angry with frustration.

We couldn't drop our rope over fast in coils without its knotting hopelessly; when we did get a water-lifting bag full we couldn't get it up on board without losing most of the water! On our ability to pull up ballast from the sea depended the whole success of the flight, and I seriously doubted whether we would be able to combat those two failures before we were forced down like all other balloonists by having lost too much lift.

We knew, of course, what was needed — some sort of non-return valve in the water-lifting bag, while it was lying mouth down on one of those long Atlantic rollers, which would let the water in but not out. We were not equipped to make anything like that, though. Then Rosemary had her bright idea.

"Why not sew a sort of sock inside like a wind-sock that will let the water in but bunch up and stop it if it tries to flow out?" she suggested.

It was a brilliant idea, but it was easier to say than to do. Tim and Colin each got down to designing a water-lifting bag with Rosemary's lobster-pot trap in it. They worked at it on and off for the next two days.

But before that there were many other things to do. Tim was worried about the gas blowing down on us from the open neck, particularly as the wireless was not enclosed, and he wanted to climb up and fix our baffle cloth to deflect it. I insisted that he put on his safety harness and showed him how to get into it. He then scrambled up and fixed the screen in place. Rosemary got her cameras out and took some pictures; Tim sent a wireless message. Until the late-afternoon sun hit us everything seemed to be fine.

On the way down after our second climb to eighteen hundred feet we had to get rid of some ballast to make up for the gas we had lost, and overboard went eighteen pounds of nut pemmican, twelve pounds of chocolate powder and all the less essential of our heavier tools, but it wasn't enough, and we had to throw over twenty pounds of sugar as well. I realised that many more such unwanted ascents would mean the end, for now we had only a few things that we could throw over. It was obvious that we were a long way from solving our problem of height control and that any sudden thermal would carry us up faster than we could take on water. We were determined to jettison just about everything on board, including the pedalling apparatus, the hydrogen generator and the safety rail before we gave up and came down because of lack of lift. Now I had to decide what to get rid of next.

It seemed that we wouldn't be using the radio receiver at all, for we had no time for listening, and it seemed certain that before long the transmitter would have to go too. The propellers were useful in stopping us bouncing too hard, but useless against a thermal, so they would have to go. No doubt there was still some food too that could be spared.

But that night we trailed along quite comfortably, and Tim and I had four glorious hours of sleep; Colin, too, dozed off in his pedalling chair about three o'clock in the morning, leaving Rosemary the only one awake. She kept a weather eye on the altimeter and over the stern at the sea and kept herself awake by writing up her log and getting the films in her camera changed.

CHAPTER TWO

JUST before dawn Rosemary woke us all up so that we should be ready for the fight against superheat. We were riding along about fifty feet above the waves, at an average, which was just right for taking on extra water ballast in a hurry.

But once again it was an overcast sky, and the morning sun was no problem. It was squally, and several times during the morning the rain pelted down with tropical force for twenty minutes or half an hour. At the peak of the heavy shower it felt as though we were flying through a waterfall, and the rain poured off the gas bag and filled the baffle cloth under the open neck. When it got too full a sudden lurch would spill it down the neck of whomever was underneath. It was very funny when it happened to someone else.

But what wasn't funny was all the extra weight this water meant, which we didn't want at all. The surface of the balloon picked up quite a lot of weight just with its film of water, but it was the rain that poured into the boat that was even more serious. Unfortunately, the bungs in the draining holes were not in the most accessible position, and they had to come out every time the rain fell. They then had to be put in again as soon as the rain stopped, and before the water had completely drained away. This was because while it was raining and making us heavier we wanted to get rid of weight, but we knew that as soon as it stopped the sun would come out, dry off the balloon and start heating the gas, and then we'd want the extra weight. So the order was "Out bungs!" then "In bungs!" and so on as the rain squalls came and went.

Everything got sopping wet and the labels came off the tins, so that from then on opening a tin was a lucky dip. With more time we would have followed the yachtsman's practice of writing on each tin in black paint, but we were too rushed. But it was already warmer, and our special suits kept us beautifully dry. Also the sun dried everything out remarkably quickly, so that it wasn't really too unpleasant.

Tim dutifully sent his radio message, but left the transmitter on and ran the battery down, which, as it meant pedalling the dynamo, made him pretty unpopular for a bit.

Rosemary had taken aboard a kind of flour called Gofio which is peculiar to the Canary Islands, I think. It is made out of parched wheat and is supposed to be of great nutritional value. I didn't like it much — we had it for breakfast with tinned milk every day — but Colin thought it was fine, and the others ate it too. I found that I wasn't awfully hungry, and I never eat when I'm not hungry, so that I had less than the others. I remember on Saturday our lucky-dip tins turned out to be carrots and mandarin oranges. I didn't think this a particularly appetising mixture and had only the carrots. A week or so later I remembered turning down those tinned oranges and simply could not believe that I'd ever been so foolish.

The rain stopped in the afternoon and the sun came out. We managed to stay ahead of superheat lift by lots of little grabs of water, and by 4 o'clock or so I thought the worst of the heat was over.

"It can't get any hotter now, can it?" I asked the others. They agreed that it couldn't.

We passed under a cloud. That's a dangerous place to be, but as we were only at two hundred feet I thought the thermal wouldn't influence us. I was wrong, for this one caught us off guard and we started to go up like a lift. We tried feverishly to get our water-lifting bag down to sea-level in time, but we rose faster than we could pay out the line.

"Damn!" I said, when I saw that we were free ballooning and there was no hope of picking up water, "Oh, well, we might as well enjoy a couple of hours of free ballooning and not worry about it."

I knew that we had gone to eighteen hundred feet twice and that we'd probably go about the same again. One of the quite encouraging things was that, although we had lost gas on our first ascent about half an hour after take-off, the following day the remaining gas had expanded when warm and we still had a full balloon. Even if we hadn't gone high and so lost gas that first night, we should have done so when the sun warmed the envelope the next day, for it would have expanded on heating and come out the open neck. This second day, Saturday, was hotter than the first, and once more, even though we had lost gas on Friday afternoon, the expansion had filled the balloon. We really weren't doing too badly as far as conserving gas was concerned, but the serious thing, of course, was that we still didn't have a water-lifting bag that worked.

Once again we levelled off at eighteen hundred and then, slowly over a period of two hours, started to come down. What happens is that the momentum of the balloon carries it beyond the point where it is heavier than the air it is displacing, and when it is so heavy that it has to stop, it starts coming down, only remaining at its peak altitude on the rarest occasions. Unless its descent can be checked, its downward momentum will continue until it hits the ground.

So, as soon as we started to fall, I ordered ballast off fast. We had decided that the propellers were not worth their weight, and already had one and its supporting outrigger unshipped. This was the first thing to go. It didn't seem to make much difference, and so over went the radio receiver, more tools, our knotted Terylene rope that had defied all the efforts of the Mudie knitting team, the grapnel — when we reached the jungle we'd just have to come down on the tree-tops — and more of our precious food. All this slowed us up and stopped us hitting the water hard.

By this time the sun really was cooling, and once again we sailed on through the night oscillating from just above the waves to a couple of hundred feet.

Tim had designed a water-lifting bag with a rather heavy device inside to stop the inlet sock from coming out and spilling the water, but was having difficulty in actually making it. I asked Colin to give him a hand, which he did rather reluctantly, because he didn't think much of Tim's design, but I was at the stage of grabbing at straws and insisted. They got it made late that night, and we were able to test it the next day, Sunday.

We were all up, of course, before dawn, which was another squally, cloud-patched one. But an hour after sunrise the clouds cleared and we felt the superheat within a few minutes. We plopped over Tim's water-lifting bag as soon as we saw our tow hose start to lift out of the water. The bag sank quickly and we began pedalling. It was very heavy, and by the time we were able to get it up to the level of the boat we were at four hundred feet. But it was chock full of lovely sea-water — about a hundred pounds of it. It was so heavy that I had to rig up a three-way pulley from the leading lines of the net to get it inboard. I was immensely elated, for it had done the trick.

We floated along for an hour or so still trailing, and I thought that the best thing to do would be to test our new bag once or twice more and then, if it worked every time, to let the balloon rise until our trail was right out of the water and we were free ballooning at just above five hundred feet. We could have the water-lifting bag half lowered too, so that as soon as we hit a thermal we could plop it in and pick up a hundredweight of water at a time, which would surely be enough to stop us. It was an exhilarating thought, for this was how we originally intended to make our crossing, and it meant that we could get on so much faster.

Not that we had been doing at all badly as it was. Colin had done his navigation and told us that we were making a steady three hundred miles a day, which was most encouraging.

But the next time we tried our water-lifting bag it sprang a leak; Tim repaired it, but it was a blow. The rain squalls came again and once more we had the hectic 'out bungs' and 'in bungs' and the scrambling about for ballast. We had a ballast bag into which we threw every little thing such as the lead insulation around the wires, bits and pieces of metal, plastic and anything else we could do without. But, of course, unless we could pick up water we were dissipating our limited supply of ballast and bringing nearer the hour when we would have to come down.

So far we had hung on to the hydrogen generator and most of

the calcium hydride, for the use of them was to be our final effort. The smaller amount of gas in the balloon, the less we lost if we were sent soaring by a thermal, and unless the sun had so heated the gas that the balloon was full to capacity we wouldn't lose any until it went higher than the last time. But if we now generated hydrogen and filled the balloon we might lose most of it on the next thermal. My plan was to get rid of absolutely everything we could spare, thus lightening the craft to the minimum. At that point I calculated that even if the balloon was no more than half full it would keep us up. Then I would keep it aloft by making new hydrogen. When all our calcium hydride was used up and the hydrogen generator thrown overboard as well we would not be able to do anything more, but this plan should keep us aloft for the maximum time.

The rain that Sunday morning was heavier than we'd yet known it, and we worked like slaves to offset the effect of the water pouring in. Then, as is the way with tropical rains, it stopped suddenly and the sun came out. Instantly our efforts were reversed from trying to keep light to trying to become heavy. Over went Tim's heavy water-lifting bag, which, fortunately, he had repaired, and we started to haul it in. For a few moments it was slow and heavy, and then it started to come quickly; I didn't have to look and find out what had happened for I knew — the bag had burst with its weight of water. We started to go up with alarming swiftness: I looked up, and sure enough we were under another damn cloud. When I looked down again it was to see the last few feet of our heavy hose whip out of the water. I jumped for the variometer which shows rate of climb. The needle was jammed right over — we had run out of dial and were rising faster than ever before. With that kind of momentum I knew it was unlikely that we would level off at eighteen hundred feet this time.

I grabbed the line to the gas valve. The others were looking at me waiting for instructions.

"What do you think, Tim?" I asked. "Do I valve out a bit of gas?"

"Yes, the earlier, the better. If we wait, we'll lose much more."

I pulled the valve for three seconds. I knew from experience how easy it is to valve out too much, for apparently it has no effect. It takes time for the loss of lift to overcome the momentum, and one is inclined to overdo it. Tim, of course, hadn't experienced this time lag, and kept telling me to valve out more.

We hit the cloud at eight hundred feet: again rain fell heavily.

"In bungs!" I yelled, for we needed every ounce of weight we could catch. Colin scrambled under the foredeck and got the bungs back in, but we kept on rising right through the cloud. The rain stopped.

"How fast are we rising?" I asked. Tim had got hold of our sensitive altimeter and was using it with his stop watch.

"A bit slower," he said. "I think we might steady off at about two thousand feet." If we did it wouldn't be too bad, although we should then start to lose gas through the open neck, for the balloon would have expanded to capacity. But at eighteen hundred feet we were still rising fast. I pulled the valve line again, but didn't dare do it for too long. Not only did I not want to lose unnecessary gas, but I was afraid we'd be so heavy that we'd fall like a stone.

Rosemary was standing by the altimeter calling out the height. "Twenty-seven . . . twenty-eight . . . twenty-nine" — it was like a damn helicopter! I pulled the valve line and counted the seconds "one little second; two little seconds; three little seconds". There — that had lost us forty pounds of lift. Surely it *must* make a difference.

"Three thousand feet . . . thirty-one hundred . . . thirty-two hundred . . ." Thank God we were slowing up. "Thirty-three . . . thirty-four . . . still thirty-four . . . no!" Rosemary shouted, "thirty-three — we're going down!"

Tim immediately climbed up into the load ring and tied the neck, for unless, at some later time, we went higher than thirty-four hundred feet, which seemed highly unlikely, the balloon wouldn't burst and the tied neck would prevent air perpetually mixing with the gas.

Now, I knew, we were going to fall like a spent rocket. I had valved out over a hundred pounds of lift, and we were heavy with rain.

"Out bungs!" Colin had them out in a jiffy and water poured out, but our fall was accelerating.

"We'll have to be ready to hit the water hard," I warned the others. "I'm going to prepare the quick release, just in case." I made sure that there were no extra ropes holding the craft to the balloon, and I cut the lashings of cord that were kept on the triggers to prevent them operating accidentally. At the same time I told the others to get the emergency ballast ready.

"Two thousand feet . . . eighteen hundred . . . sixteen hundred . . . fourteen hundred," Rosemary shouted out: we were falling so fast she could only call at two-hundred-foot intervals.

"Wireless transmitter ready to chuck over, Tim?" I asked.

"Right — in twenty seconds," he replied.

"Get one of the batteries ready for chucking, Colin." Colin jumped to it. I gathered up the sleeping-bags and looked around for anything else.

At eight hundred feet we plummeted through the cloud. At five hundred our seventy-five pounds of hose would hit the water and relieve us of that much weight, but our momentum would overcome the added lift. We'd have perhaps another twenty seconds to get shot of enough weight to avoid being smashed up when we hit the water.

I had shouted to Colin to get the starboard propeller unit undone; we were all struggling in the wet and cold with slippery gear. At five hundred our hose went back into the water and we started to drag: the cups of our wind-speed gauge span round madly. That meant that we were now going slower than the wind, and therefore that the surface of the balloon would be cooled, the gas contract and we would lose even more lift.

"Ballast off!" I ordered and overboard went the transmitter, one battery, the propeller unit and our sleeping-bags. Still we kept on falling too fast. Rosemary dived for the food bags. We had ten tins of peaches and pineapples, and the whole lot had to go. A few seconds later we hit the sea hard.

We all hung on to something to keep our feet. I was relieved to see that the hull was still in one piece. The tension wires were howling as they were dragged through the water. In a few moments we bounced high out of the sea again. We had to be lightened still more somehow, and over went the other battery and the electric generator. The bounce wasn't too bad. Up she went again, and next time we bounced quite lightly. There wasn't much more to throw over, but we sacrificed a few tins of our nut pemmican, and she stayed up with the hose trailing comfortably.

I had noticed the time when the rain stopped and our troubles had begun — it had been 10:50 on Sunday morning. Now it was 11:15. It had been an eventful, exciting and fateful twenty-five minutes.

The wind dropped considerably, and we continued on our south-westerly path, still making good progress but with frighteningly little spare ballast left. We were low on gas too, for the lower quarter of the envelope was flapping madly, as if to advertise its ugly emptiness. We went back to the water-lifting bag problem.

All in all, we had very few quarrels and very few personality clashes, but we were all very tired all the time we were in the air, for there was too much to do to allow us to get enough sleep, and we had started exhausted. Also the feeling of likely defeat was somewhat embittering.

Despite my talking to him at Médano, Tim was still arguing about every damn thing. It didn't matter what was suggested — he always came up with a criticism and what he believed was a better suggestion. He hadn't realised that the most efficient way of doing something is not always worth attaining, particularly at the price of peace and good crew relations. I know that he was anxious to be most helpful in every way, but it got so that I dreaded ordering anything to be done, for I knew that I was going to have an argument. One such occasion was too much for Rosemary.

"Look here, Tim, Bushy is supposed to be in command. Why do you keep trying to take over?" she asked angrily. "We came along on the understanding that Bushy is Captain in the air — not you."

I had asked Tim to be responsible for anything to do with the physics of ballooning or meteorology because I just hadn't had the time to swot them up. This covers a lot of ground while ballooning, and I had asked his advice many times. Now I felt that I had to defend him, although I realised how Rosemary felt. Anyway, as a result of bringing this particular irritation into the open it was agreed that Tim was Balloon's Physicist, and we would listen to him on that subject: he agreed to try to curb his criticisms and suggestions on all other subjects.

This, unfortunately, had the effect of confirming the division of the crew into two which I very much regretted. Perhaps it was that I had piled too much responsibility on to Tim, I don't know; I only know that he felt the strain more than any of us.

That day, like all days in the balloon, I seemed to be looking at my watch every ten minutes willing the hands round fast so that night, with its comparative peace, would come quickly.

For the rest of Sunday we oscillated between fifty and two hundred feet, throwing out a little water when it threatened to bounce or scooping up a little in a small water-lifting bag if it looked as though we were going over two hundred and fifty. The only difference between a thermal and our normal rising and falling was that at the top of one oscillation we kept going up, despite the added weight of our hose as it lifted out of the water. This could be quite a gentle movement, and to guard against it meant that someone had to do nothing else but stand astern and keep watch every minute of the day.

Our first great tangle of line had not been our last by any means. One of the difficulties was that there were already three lines suspended beneath the boat: the tow line, the mast and a ballast bag of emergency food designed to stop us bouncing too hard. It worked all right, but when we dropped a water-lifting bag over and it filled up it pulled us down as planned, but then took up a position in line with our tow rope and, as often as not, wrapped itself around it. Or, if we were lower, around the mast. The line to the bag full of water could then be freed only by leaning over the stern and carrying it around and around the tow line. With a weight being towed behind, the line was stiff and all our hands got like raw meat. Mine were the worst, because in the excitement I hadn't noticed what I was doing to them on the first night. While trying to pull in the knotted line I had taken the skin off and exposed the flesh in three places. They never had a chance to heal, and it made playing about with a wet, taut line uncomfortable.

Meanwhile, all Sunday afternoon and evening Colin worked at his own design of water-lifting bag with non-return valve. We watched him anxiously, because now that Tim's heavy bag had burst we had nothing with which to combat the sun's heat at dawn the next day.

Colin finished it about midnight and showed it to us while we were waiting for the sunrise. It looked almost too light and small to be effective, but we knew Colin too well to be fooled by that. It was a beautifully simple light construction with a narrow mouth of only three inches diameter and the weight just in front of the entrance instead of at the base. He had sewn a wind-sock-shaped funnel inside and then woven a grid of string across the mouth. Water could flow in, but when it tried to run out the funnel piled up against the grid and stopped it. We passed it around and admired it. If it works, I thought, we might make an Atlantic crossing even yet.

If it didn't work I couldn't see how we could stay up more than one or, at the most, two more days.

But in fact it did — perfectly, and we called it 'The Weightless Wonder'. We overcame the sun's heat at dawn with nothing worse than more skin off our hands from hauling the water aboard. The Weightless Wonder sank quickly, filled up and lifted thirty or forty pounds of water each time. By 9 o'clock we could relax in the sunshine while we scudded along.

Tim suggested putting the mast on the same line as the tow right down where the hose began, in order to increase the weight in the water and also to do away with at least one of the lines dangling beneath us. It was an unpleasant chore, but we pulled ourselves down to just above the sea and hauled mast and hose inboard and then tied them together. We used two completely independent lashings of Terylene cord, so that if one frayed through we wouldn't lose our mast, which, we well knew, might be the most important thing we carried. When we put it all back in the water the added weight at the end of the tow did level off our oscillations surprisingly.

The heavy bag dangling beneath the boat to act as a shock absorber was one of Tim's ideas, and it was a very good one. It always hit the water first and relieved us of its weight, which either stopped us from bouncing at all or, at the worst, took the shock out of it.

But the bags had not been designed to withstand such a beating, and tore themselves to pieces. One, which we had filled with everything we could possibly find as ballast, such as the electrical wiring, spare magazines of film for the electrically run camera, the electrical instruments, some of Colin's navigation books and the contents of our pockets, ripped open and dumped them all in the sea. We had to take on water quickly to make up for the sudden loss of weight. Tim set to work cheerfully making another one of two thicknesses of rubber protected by canvas which would just hold sea-water but do the same job.

Hour after hour went by on Monday without our losing either gas or ballast, and I began to feel that perhaps, after all, we had a chance of making it. Tim had always been supremely confident that we would, and when I had expressed a cautious doubt once or twice had promptly offered to bet me. He even wanted to give me three to one that we'd cross the Atlantic by air.

"No, I'll give *you* three to one, Tim," I said. "And I certainly hope you win."

Colin, too, was quite hopeful that we were going to make it. I knew that I had more ballooning knowledge than either of them, and so could see more clearly how slim our margin of gas and ballast was, but their optimism was most heartening. When the hours slipped by without any more thermal troubles and with Colin's bag working beautifully I, too, started to let myself believe we were going to do it.

For the first time we had the odd hour or so to get other things

Aloft. Rosemary, dressed for the cold, takes her turn at the winch.

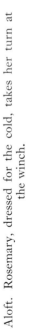

In the sea. Tim, dressed for the tropics, opens the tin of milk for the birthday party.

Life at sea. Tim is mixing chemical
sea-water to remove the salt. Colin
up another message balloon.

Trying to attract attention from a pa
ship with a flare. It was not seer

done besides sleeping, eating and wrestling with the balloon. We washed and shaved, cleared up some of the untidiness and generally made things shipshape. Tim got out his meteorological instruments, which he had clung to through all demands for ballast, and it was decided that the next day we would start in earnest on the heavy programme of observations we had undertaken.

I also checked on everything and, with Colin, made sure that we were all prepared for a sea voyage if it became necessary.

We had all been watching the chronometer, and at 5 o'clock we took time out for a little quiet congratulations, for we had broken the world's record for duration for free balloons of any size.

"What's almost more important," I said, "is that we've been flying for the last twenty-six hours or so at between fifty and two hundred feet, and we haven't lost any gas. If we can keep on like this we'll be there in another five days."

Colin had had time to get a fix at noon and had told us that we had come nearly eleven hundred miles in three and a half days.

At dusk I had a last look around and then got down for some sleep. Normal watches had had to go by the board, and now mine was to be from nine until one, ship's time, which was two hours behind Greenwich.

Tim woke me quietly at 9 o'clock — I say 'quietly' because the night before he hadn't been quiet but had argued with me about something and had got a rocket from Rosemary for it.

"She's been going like a train, Bush," he whispered. "Oscillating between one hundred and three hundred with occasional four-hundred-foot peaks." He handed me the altimeter, bearing compass and a bucket. "I don't think the gas has finished cooling yet, so I should chuck over a cupful or so of water when we seem like touching. It's set fair for America!"

I made myself as comfortable as possible in the stern and got the feel of her. She was oscillating smoothly: down again; up again; down again; up . . . the rise and fall was rhythmical and so gentle that there was never that feeling in the pit of the stomach you get on a scenic railway. At the bottom of each down-swing, despite the darkness of the cloudy night, I could see the ocean, and a swinging motion was set up in the boat by the waves catching the trail with greater strength. But again it was such a gentle movement it couldn't have upset even the queasiest stomach. It rocked the boat like a lullaby.

Up again; down again. We had no light any more to see the altimeter because we had no batteries, but we had worked out another method of keeping a watch on our height. Whoever was on watch kept one hand outboard on the taut trail rope. The angle it made to the sea changed as the boat rose and fell, becoming almost horizontal at the lowest point and almost vertical at the highest. So long as it moved between the two accustomed positions we were neither too high nor too low.

It was moving slowly back and forth in its familiar arc. I let my mind wander on another tack, trying to solve tomorrow's problems.

We were doing remarkably well. It was a long time since we'd been carried up in a thermal, and it looked as though we'd got the water-lifting problem licked, for we'd been able to oscillate just above the water ever since yesterday afternoon.

Of course, there wasn't much margin of gas or ballast left, but we'd carried on like this for — what? — thirty-four hours, and there was no reason why we shouldn't keep on doing it.

Down we went again until, when we were just above the waves, the line was nearly horizontal to the hose trailing behind. Then up again until it was nearly vertical. Down again; . . . they were all sleeping soundly, for we all still had many hours of sleep to catch up. . . . Up again . . . up . . . up . . .

My left hand was carried down as the tow rope went vertical. It couldn't be! But it was, for I could feel the vertical surface of the transom against my hand. I squinted in the darkness to see the worn, luminous figures on the altimeter — six hundred feet! But how?

Never mind how — I had to pick up water ballast quick!

The Weightless Wonder was on the short line. Damn! — I'd have to get it off and on to the long line. I started to untie it rapidly.

I wasn't holding on to anything, for we were ballooning free and there was hardly any movement, and I expected none. Then quietly, and so quickly as to be incredible, the bows of the car lifted a good forty degrees and I was tumbled backwards, crashing hard against the transom. I grabbed for the safety rail, but the movement, thank goodness, was over and the pendulum started to swing back. I adjusted my stance and grip to allow for the contra roll, as one does on a ship, when, breaking all the rules, the car stopped its counter swing and up, up, up went the bows to an angle of sixty degrees this time, and back I was hurled again on to the transom. I held on to the safety rail so tightly that at that moment I wouldn't have been good for anything at all. Something was very wrong, and the one thing I could do was yell.

"Quick!" I shouted. "Get up quick! We're in trouble! Hold on tight!"

But the only solid thing to cling to was the safety rail, and they couldn't grab that until they were standing. Before they were able to get to their feet the port rail rose abruptly high above us. The Mudies, who were on that side, were thrown down on top of Tim on the starboard side. Once again, just as we started to swing back, the downward movement was broken in a series of jerks and up went the port side again even higher. I don't know if it was the new motion or fear, but I had a horrible feeling in my stomach.

This time it swung back, and for a few moments we were horizontal and steady, and the others scrambled to their feet and caught hold of the safety rail.

"Hang on tight!" I warned them. "Here it comes again." A steep roll threatened once or twice — it was as though there was a strong upward thrust on one side of the balloon only. We must be on the edge of a strong updraught, I thought to myself, and the side of the boat that is closest to it gets pushed up and the other side doesn't. It spins us around and a different part of the boat gets biffed up next.

Tim dived for the altimeter, but it was too dark for him to read it. He got one of our 'marker' torches and holding the contacts together directed the weak light on to the altimeter.

"We're at twelve hundred feet already! Valve out some gas, Bushy, for God's sake valve out some gas quickly!"

I hated the idea of valving gas, for we hadn't lost a drop since we'd gone up to thirty-four hundred feet in the thermal the day before and tied the neck. . . .

Tied the neck?! Then it was still tied, and we were rising at a tremendous rate. If we went over thirty-four hundred the balloon would burst.

"Get up the ladder quick, Tim, and untie the neck! Quick — before we get to thirty-four hundred!"

He gave Rosemary the altimeter and marker torch and reached up for the rope ladder. At the same moment the stern rose sharply and Tim fell backwards with sickening speed. For a fraction of a second I imagined his head striking the jagged edge of the pedal unit, and then I saw the rope ladder go tight and knew that he had just managed to grab it. The rest of us were all right, for we had been holding on, but Tim had been lucky to avoid injury.

Tim pulled himself up the ladder to untie the neck. Colin held tight to the safety rail with one hand and supported Rosemary with the other, while she held the marker torch and the altimeter.

"Fourteen hundred . . . fifteen hundred . . . sixteen hundred . . ." she shouted.

I gripped the safety rail with my right hand, braced my feet and wound the valve line round my left hand. But I didn't pull it — I couldn't, for if we lost any more gas we couldn't possibly make it across the Atlantic by air. Tim was shouting for me to valve out gas quickly; Rosemary had reached eighteen hundred feet, and we were obviously still rising. Still the boat wasn't being shaken so violently now, and I had time to take a rational view of our situation.

"If we lose any more gas we're sunk, Tim," I shouted up to him. "Isn't there a chance that we can ride this out?"

"There's not a hope in hell!" he shouted back. "If you don't valve us down quick we'll get carried to twenty or thirty thousand feet."

At that altitude, of course, we'd not only lose most of our gas anyway, but might well blackout for lack of oxygen. It looked as though I didn't have any choice, but it would be a bitter decision. For two long years we'd ignored depressing news and insurmountable obstacles, and I couldn't make up my mind that this was something different, that this time there was no juggling our way round it.

"It's getting stronger every second, Bush!" Tim shouted urgently. "The quicker you valve, the less gas we'll lose."

I was holding the valve line high over my head and trying to make up my mind to swing on it with most of my weight.

"Nineteen hundred . . . two thousand feet!" Rosemary said.

I swung on the valve line for the normal three seconds, and for that short period it was quiet enough for us to hear the gas hiss out of the valve. For us all at that moment there couldn't have been a more depressing sound, but I had no time to dwell on that, for Tim, perched up in the load ring, was criticising my half-hearted valving in no uncertain terms.

"That's no good at all, Bush. This is a hell of a thermal we're in, probably a cunim — we're rising at twenty-five feet a second! You'll have to valve like hell."

My disappointment made me angry. "How do you know how fast we're rising? — we haven't had a variometer since the batteries went."

"I'm counting the seconds between Rosemary's hundreds."

"Twenty-three hundred . . . twenty-four hundred . . ." Rosemary's voice went steadily on.

I was just about to continue the argument with Tim — after all, it takes a bit of ballooning experience to realise how long the interval is between gassing and losing height — when the craft gave a real jerk. It was the most violent yet, and the starboard side rose so fast that the suspension ropes went slack and then snapped taut as they took the weight again. No matter how strong a rope is — and ours were supposed to take twenty times their normal loading — it can't stand much going slack and being pulled hard. The loosening and sudden tightening of the suspension ropes gave me the worst feeling of fear that I had so far experienced. We had to gas our way out of this before the ropes or the netting started to part.

I put both hands on the valve line and swung on it with all my weight. At the same time the starboard side rose higher and higher, and my body was bounced hard against the Mudies. Rosemary kept a grip on both the altimeter and the torch somehow. It would have been terrible if she'd lost either in the dark corners of the boat, for the one thing that was perhaps more vital than anything else was that we should know our height at all times.

I swung on the valve line and counted ten seconds. Ten seconds! I'd never valved so much before, and I wondered if I'd been too impetuous because of Tim's impatience. Keep your own counsel and go easy, I said to myself as I let the valve close again. Ten seconds of valving meant we must have lost a lot of gas, and any moment we might find ourselves dropping like a stone.

"Twenty-six hundred . . . twenty-six and still going up," said Rosemary. Thank goodness she was still able to tell our height.

For the simple reason that you just have to wait for the effect after valving, I waited.

"Don't stop, Bush — keep on valving!" Tim's voice came down, telling me that he was still with us, that he hadn't been shaken off by those frightening lop-sided jerks. But I couldn't leave the timing to him. The one thing I knew that none of the others did was that you had to wait. You simply had to wait.

"Three thousand and still going up . . . three thousand one hundred," came Rosemary's voice. We were still rising as fast as ever, but I didn't dare valve again yet.

"Shut up and come down, Tim," I shouted. "If I keep on valving until we start to drop we'll finish up falling like a stone, and that will be our lot. You must have untied the neck by now — come down."

"I haven't untied it — I pulled the wrong end, and it's knotted."

"Thirty-two hundred feet . . ."

"We burst soon after thirty-four hundred, don't we, Bush?" Colin shouted.

"No, I've just valved out some gas but it's urgent — take a knife up to Tim quickly."

"On my way!" he said, and in two seconds he had grabbed one of our four emergency knives and was up the rope ladder.

In another few seconds the codline binding the neck had been slashed. There was a slight puff and a sigh as the gas, already under some pressure, billowed out of the neck. We all sniffed the sweetish, sickly smell of hydrogen.

Tim and Colin came down, and I noticed how Colin scrupulously observed a point of discipline we had all agreed to adhere to whatever happened. He put the knife back in its sheath by the suspension rope. There was one by each rope, always kept razor sharp, always ready for instant use. If we had to ditch and the quick release didn't work perfectly our safety would depend on one of us being able to cut through a jammed suspension rope in seconds. The craft was beginning to heave again, but Colin was determined to get that knife back in its place, come what might.

Rosemary had had to crook one arm round the safety rail while Colin went aloft, but she was still able to hold the marker torch and the altimeter, although the violent movement was banging her body against the rail.

"Thirty-seven hundred feet . . . thirty-eight hundred . . ."

"Why don't you valve, Bush?" Tim said. "We're rising as fast as ever!"

"Shut up!" I said, but unfortunately he was right. I'd waited long enough, and we were still rising and our movements were as violent as ever. It was something extraordinary in thermals, and it put normal ballooning practice right out of court. My ten seconds of valving had apparently had no effect. I swung on the valve again. Now there could no longer be any doubt — we were finished as a flying craft.

"Start cutting the auxiliary suspensions, Colin," I said. "And the quick-release preventers to get ready for ditching. Right?"

"Right, Bushy, clear all lines ready for ditching." He got on with the job immediately.

While I was swinging from the valve line counting up to ten as slowly as I could bear it, our ship took on that frightening, jerky, swinging again. We simply had to get out of it, and I valved a bit longer than the last time.

Then I let go of the line and got hold of the starboard aft knife. I cut the auxiliary suspension there and the preventer on that quick release. I was glad that I had sharpened the knives just the day before.

"I've cut this one — how about the other three, Colin?"

"Yes, I've cut all three auxiliaries and all three preventers. We're only connected to the load ring by our four main suspensions. The quick releases are all ready to go." As he was speaking I noticed that he checked the starboard aft suspension that I had prepared myself. Bloody right too, I thought, on anything as important as this there can't be too much checking. I'd do a bit myself.

"Is the rope ladder clear?"

"Rope ladder cleared."

"Filling tube cleared?"

"Filling tube cleared."

"Rip line?"

"Rip line cleared."

"Valve line?"

"Valve line cleared."

"Neck line?"

"Neck line cleared."

I could tell by his voice that he was glad that I was covering the ground again. It wasn't as though this was a routine job, for this was the first time any of us had done it, and Colin felt the same need for checking as I did.

"Can you think of anything at all that could tow us behind the balloon after I've pulled the quick release?"

"Not a single thing, Bushy, I assure you."

"Forty-two hundred and still rising . . ." said Rosemary. "Forty-three . . ."

Then came the most violent of all the tossings we'd had. The craft felt like a rag doll being shaken by a dog, and we all clung fast to the rail. As we'd cut all our auxiliary suspensions this violent shaking was being taken by our four main suspension ropes only. I thanked our stars we'd taken the precaution of keeping our quick-release triggers in place with strong shock cord which could be overcome only by pulling the quick release hard. Everything seemed to be holding, but ropes under strain don't give slowly — they snap suddenly. Before that happened we just had to get down out of this nightmare turbulence.

I swung on the valve line for another slow, slow ten. I must have let out about six hundred pounds of lift in all — surely it must have an effect!

We hung on to the rail while the worst of the swirling, jerking movement died down.

"We're steady at four thousand six hundred, Bushy!" Rosemary shouted delightedly. "Do you hear that — steady at forty-six hundred . . . now she's starting to come down!"

"O.K., Rosemary — but don't stop shouting out our height."

"Forty-five hundred . . . forty-four."

We weren't coming down quickly yet, but I knew that before we finished we'd be dropping fast. One good thing was that our neck line had been let go and the lower part of the balloon had blown up into a sort of parachute shape which would slow our descent.

"What have we got left to throw over?" I asked.

"More than a hundred pounds of calcium hydride," Colin said.

"O.K., get ready to heave it over."

"Not yet," said Tim. "We're still only falling at ten feet a second."

"Are you still counting the interval between the hundreds?" I asked.

"Yes — I have been all the time."

"Thirty-eight hundred . . . thirty-seven hundred . . ." but the intervals weren't frighteningly close yet.

There would be no more valving now, so I left my position by the valve line and moved round to one of the bags of calcium hydride tins.

"I don't think we'll come down fast as long as we stay in this strong thermal," Tim said.

"How do we stay in it?" I asked.

"We can't do anything about it, of course, but at least we know we're still in it because of the buffeting we're getting."

He was quite right, but the buffeting was so much less than it had been on the way up that I hadn't really taken it in. Now the intervals between the hundreds started getting shorter and shorter.

I started to throw over tins of calcium hydride, as did Colin and then, last of all, Tim started. The faster Rosemary called out the hundreds, the faster we threw over ballast. At last, at sixteen hundred feet, I had none left.

"How fast are we falling, Tim?"

"I make it less than twenty feet a second."

That wasn't desperate, but it was still fast enough to give us quite a crack when we hit the sea.

"Mine's all gone," said Colin. Tim still had some left.

"Thirteen hundred," said Rosemary. At that moment the craft gave a violent lurch, and she and Colin were thrown so hard that it broke their hold on the rail and sent them crashing.

"Are you all right, Rosemary?" Colin asked.

"No — I've lost the blasted torch. I can't see the altimeter any more." She was groping about on the floor, trying to find it, and we were still dropping.

"I've got it!" she said. "Eight hundred . . . seven hundred . . . six hundred . . . five . . . Oh lord, it's gone out! It's the switch — I can't see, I can't see!" There was real dismay in her voice as she held the altimeter up to within three or four inches of her face.

"It's all right, Rosemary, I can see the water now," I said. We had come out of the low cloud and were at about three hundred feet. It was light enough to see the waves.

Our trail was in and had turned us so that our bows were pointing in exactly the same direction as the waves, but we were travelling fast and coming down fast.

After all the turbulence aloft I had half-expected we'd come down in a howling gale, but as I looked over the side I saw that although there were big, white-topped waves they were not the monsters of a real storm. The wind was about force six, and we were moving exactly right. If the quick release worked it should be a piece of cake. The quick release should be all right — we'd tried it a hundred times at Tenerife, and it had always worked perfectly. If Colin had done his clearing of ropes up aloft without a mistake we should be all right, and if anyone knew how and what to do, he did.

I knew Colin's job had been done all right; I knew the quick release would work — now it was up to me. Fifty feet above the waves . . . thirty . . . twenty . . . ten . . . six . . . four feet . . . PULL!

The quick release worked instantly, dropping us into the water, and the balloon was whipped away and disappeared through the clouds.

CHAPTER THREE

"Now we're at sea in a boat again — and a damned good thing too!" I think those were the first words I said when I knew that everything had worked as planned and we were floating. After the nightmare of the balloon in the storm I felt that I'd come home again. "Is everyone all right?" I asked.

Colin was a casualty. In that last bit of fierce turbulence, when he and Rosemary had been thrown violently from one side of the craft to the other, his foot had caught on something and turned his ankle. It was now so badly wrenched that he could put no weight on it at all.

"What bloody awful luck — do you think it's broken?" I asked.

"I shouldn't think so. It's pretty painful, though, and I can't find any position for it where it's comfortable."

Since, when we finally were able to get it X-rayed, we found that two bones were broken, it's not surprising that Colin found it difficult to get into a position where it was 'comfortable'. But at the time all we could do was to give him one of our strongest pain killers. Rosemary was on to this even while we were talking.

It was bad luck that the one member of the crew to be put out of action was Colin. He was far and away the most experienced blue-water sailor, and the decision that he should skipper the craft, if and when we came down, had been unanimous. And here he was more or less out of action.

"How about skippering?" I asked. "Do you think you can take it on, or would you prefer to groan quietly to yourself in the corner while we manage the best we can without you for a bit?"

When a man's job is to lead it is difficult for him to do so if he is out of action himself, particularly if the situation calls for vigorous and decisive action, but I needn't have had any doubts about Colin.

His reply let me know in an instant that he was still very much on the ball, despite his obvious considerable pain.

"My dear Bushy," he said. "It has been my secret ambition for years to be an armchair skipper and do all the shouting and none of the hard work. It's an opportunity that may never come my way again, and I intend to take it firmly with both hands, Mr. Bush."

"Then in that case she's all yours, Skipper," I said, and with as much solemnity as our rolling and pitching allowed I went through the motions of removing from my head the tricorn of an admiral and handing it to Colin. Just as solemnly he took it, placed it on his head and adjusted it with the help of an imaginary mirror. As a last crack, before descending to the ignominy of the lower deck, I said, "I did my half of the Atlantic in four days — I bet you take longer with yours!"

"What we want now is a long restful cruise," said Colin. "But the first important thing is to remember to keep her balanced . . . We must never forget for a moment that we don't have a keel and that we can be sure of keeping her right side up only if we keep her balanced. From now on it must be two on this side and two on that at all times." From that moment the port side of the boat became the Mudie side and the starboard the Eiloart side, and we religiously adhered to the rule for the rest of the voyage. If one of us had to cross to the other side for any reason his place was taken by one of the others. Whether she would really have capsized with all four of us on one side was something we never found out and never wanted to find out in mid-Atlantic.

"We must get the food bags inboard while we still have some dry and eatable food," Colin said.

The food bags, of course, were still hanging from the safety rail as they had been when we were a balloon. They had been well enough covered to keep out the rain, but spray was a different matter. Tim cut free the starboard bags and Rosemary the port, and I took them and put a temporary lashing on them — just enough to serve until morning when the job could be done properly. We wanted to make dead sure that we weren't going to starve even if we capsized. As they cut them loose and handed them down to me I was afraid that a sudden movement might cause us to lose one, which would have been a major mishap, but we got them inboard safely and soon had them secure.

I noticed that we were not quite stern to wind as I had expected, from trailing three hundred feet of warp, two hundred of hose and our mast. We had settled exactly right into the sea, but now we were drifting with our port quarter to the wind, which meant to the waves too, and so were pitching about the same extent as we were rolling. It was uncomfortable, but we were shipping remarkably little water, despite the force-six wind, which was making plenty of white-tops. If we had been a round-bilged boat our movement would have been much greater. The fact that we were shipping very little water and riding fairly steady was encouraging, for it meant that we had every chance of being comfortable for the next two or three weeks.

Nevertheless, I dreaded what I was pretty sure was going to be Colin's next order — to get the mast hauled in and stepped in its socket. With him able to help us it would have been one thing, but for me to take it on with help only from Tim and Rosemary was quite another.

I knew Colin was tough, for he sails in the smallest class of ocean racer — the Junior Offshore Group — and JOG men, as they are called, get so tough that they are completely out of touch with routine sailing. If Colin's foot were all right, I said to myself, he'd probably have the mast almost in by now. With that sort of standard in mind, he'd be telling us to get cracking any minute. If he did, the last thing I wanted to do was to start arguing about his very first order, so I thought I'd better let him know what I felt before he gave the order.

"Do you think it would be all right if we just drifted tonight and started sailing tomorrow?" I asked. "If it's all the same to you, I'd much prefer tackling the mast when we've got some daylight on the job. What do you say, Colin?"

"Good idea, Bush. There is one thing I'm keen on your doing now, though, and that's lashing yourselves in with some sort of life-line. When you've done that you can all go to sleep. I'm comfortable propped up here, and I'll just sit and freshen the nip on the tow-line from time to time so we don't lose the mast."

The hull of The Small World rode high on the water, and the windage on her stern was considerable. This meant that the tow-line was under strain, particularly where it was bent round the cleat. This is called the nip, and its position must be altered every half-hour or so to prevent it chafing through.

We offered to spell him at the job, but he explained that his ankle wouldn't let him sleep, anyway, so he might just as well stay there until dawn. Our turn would come in the morning, he said, and since there would be more than enough to do then, our best plan was to get in as much sleep as we could.

Tim and Rosemary were seasick, and neither Colin nor I felt too good. Rosemary passed seasick pills around, which helped, though.

Tim and I stretched out on our side and Rosemary on the other. The waterproof cover was just large enough to keep the worst of the rain off, but as we had no sleeping-bags we couldn't expect any real comfort.

Because our stern wasn't square to the wind we shipped some water — not much, but more that first night than the whole of the rest of the voyage, for, once we were sailing, she was an exceptionally dry boat. So it was cold and wet, and although we were extremely tired, we were unable to sleep except in fits and starts.

I closed my eyes and tried to sleep, but couldn't. For one thing there was that frustrating, disappointing fact that we were down for good, the balloon was gone, and our dream of a complete trans-Atlantic flight from land to land was shattered. The irrevocability of it was hard to absorb. Half an hour before we had been up and moving at twenty knots or so: now we were down and drifting at half a knot and all we had in front of us was a long, uncomfortable sea voyage. I had begun to be infected with the others' confidence, too, as we had continued on hour after hour without difficulty, and it was difficult to realise that in such a short time everything had changed and the two-year-old project was as dead as mutton.

But there were consolations — we felt happy and secure in the sea, and now that Colin was in command I no longer had that load of responsibility on my shoulders. All I had to do now was what I was told. Colin was a good seaman, and with reasonable support from us he'd plan a landfall and make it without any fuss at all.

I must have dozed off in the end, for, just before dawn, I remember waking and seeing that Rosemary had taken Colin's place and was looking after the nip of the tow-line. Colin was dozing in exactly the same propped-up position. Of course, I didn't know that his ankle was broken, but there was now enough light to see how enormous it was. Every time a big wave caught us more broadside on than normal and jerked the boat I could see his face twitch with pain even in his sleep.

"It was hopeless having him sit there in pain hours on end without any rest," Rosemary explained. "So I gave him so many pills he had to go to sleep."

I asked her if she would like a break. She said that she would, and I took over the tow-line from her.

The rain had stopped, but it was a cloudy day with plenty of wind and white-tops. I marvelled at the way we were riding the seas. A round-bilged boat would have been rolling all over the place in that sea, but we were sailing far more comfortably than many a boat I've sailed in Chichester Harbour. If only we'd been lying square to our tow-line or better still had the steadying influence of a sail, we'd have had even less movement and probably not shipped any water at all. If only the sun will come out, I said to myself, we'll soon be enjoying a pleasant sail.

Down in the troughs, it was as though we were in a room with high walls of water, so high we could hardly feel the wind at all; on the crests we got a glimpse of the immense ocean all around us and felt the full force of the wind. This was the way it was going to be for two, three or even four weeks, and the sooner we got used to it, the better.

Colin woke up and took over from me again. Tim got up, chilled and stiff and started slapping his body with his arms to get warm. Colin obviously couldn't move, and I sensed that it was outside his

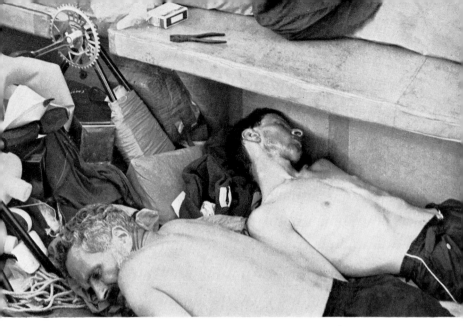

After two weeks at sea. The Eiloarts resting in their half of the boat.

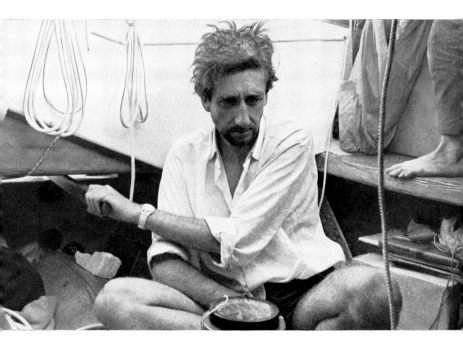

Colin at the helm on Christmas Eve — only a thousand miles to go.

Last lap! Barbados on the horizon.

Welcome to Barbados.

character to sit doing nothing himself while issuing orders to others, so I tried to think of jobs to suggest we do. It seemed a pity for Tim to waste his energy, so I told him to stop and help me get the craft ship-shape — to change it from an aerial car into a sailing-boat.

"Odds and ends in the bath for the time being, Colin?" I asked while Tim threw litter and other débris at me from all directions.

"Just so, Mr. Bush, all in the bath. We'll sort them out later. As soon as you get the decks cleared for action we'll get the mast stepped and rigged. The sooner we get her sailing, the quicker we'll be able to give Tim and Rosemary their first West Indian punch."

We had the boat cleared quickly, and then Tim dismantled the seats of the pedalling apparatus. No more pedalling! We were all glad about that. We decided to keep the lengths of Dexion from which the seats were made in case we had to make a jury rig of some sort later.

We were warmer now, and I went to the stern and started the long business of hauling in the mast.

It would have taken half a dozen men to pull in three hundred feet of line plus two hundred of heavy hose and a mast in that sea with that wind. The method was to keep the line taut by taking in a foot or two of slack every time the boat lurched, making it fast to a cleat and waiting for another bit of slack. After about an hour and a half of this my hands, which had never had a chance to heal properly, were about as bad as they had ever been, but at least the mast was within reach.

Getting it inboard could have been managed by one person in calm water, but it was just about all Tim, Rosemary and I could do in that seaway. It was wrenched out of our hands twice and splashed back into the Atlantic, but finally we got it in. The high-pressure hose still streamed astern.

"I hate to cut the hose loose, Colin," I said. "It cost fifty quid — shall we pull it in and stow it somewhere?"

"Let it go," said Colin. "We're much too heavy for fast travelling to carry that."

P 225

With great reluctance I cut it loose. There wasn't even a chance of someone finding it as flotsam and putting it to some use, for it sank out of sight.

While I had been slowly getting the mast in, Tim and Rosemary had been doing the very important job of lashing firmly and separately every bag of food or water so that we would still have provisions if we capsized. They secured the last one and turned to help me.

We fitted the sail on the mast and then wrapped it tightly around it with a spiral of rope from head to foot. No matter what happened, we didn't want the wind catching the sail while we were struggling to get the mast stepped. Then we bent sheets to the clew of each sail and led them through fairlead pulleys to the stern-cleats. Now if we should lose our grip on the mast and let it go overboard we wouldn't lose it.

The most difficult part of all the jobs we ever had to do on the whole of our sea voyage came next — getting the mast stepped. If it had been a matter of stepping it in the middle of a deck the way most masts are we shouldn't have thought twice about it, but this was a very different matter. Our mast socket was right at the top of the bow self-righting hump, and for'ard of it. Apart from the few square feet of space at the top of the hump itself, there was no possible foothold. To hold an eighteen-foot mast upright while you lift and drop it into a socket on a ship with a twenty-five-degree roll needs the best foothold possible.

First we lashed the foot of the mast loosely to the socket, so that it could pivot but not stray. Rosemary was posted here to direct the foot into the socket when Tim and I got it up.

But getting it up was easier said than done. Tim on the starboard side and I on the port deck tried walking for'ard, slowly raising it higher and higher as we went along. With both hands on the mast it would have been difficult to keep our balance, and so we walked five feet apart and leaned towards each other. The theory was that we would then have the firm stance of a triangle with a five-foot base. The theory was all right — I can't to this day see any alternative — but as we walked farther and farther for'ard the boat's movement worked more strongly against us, and time and again one or both of us fell.

I couldn't for the life of me see how we were going to get our mast up, for every time one of us had to climb up on the hump to finish the job there was nothing to support the other, and over he would go with a crash. We never hurt ourselves, and we didn't fall overboard, but we got weary to the point where we didn't think we'd ever succeed. The trouble, of course, was that Colin designed the mast and placed its socket thinking that there would always be four people to get it put in. But we were only three, and with that sea running I couldn't see how we were going to do it.

"Shall we wait and see if it gets any better, Colin?" I asked.

"Wait for a lull, Mr. Bush?" he asked me cheerfully. "How long do you think we might have to wait?"

He was right, of course. It might take weeks before we'd get the sort of sea to make it easy. The trades often blow month in and month out without a lull, so we'd have to get that mast up.

"All right, Colin, we keep trying — but how do we do it, what's the secret?"

"Simple, Mr. Bush, you have four on the job instead of three," he said, grinning wickedly. I threatened to break his other ankle.

"Oh, just wait until we get this mast up!" Rosemary threatened. It was hard to indulge in self-pity for long with Colin about, so back to the job we went.

"One of these times, Mr. Bush," Colin said. "Just when you need a roll to port to make the job possible she actually *will* roll to port. Your mast will be stepped, and you'll probably be so surprised you'll fall overboard in a dead faint."

We failed once or twice more and then, sure enough, just as Tim and I had walked the mast up and Rosemary was carefully holding the foot of the mast to the socket mouth, the boat gave a roll and the mast lurched up dead in line with the socket and dropped six inches down as though by magic.

Before it could hop out again Tim and I jumped up on to the hump and screwed it down well and truly by exerting all our weight and strength. Then we flopped down on the deck to rest. The hoisting must have taken a solid hour — perhaps more.

I was tired out and thirsty — my mouth felt bone dry.

"How's the water situation?" I asked.

"Bad, I'm afraid," said Colin. "Rosemary and I were talking about it in the night. We've got six gallons of fresh water, and we can make another four with the Permutit. That's forty quarts in all. If we allow a quart a day among us — that is a half a pint each — we've got enough for six weeks. That's what we've got to allow for."

"Six weeks!" Tim said. "How far is it?"

"Fourteen hundred and fifty miles — sea miles that is, or nearly seventeen hundred statute miles."

"But if we average four knots, a hundred miles a day, it'll be just over two weeks for the whole trip," I said.

"And very nice too, Mr. Bush, but it's about as likely as getting that mast up first time. All kinds of things can happen — if we lose our mast we'll be six weeks or even eight. No prudent mariner would dream of a bigger ration than a half a pint each a day at this stage."

"But that's not enough!" Tim protested angrily. "We can't get by with so little water — we *must* have more. It's a number one priority, and we should get on immediately with testing the stills or even improvising one somehow."

Tim carried on like this for quite a bit, but failed to rouse our sympathy. Tim knew that he needed more water than most people, and probably should have told us this, although I don't suppose at the time we should have believed him. A few days later he became ill, and all during the voyage suffered much more than the rest of us from lack of water.

But none of us knew any of this then, and when Tim kept on and on we squashed him again and told him that he would just have to make do with his half pint a day.

I hadn't intended to raise the big issue of water rationing. All I had wanted to know was if I could have a drink of water before we got on with fitting the rudder and tiller. The consensus was that it would be better to do the work first and then have an eighth of a pint each when we could afford to rest and enjoy it. We all agreed that if we had a drink and then exerted ourselves with the rudder we'd be just as thirsty and not have any ration to help us through the morning.

We started on the rudder. It was a job that would have taken about twenty seconds on land, but was not so easy in those seas. First, we put a loose lashing on it. Again, if it broke free from our grip we were determined that we wouldn't lose it. Then Tim and I checked that the life-lines round our middles were securely fixed inboard. Then, with Rosemary holding our legs (come to think of it, finding the four legs rather an armful she put a lashing round them as well) we leaned as far over the transom as we could. We could only reach the top of the rudder, and we tried to hold it upright for just those few seconds needed to slide it on to the pintles. Time and again we got one pintle on, but getting the second continually beat us.

The main difficulty was that the following seas kept coming up and swamping the transom so that the rudder and pintles were under water — not to mention our heads and shoulders! Because we could hold only the top of the rudder, it was impossible to stop the waves moving it about. Colin called us back inboard.

"Let's start again," he said. "First of all shift all that stuff away so that I can take up some sort of position inboard and up close to the tiller port" — this is the horizontal slot the tiller comes through — "with three of us holding it we must be able to get it on."

We cleared away the bath full of odds and ends and helped Colin take up a new position where he could get his hand through the tiller port and get a grip on the rudder. It was painful for him, but the only way we could to it — it needed three pairs of hands, and no matter how much it hurt his ankle, we had to agree with him that it was the only thing to do.

We checked our life-lines again, hooked our legs under Rosemary's arms and leaned down outboard and grasped the rudder again. The trick, of course, was to time our attempt to take place when we were right on top of a crest so that the rudder was half out of the water.

Colin had the best grip, but couldn't see the rudder pintles and had to move according to our directions. If we didn't give him exact instructions at the precise moment we would find him working against us instead of for us. It's not easy to give good clear directions while lying on your stomach leaning overboard, but, after a half a dozen failures, suddenly we found the rudder safe home and I swung a leg over the stern and put my foot on it until Colin and Tim got the tiller in.

Now at last we were ready to sail. We unwrapped the spiral of rope which had been keeping the sail furled round the mast and had the thrill of seeing the wind fill the twin sails with a flap. Our boat began to move forward in the water, the rudder became alive and we were on our way to the West Indies.

We enjoyed our reward — an eighth of a pint of water — and rested from our exertions. We knew that we had a long way to go and that we should have to husband our energy on so small a water ration. Fortunately it didn't look as though there would be much work apart from six hours out of every twenty-four at the helm and we could catch up on some of the sleep we had been missing.

We sailed on all day in a force five or six wind, and I see that I wrote in my log: "The boat sails well and is stiff and dry. We shipped no water at all."

CHAPTER FOUR

Wednesday, 17th December. My watch was from four to eight this morning. The day broke with bright sun. Rosemary is pretty well recovered from her seasickness; Colin's foot seems less painful and so are my hands. Tim complained of a slight headache earlier, but it soon went.

We finished lashing down all our food and water so that a capsize will be a discomfort and not a disaster. We are now set for the siege — low input of food and water and low output of energy for thirty or even forty days. So we lazed most of today except that during my afternoon watch I did Tim's stint at the helm while he made a water catchment for supplementing our supply with rain when it comes. I found four hours of steering to be plenty.

Tim also let off a balloon message.

A nice day, little rain, hot sun, some overcast.

So reads my log. Rosemary also kept a log, and I shall quote from hers from time to time too.

Watches were arranged so that two of us should be on for four hours at a time and the steering shared, so that normally one only steered for two hours out of eight. It naturally fell into a Mudie Watch and an Eiloart Watch, with dog watches from four to eight in the evening to vary the times.

The idea of the balloon message Tim let off was that the wind would blow a four-foot air-filled* meteorological balloon over the waves ahead of us much faster than our boat. We put a message inside giving our position and saying that we were all right and happily sailing on and let the balloon go hopefully, but for some reason it didn't make much better time than we did. After an hour

* We no longer had any means of making gas.

or so we could see it about a hundred yards ahead of us. We sent off two or three of these during the voyage, but have never heard that any of them have been picked up.

We weren't worried about food, for we had nuts, raisins, cheese, chocolate, Vita-Weat, ship's biscuits and Gofio from Tenerife. There was plenty of butter, Marmite, some dried milk, a few tins of evaporated milk, one tin of tomatoes, two tins of lemon juice, sugar, honey and jam. With only a half a pint of water each a day it was never necessary to ration food, for we couldn't eat much, anyway.

The weather improved, and the next day, Thursday, our third at sea, started off magnificently, but by noon it was uncomfortably hot. It was so hot that we changed our big piece of waterproof material from a protection from the rain to a shelter from the sun. The rain was warm, anyway, and we welcomed it. As soon as we got into the shade our spirits picked up. We were now dried out, had some sleep and hadn't felt cold since the first night at sea.

Colin got his fixes that day and told us that we were about half-way across the ocean.

Tim was suffering more than any of us from lack of water, and he rigged up a speedometer and discovered that we were making about three knots. He pointed out that if we had the equatorial current with us we should make Barbados in twelve to thirteen days, and he asked for an increase in the water ration, but Colin was adamant. Tim collected two cups of water from his catchment, but it tasted vilely of Neoprene from the fabric. We had a jar of foul water which we kept for emergencies, and we added this to it.

Our beds were sheets of the P.V.C. foam and were not exactly soft, but we discovered that you can sleep on anything. I wrote one day in my log about this:

Someone takes the helm to relieve you and you flop down on a bundle of clothes spread out on the deck just like a dog would — a gypsy's dog at that! Yet you feel that it is pretty luxurious and you are damned glad to be able to flop down and wallow in the comfort if you are tired enough. Normally you are pretty tired not because the work is hard but food is low and energy low too. It can be hell to have to go on watch when you are having the only bit of deep sleep in days and it is amazing how often that seems to happen. At 11:45, say, I am awake turning things over in my mind and at midnight I am in the middle of a deep sleep and find myself being shaken to go on watch. I curse my luck and feel convinced that I could have gone on sleeping for hours.

Yet at other times when sleep is not so easy I come out and take the helm on a moonlight night and watch the wake of the boat in the track of the moon and feel it is quite a privilege to be there. I even pity all the people who have never known what it is like to be stranded in the middle of the Atlantic in a 15-foot open boat.

The wires under the hull made a constant humming noise for the first week or so at sea and then first one, then the other rusted and parted and the only sound was the wind and the waves.

Friday, 19th December. This was our first full day under the new shade and we all felt much better for it, but Tim was still suffering badly from thirst, so he was given permission to drink his fill from a new catchment of Neoprene-flavoured rain-water which was evaporating rapidly, anyway. He drank nearly a pint of this and said that he felt much better.

Colin told us that we still had 1,140 miles to go, which was a disappointment. It meant that we were only doing seventy-five miles a day and gave us another fifteen days before reaching the West Indies. Colin pointed out that it could be a lot worse — we could lose the mast in a storm, in which case we would drift at about half the speed and take another month.

But except for the shortage of water, it was really very pleasant. The wind had dropped and was only strength three or four most of the time, the boat was dry and sailed well, and we were warm.

Tim and I soaked our shirts and pants in the sea and put them on wet so that the moisture would stave off a bit of thirst. He and I must be two of the untidiest people who ever put to sea and the

Mudies two of the tidiest, so that there was a tremendous contrast between the starboard and port sides of the boat.

None of us wore shoes, for we found that our feet stayed wet and soft if we did. At night we put on our flying-suits at first, but gave this up as it got warmer, because they made us sweat and we couldn't afford to lose the precious moisture.

We made a couple of new catchment rigs, but now that we wanted some rain it stopped, of course. We tried out our Permutit chemical for making fresh water out of sea-water, but it tasted so unpalatable that I should have to be a lot thirstier to drink it. Colin mixed some with his precious Gofio, though, and got it down, and Tim drank his share.

Sunday, 21st December was a landmark. Rosemary wrote it up in her log:

> 980 miles to Barbados! — it seems so much less than 1000. We decided to celebrate and had a tot of brandy each and our one and only tin of tomatoes — delicious! Tim had been keen to eat them for days — saying if we don't they might go bad but ironically he found that his stomach had shrunk and he couldn't eat all his share.
>
> I expect that all our stomachs have shrunk by now for we only eat two or three biscuits each at 'watering times' and little else. Perhaps some nuts and a few boiled sweets. The result is that it is a great effort to do anything and we sleep most of the time and flop down after any particular effort.

I remember that the tin of tomatoes had been a bone of contention for at least two days. Tim insisted that it might rust or go off in some way and that we should eat it before it did. I didn't think it very likely, but I couldn't see why we shouldn't eat it now. Colin, however, was against it and spoke of the moral value of holding something back, but it obviously meant so much to Tim that in the end he gave in and we had it for our less-than-a-thousand-miles celebration.

We had the tot of brandy first, which, because of our dehydrated state and empty stomachs went straight to our heads. Tim took the tin of tomatoes and started a speech about how happy he was that we had allowed the scientific outlook to prevail, and we shouted him down in a friendly way and told him to get on with opening it, or we'd change our minds. He made dead sure that not a drop was spilt and divided it among four cups. It was amazingly good, but all Tim could manage was the juice and half the pulp, so he gave the rest to me.

Colin's ankle took a long time to get better (we did not know it was broken, of course), but he managed to get about the boat, anyway. He and I grew fairly heavy beards and began to look like cast-aways. The days passed and the miles were slowly covered.

On Tuesday, 23rd December at 4:30 in the afternoon Colin, who was at the helm, said, "I think we are being followed," and pointed astern. There, quite plainly, was a submarine coming towards us.

For a long time we thought that it was going to come alongside and have a word with us, but it lay about a mile off astern of us. Then it turned and chugged along on a southerly course. We felt sure that they saw us, but they made no sign. We could hear the throbbing of the engines quite plainly and kept expecting them to change course and bear down on us. I could almost taste the fresh water and Coca Cola, but she kept right on southward and out of sight. It was a rusty colour and very modern looking, and we now think it was probably a Russian submarine with orders not to make contact with anyone.

It was very disappointing, and we had one of our tins of evaporated milk to cheer us up.

Colin announced that we were eight hundred and fifty miles from Barbados.

The weather had been fine for about a week, but on Christmas Eve it changed, becoming wet and stormy. We tried to make a polythene rain-water catcher that wouldn't make the water taste, but to do so we had to get the food under cover and clear away one of the old seats to make a space for it. Rosemary and I cut it off with a hacksaw, but the long session with her head down made her seasick again. She said that it was such a waste, because it took so long to get her stomach filled again.

Tim told us that he had diarrhoea, which I thought was probably due to his drinking the Neoprene-tainted water. He was obviously pretty ill, and so I told him that I would take his watch. Colin and Rosemary wouldn't hear of it, though, and so we divided the night up into two hours on and four off. By dawn on Christmas day we were all very tired.

We were all awakened at 7:50 on Christmas morning by a loud crack and the sound of Colin shouting for all hands. We jumped up and saw him struggling with the tiller, which was breaking after a night of heavy seas. The first thing to do was to take the strain off it, and Rosemary and I uncleated the sheets and furled the sail around the mast.

Tim went to help Colin, and together they lashed lengths of Dexion on each side of the tiller, but by the time it was ready we were all pretty exhausted and we decided to leave the sail furled and rest. So we trailed a long warp astern to keep ourselves headed in the right direction and all lay down for a four-hour rest. The night of extra watch duty had come after a particularly tiresome day of rain squalls, and we were beginning to feel the worst of the effects of dehydration, little food and short snatches of sleep.

We all remember Christmas Day as one of the most miserable of the whole voyage. Rosemary was seasick and Tim's diarrhoea was no better, and we all felt tired out by the extra effort and were wet from the rain. Even worse was the fact that we needed more drinking-water and didn't seem to be able to work out a method of catching any that didn't taste awful.

But as it was Christmas we had an extra quarter of a mug of water all around. None of us felt it made a festive occasion of it, though.

We were to have had our one and only tin of cream, but none of us felt like it, and we decided to save it for a more cheerful day, when we would appreciate it.

I knew that we had another ten days at least, and these seemed to stretch ahead of us like so many months. Also, we knew that something could still go wrong and that it might take us three weeks more.

Rosemary's and Tim's illness accented the crampedness of our living-room — four of us were sharing a space five and a half feet wide by eleven feet long, which also contained all our supplies. Not to mention the pedal unit, which we were too tired to cut free. Our small world seemed to get smaller as the voyage went on.

The awning divided the boat up so that there were a few clear feet for'ard of it, and this was the bathroom. While we were in the air we had used a bucket and polythene-bag system for a lavatory, and these were now put in the 'bathroom', from where all in turn got a very fine view of the sea.

We washed in sea-water, of course, which leaves a sticky salt deposit, and we washed our clothes by towing them behind us for a bit. We washed our cups this way too until we lost two of them.

About noon on Christmas Day we decided that we were rested and unfurled the sail and got going again. Tim did a two-hour watch in the afternoon — it was tough to drive him, and it made me feel like a Bligh, but a man off watch slows up the works, as we had seen in the morning. So as long as he was able to drive himself to do even a part of his turn at the helm I felt that he should.

The night watches were the worst, and I had to discipline myself not to look at my watch, for it seemed impossible how slowly the two hours were passing if I did. At one o'clock in the morning of 26th December I realised that it was just two weeks since we took off and that we'd been down in the sea for ten days only, which seemed quite unbelievable.

But the next day, 26th December, the sun was shining again and we all felt much better. Rosemary writes in her log:

Sun again. Still not quite over yesterday's exertions, but feeling better. Massaged Colin's ankle which seems to be improving — he is anxious not to have it out of action for skiing! We now have less than 700 miles to go and can turn the chart over so that we can see the West Indies which make them seem nearer. We are afraid to tempt the fates by banking on anything, though.

We had our Xmas tin of cream today. Colin had his in his Gofio mixture, Bushy mixed his in a cup with jam, Tim likewise, and I had mine on Vita-Weat with jam. We had all suddenly 'discovered' jam. The red plum is particularly good, just slightly acid and we eat it by the spoonful. Strawberry jam not so popular but we have a spoonful each per day.

A flying fish committed suicide on board during the night but we are not short of food and threw it overboard — couldn't have cooked it, anyway.

We have two tins of evaporated milk left and four tins of lemon juice which is very nice with sugar and water for a change of taste.

I saw another flying fish and a large fish about four feet long jump out of the sea during my watch. Colin says it's a dolphin.

I remember that Tim seriously considered eating the flying fish that came aboard, but gave up the idea, which was probably all to the good. He didn't get over his stomach trouble for some days, but did his full watch from 27th December onwards.

Lemon juice and water seemed to us to be one of the most wonderful things ever invented, and we couldn't think why we hadn't had it regularly on land. We promised ourselves that we'd always have a big jug full in the ice-box once we got home again.

Saturday, 27th December. Colin decided that there was enough water to unration Permutit, and Tim immediately got working and made himself nearly a pint. It still tasted horrible to me and Rosemary, but to Tim it made all the difference, and Colin managed to drink his by mixing it with his Gofio.

We could see by now that Tim was not exaggerating about his need for more water than us, for he was beginning to look like a particularly bad example from a concentration camp. He is six feet tall and weighed ten and a half stone (147 lb.) when we took off. When we arrived at Barbados twenty-four days later he was down to eight stone three (115 lb.). But this was not all caused by lack of water and food, for he did, in fact, have more water than the rest of us, because he drank the Permutit water. He also worried much more than the rest of us, and he now says that he thinks that it was his worrying that upset his stomach.

The fact was that Tim had quite a strong sense of danger since the balloon came down and we started sailing in our fifteen-foot open craft. I asked him about this once. He said that he was worried because he didn't think that we were being careful enough. I asked him what, in particular, he wanted done, and he made several points, some of them fairly sound, but some seemed to me to be completely cock-eyed. For instance, he was keen to have a capsize practice.

"It seems silly to me to have a capsize practice every day just so we don't have to worry about capsizing," I said a bit unkindly.

"It's all very well to laugh at capsizes, but we've never sailed this boat in a gale," he said. "I did meteorology research, Bushy, and there's likely to be a gale at least once a month here. Colin has admitted that he doesn't know how she would behave in a gale."

This puzzled me, and then I found out that Tim and Colin meant different things by a 'gale'. For Colin it is a very strong wind — strong enough to tear trees out of the ground — and they are rare. Meteorologists give the name to a much less powerful wind, the kind that Colin was quite confident we could ride out. When this was explained to Tim he said that it stopped some of his worries but obviously not all.

I wasn't really worried about our actually surviving and nor, I think, was either Rosemary or Colin. We didn't like our discomfort and thirst, but we were pretty sure that we were going to make good our passage. Tim, however, was not. He didn't place our chances of survival very high, and the effect of that was to make him extremely impatient with any inefficiency. He felt that we might miss complete safety by a fraction, and that every tiny fraction counts. The rest of us were more fatalistic about it, feeling that if our luck was in we would be all right and if it wasn't we wouldn't. That, of course, was only to a certain degree, for we were heading on the best course we knew, we wore safety lines constantly and we had our food and drink lashed in. After that we were resigned, and resignation is no big part of Tim's character — for that kind of trip a certain amount was a good thing.

But I was sorry that Tim wasn't well and that he felt that we weren't being careful enough, but there wasn't much I could do about it. He certainly didn't let it affect his work, for once he was well again he was always the most active of us.

Monday, 29th December was Tim's twenty-second birthday, and we decided to have a party. Everyone who was anybody was invited to the feast, which was a tin of evaporated milk. It was too strong for us neat, and we had to dilute it with water, which is an indication of how our restricted diet was affecting us. It was very good though, but we now only had one tin of milk left.

This was our roughest day, with exceptionally big waves. One during my afternoon watch was a monster. All I had time to do was shout a warning, and then it hit us hard, and the next moment the other three, who were sitting down, were knocked flat. After that we had some quite deep troughs, some so deep and steep that seventy degrees of sky were blotted out. Oddly enough, all this seemed to be caused by a wind which could not have exceeded force six.

We were making good time, though, for Colin's fix in the afternoon showed that we had covered a hundred and eighty miles in the preceding two days, which was our best run. We were only four hundred miles from Barbados, and we had two and two-fifths gallons of fresh water left and enough Permutit to make another three and a half gallons.

We discovered that Permutit made in polythene bags instead of the rubber ones supplied doesn't taste so bad, and if it is then mixed with Marmite the taste is almost hidden.

Sailors are well known to be superstitious, and Colin is no exception. I remarked that our cramped living would last only another five or six days and he was horrified. He said that it was asking for trouble and that to be superstitious is part of being a good seaman — if that is so, then the crew are all good seamen except me, and I must try to improve my seamanship in this respect.

Any little chore we tackled seemed to use up so much energy. On Tim's birthday I looked over and re-wrapped and then re-lashed the ship's papers. It took about fifteen minutes, but when I was finished I felt that I'd done a day's work. With little water one takes but little food — I reckoned a typical day's diet for me and put it in my log:

Breakfast	Three ship's biscuits	about 1 oz.
Lunch	Nuts and raisins	2 oz.
Supper	Dried milk and biscuits	2 oz.

Total five ounces — how to live on a shilling a day!

The others force more down on principle to keep their strength up, but I don't agree with that, and only eat as much as I want. We should be not more than five days away from all the food and drink we want, but no one dares assume that this is so. We might drift through the islands without a wind and have to go another thousand miles to the mainland of the continent if we are unlucky. That *would* set us back — it would mean another twenty days at half a pint per day of water each, and then we'd be in pretty poor trim.

With that possibility in mind I can't assume that I'll have all the Coke and beer and water I want this time next week. It's too good to contemplate, anyway!

I can see that I was beginning to be influenced by the 'don't tempt fate' superstition. The wind did in fact drop soon after-wards and we started to crawl.

But the next day, 30th December, we had our second bit of excitement. Rosemary's log tells the story:

Tuesday, 30th December. Not making very fast time but nice gentle sailing. Very hot in the 12 to 4 watch which made it a long, long afternoon. Lots of fish around us — all apparently trying to jump out of the sea.

Soon after Bushy took over the helm he said the now classic words: "We are being followed!" This time it was a small white patch coming up astern that we thought was a sail at first but then saw was the superstructure of a small cargo boat. She seemed to slow down a mile or so from us but did nothing else. We got a cable ready for them to send saying that we were all right and we let off two flares to attract attention but apparently they didn't see us for they sailed away again much to our disappointment.

We certainly were disappointed, for it didn't seem possible that they could miss us, and I could taste the fruit and cool drinks we were going to beg. Colin held a flare aloft, and Tim waved his shirt like mad. We waited and waited to see her bows swing towards us.

"It all takes time," said Colin. "The mate has to report to the captain, and the captain has to get up from his tea and find his glasses. Then he has to have a chinwag with the mate. All that takes time." We stared the skin off our eyes, but she kept to her course.

After ten minutes we had to admit that she couldn't have seen us, and we watched her steam away. Tim got quite cross with me because I didn't wave my shirt too, but I felt that if they didn't see our flares or our sail it wouldn't do much good. Still, I felt sorry for Tim, because he looked so despairing as she sailed away from us.

The last day of the year found us making not much more than two knots, but Colin placed us only 280 miles from Barbados, so we weren't worried.

Having a Scot for a captain, we had to have a New Year's Eve celebration, so we let ourselves go with an extra tot of water *and* a tot of brandy.

CHAPTER FIVE

O N New Year's Day 1959 we had been down in the sea for seventeen days and had come about twelve hundred nautical miles. We had about two hundred and fifty more to go. We were not exactly bursting with energy, but we were pretty fit, though very thin, especially Tim. He had got over his diarrhoea, though, and with the extra ration of Permutit water was feeling much better. Colin's ankle was not bothering him quite so much, or at least he didn't complain about it. Rosemary had found her sea legs and hadn't been sick for days. I felt fine except for a feeling of wobblyness in my legs sometimes which I put down to not using them.

We were going slowly, but the main thing was that we were still going and in the right direction. Realising, although we didn't say so, that we probably only had a few more days, we decided that we would have to raise enough energy to get some films and still photographs.

Because we had colour film it had to be shot in the hottest part of the day when the sun was at its brightest. Also we had to take the canopy down and do without shade, which, in our dehydrated state, was an ordeal. It made us realise what a tremendous difference the shade had made — with it, and a reasonable amount of Permutit water, life was easy, but in the sun we all sweated and wanted a drink badly.

First we filmed the making up, filling and inflation of one of our solar stills and then the writing of a message, putting it in one of the big air balloons and letting it go, to be blown ahead of us. Everything had to be photographed four times, for we had one movie camera and three stills, and those two operations took two hours, at the end of which we were all hot, tired, thirsty and irritable.

243

We found that it had taken a great deal out of us, and none of us was good for anything else much for the rest of that day.

We did, however, have our last shot at making fresh water out of sea-water with a solar still. These are supposed to be able to make about two pints of fresh water a day in sunny weather, and are used by airmen who are forced down and drift about in their rubber dinghies. We had five of them and, relying on them for an emergency, took too little fresh water.

Jenny and Rosemary had tried to make one of them work on the beach at Médano, but without success. We decided then that it was because they had tried to do it with the still in a bucket of sea-water instead of floating in the sea. Anyway, the instructions said, "If there is salt in your fresh water at the first attempt try again." So we weren't unduly worried. It never occurred to any of us that we would get nothing from them at all.

Probably the reason was that we were sailing and they were designed to be used for drifting conditions. We could see, as we towed them behind us, that the hot, evaporated surface got jogged against the cooling surface, which mixed salt with the fresh water. So after one more unsuccessful effort we put them away as a secret weapon against thirst if we ever got becalmed. Then we should be drifting, and they would certainly work.

As we got nearer to land our escort of fish increased and we had the regular companionship of some lovely ones between three and four feet long, beautifully coloured with brilliant blue/green bodies and golden yellow fins. We found out later that they were dolphins. They were very curious, and whenever we did anything unusual, such as trailing our washing or trying to make the solar stills work, they came around to investigate, six or a dozen at a time. They kept us company, jumping four to five feet high in a long arc of glittering colour. On moonlight nights it was as though a big silver ring had suddenly been thrust out of the sea. We grew to feel quite affectionate towards them and the stormy petrels and bo'sun birds that travelled with us from time to time.

Four out of five days dawned clear, with just a few clouds, and we would know that it was going to be a scorcher; the fifth day would be cloudy, and that meant short, sharp rain squalls. These were uncomfortable because our awning was rigged as a sunshade and not an umbrella, but it wasn't worth changing for the occasional shower, and we just got wet.

The 2nd January was one of the clear, hot days, and our spirits were high because we knew that the miles between us and Barbados were dwindling. Rosemary's log hits it off:

> *2nd January.* A lethargic day and no inclination to do very much after yesterday's strenuous efforts. How any movement takes it out of us! Two days' anticipation of a job and one day's rest afterwards is about the proportion. Even lying down can be pretty uncomfortable for every bone sticks out and if one part of you is comfortable another is sure not to be. Circulation is poor and arms and legs deaden very easily. I wish I hadn't got such boney hips! Bushy suggested gouging out a hole in the deck for our hips but the designer of the ship wouldn't hear of it!
>
> We now have only 150 miles between us and Barbados. How close that seems! We estimate that we might just sight land late on Sunday but who can tell?

As we got nearer to land Colin took a fix daily instead of every other day and on 2nd January at 5:0 p.m. when he had finished working out our position he shocked us all by telling us that we had made exactly zero miles in the last twenty-four hours. He took his sights all over again, and his second effort showed that we had done a normal 65-mile day, but also told us that we were twelve miles south of the parallel of Barbados.

This meant that we had to start going north as much as our goose-wing rig would allow. The wind was still almost due east, so really to go north would have meant using only half our sail on one side of the mast, but we didn't think it would be necessary just to make twelve miles north on a run of a hundred and fifty west.

It did mean, though, that Tim and I on the starboard side got any seas that were shipped, but as the wind had died right down, we got only an occasional splash.

Tim had fitted an outrigger made out of the tube of our hydrogen generator to hold the starboard fairlead outboard, and in the night, when I got up to stop it squeaking, I saw a light. I told Colin, whose watch it was, and we both thought that it was a small ship, but after ten minutes or so the light turned out to be the after one of a pair of rangers; then we saw the port red come into view and a bit later she passed very close under our stern on a north-westerly course, bound, perhaps, for New York.

It was a medium-sized freighter and it must have passed within a couple of hundred yards of us. We could see the blaze of lights in her accommodation and thought of all the good things to eat and drink on board her. We were not as disappointed as we might have been, though, for we were only about a hundred and thirty miles from Barbados. Had it been the daytime they would certainly have seen us, but we didn't try to attract their attention at night, because it would have been dangerous to have something of that size coming over to us in the dark.

The next day, in a moment of carelessness, I lost my green cup overboard. We had all agreed that we would keep our green cups on our dressers for evermore to remind us that if we could just get a drink of good water from the tap we were luckier than some — those in a lifeboat, for instance.

We opened our last one-pound pot of jam and took an inventory of what we had left:

> One gallon of water
> One tin of milk
> One tin of lemon juice
> One gallon of Permutit water
> Permutit for another gallon and a reserve of two gallons of foul water drinkable at a pinch.
> Plenty of biscuits, chocolate, cheese, sugar, butter and honey.

If we made Barbados all right we had nothing to worry about; if we drifted past on the South Equatorial Current we would be in trouble.

Now that we were getting closer we wondered what sort of a reception we would get — and weren't too happy about it. After being so royally welcomed in Tenerife it would clearly be a let-down, for we would be the balloonists who didn't fly across the Atlantic, and no one would be very interested in that. We had a strong feeling of being in disgrace, but we had known that it was a big gamble when we started, and were prepared for failure. Any-way, we decided, one thing that would compensate us for the feeling of having flopped was that we would be able to have all we wanted to drink for a change.

We knew that a half a pint a day each was not at all bad as far as survival conditions in a lifeboat goes, but it was bad enough to be uncomfortable and to make us think about long, cooling drinks most of the time.

Rosemary, who had been eating very sparingly, suddenly be-came hungry and polished off five pieces of Ryvita with butter, Marmite or jam, which was more than she had eaten in one day during the whole voyage. Tim and Colin started to eat some choco-late, of which we had plenty but which they hadn't wanted before. I think the thought of Barbados tantalisingly ahead of us made us all think of the good things to eat and drink that were waiting.

Our daily fix showed that we weren't, after all, making enough northing, and we'd have to put in the leeboard and give up our goose-wing sail rig. Colin and Rosemary struggled to get the lee-board in position, but when they had succeeded we found that it gave too much weather helm, and they spent another half an hour getting it inboard again. Colin hadn't been feeling well, and this exertion made him feel all in. He tried to get a fix but missed, and so we set a course for north-west with a single sail and slogged on through the night at about two knots, hoping for the best.

The two hours in the sun for the filming took it out of all of us, but particularly Tim and Colin, both of whom looked the worse for wear. The last days were very trying, for we weren't sure that we were going in the right direction. Barbados is a small island, only some twenty miles long, and it would be very easy to miss, par-ticularly if our chronometer had been damaged in the storm. We could get our latitude on the next day's noon sight, and if we could get far enough north we could then come in on the latitude of Barbados, which could be determined with the sextant alone.

The single sail and the new course made helming more difficult and the boat was not only slower but less comfortable. We had estimated at sunset that we were about eighty-five miles from Barbados and that meant that at dawn we ought to be between fifty and sixty miles off, and we all looked and looked for a light, but saw nothing.

It was 4th January, and the morning was overcast with bad visibility. No sun all morning, but it came out just at noon so that Colin could get a sight; he got another in the afternoon and placed us thirty-eight miles from Barbados.

That meant that we should see lights later that night or at the latest the following morning. If we didn't we would know that something had gone wrong and that possibly we had gone past the line of islands, and that would be bad.

We still couldn't use our double sail on this course and were making only about two knots. We opened our last tin of milk and of lemon juice.

That was one of the nights I slept deeply, and when I was due to go on watch Rosemary had to shake me awake.

"Got any lights for us?" I asked.

"Not a one. I've been keeping my eyes skinned, but there's nothing at all. See what you can do."

So that I could keep a good look-out for lights I sat up on the side deck and steered by pushing the tiller with my foot or pulling it with a lanyard.

When your eyes are peering into the darkness looking for a distant, elusive light they do a lot of wishful seeing. You know it's going to be so faint you won't be sure it is a light at all, and, by golly, you keep seeing faint, flickering lights all the time. Your eyes retain the image of a star and reproduce it just where you are looking for your light. When you really do see it you almost refuse to believe it; you are determined not to be fooled, and you look away, rub your eyes and make sure that it is still there before you tell anyone else the great news.

I knew that Colin was sure of our latitude, which he knew purely from the noonday sight and without having to depend on our chronometer, and that if we kept on it we *must* arrive at Barbados. Unless ... unless our chronometer was very wrong, say ten minutes or more, in which case we *could* have gone right past Barbados when we were twelve miles south of it. It was unlikely, but a horrible thought nevertheless, for it would mean our having to keep on going west until we reached Central America or, at best, going southwards immediately for the mainland of South America. That would take another week; at worst — with calms or torn sails it could be a month. I knew that all this was highly unlikely, and that we would probably sight Barbados soon, but still there was that illogical feeling that we might not.

I kept my eyes traversing the quadrant of the horizon where the light should appear, and at 12:35 I saw a light. Of course, I didn't believe it immediately — I stared at it, rubbed my eyes and looked again. It was faint but undoubtedly a light. Before I called the others I looked away and then looked back again. It was really there.

"Colin!" I shouted, "I can see a light — just where it ought to be. Bright and steady!"

He scrambled up and looked along my outstretched arm, but, as I brought my finger to bear on it, it went out.

"I'd swear on oath it was there, Colin!" I spluttered. "I didn't call you as soon as I saw it, I really did make dead sure." I felt horribly guilty — as though I'd been caught out lying or seeing things.

"Not to worry, Mr. Bush," said Colin. "If it's Ragged Point it would be an occulting light and will go out at intervals. It'll be there again in a few seconds."

Colin was very good at soothing you when you found yourself protesting that you were not nearly such a fool as you seemed to be. I quietly blessed him for his understanding, and we waited. We waited a frightfully long time.

"What are the intervals of Ragged Point's flashes?" I asked.

"Can't say. We threw out the *Pilot's Guide to the West Indies* as ballast, and my small chart doesn't say. I'm sure that it is an occulting light, though."

I was beginning to wonder if my eyes hadn't invented it, after all, when it appeared again and stayed on for a long time. We got the others up to enjoy it, and we all reassured each other that it really was there, even when it went out again.

We knew by the regularity of the flashes and the steadiness of the light that it couldn't be a ship, but must be a lighthouse and the only thing to do was to steer for it and hope that it was Ragged Point Lighthouse on Barbados.

I was exhausted at the end of my watch and went back into a deep sleep. When I awoke it was daylight, and Rosemary, who was on watch, said cheerfully, "Come and see the beautiful island I've found for you, Bushy."

"That sounds like a quotation," I said.

"It is — it's what Pat said to Colin on *Sopranino* when they sighted Barbados. But it really is — come and look."

It looked about two miles away, and it was beautiful all right; a picture-postcard tropical island, with long, golden beaches, palm-trees and our Ragged Point lighthouse, all set in a clear green sea.

Colin joined us.

"How far off are we, Colin — about four miles?"

"I make it about six," he said. I knew that distances over water were deceptive, or I should have guessed two.

"Why aren't we heading straight for the nearest beach?"

"There's a coral reef between us and the beaches. We'd probably be able to sail right over it, as we draw only ten inches or so, but without the right chart we'd better go all the way round to Carlisle Bay."

"How far is that?"

"About another five hours if we have to do it all ourselves, but we might get the chance of a tow from someone who could take us across the reef. I'm all for it if we do — what do you say?"

We all agreed, and meanwhile carried on sailing parallel to the beautiful coast-line with our goose-wing sail rig once more. Rosemary was at the helm sailing a compass course, so that no one was keeping a look-out. After about half an hour I thought it was time to take another look at the island. I stood up and there, not a quarter of a mile away, was a small cabin motor boat moving towards us at a good clip. The crew were two West Indian negroes, who waved when they saw me. We all stood up and waved happily back.

"Before you start bargaining for a tow, Bushy, there are two golden rules to bear in mind to avoid any possible claim for salvage against us," Colin said. "First — don't let them come aboard. Second — don't accept their tow-line but insist on using our own. Just to make sure, you'd better get their signature to whatever terms you agree."

When the thirty-foot motor boat came close enough I hailed her and they threw us a line, which we promptly threw back. He wanted to come aboard, but we wouldn't allow that either. With Colin at my elbow saying no, no, no, I told him that we didn't want his line and would only allow him to tow us for an agreed fee. He wanted to leave the question of money until we got ashore, but we said nothing doing — we'd rather waste a few hours and sail round to Carlisle Bay.

Finally, he agreed to discuss terms. My first offer of ten dollars for the five-mile tow he rejected with a roar of laughter.

"Why man," he bellowed, "ten dollar that ain't no money at all, no money at all. For a tow we got to have real money."

While he circled around us and we shouted at each other we were obviously getting nowhere, so I went over to his boat.

"We know all 'bout you and The Small World," the skipper said, smilingly welcoming me aboard. "We been mighty worried about you, and we are proud to help you all we can."

We struck a bargain at fifty dollars to tow us through the reef and on to the beach, but first he wanted to finish fishing. As we were talking his boy hooked one of our beautiful dolphins and pulled it aboard. He slashed its head with an iron bar until I was almost sick. It was ironical that if we hadn't brought them this wonderful catch of dolphin from mid-Atlantic our tow would have been cheaper and quicker.

After about an hour he took our line and towed us at an uncomfortable two knots through the reef to Grand Bay and the kind of smooth, golden beach we had dreamed about. He picked up his moorings, and his boy stripped off his shirt and swam ashore to fetch a rowing-boat for us.

We told the fisherman that we could not land, but would have to wait for clearance from the authorities. We sat and looked at the beach about a hundred yards away. There had been three adults and a child there when we tied up to his moorings, and in ten minutes there were ten, in twenty minutes there were forty and in forty minutes there were four hundred or so. Little coloured boys swam out to us in schools, peeping through the tiller port, diving underneath us and asking for souvenirs. We had about twenty pounds of chocolate still left, and we threw it over in slabs — none of which were lost!

Meanwhile, the crowd was growing larger by the minute, and now people were waving from the beach and from the headland above it. About three-quarters of an hour later a rowing-boat put out from the shore to us carrying a tall, handsome man in khaki uniform, who introduced himself as Captain Farmer, Assistant Commissioner of Police.

"Can you telephone to the authorities so we can get health, immigration and Customs clearance?" I asked him.

"Your clearance is written on your transom, skipper," he replied. "If you're really the crew of the balloon Small World, we've been waiting a long time for you — welcome to Barbados! My only concern is to get you to the Crane Hotel as quickly as possible, so that you can get some food and rest."

We climbed into the rowing-boat and were taken to the shore, which was now a solid mass of cheering people. The original four had swollen to about four thousand and, as the boat grounded, they surged forward and carried us shoulder high up the beach.

The flight and voyage of The Small World was over.

THE END

A WORD OF THANKS

THE amount of help given to us by much-maligned British Industry was staggering, and if the full commercial price had been charged for all the research, materials and actual work we should never have been able to launch The Small World.

As well as the companies mentioned in the book there were many others, large and small, who helped: Messrs. Accles and Pollock made the load ring and safety rail for us free of charge and, when I expressed doubts about certain features, collected it, took it back to Birmingham, modified and returned it. While we were wondering what movie camera we could afford Messrs. W. Vinten gave us a magnificent one of their manufacture, because in this all-British project they wanted to make sure that we had the best available camera. When we were let down with some turning and gear-cutting two engineers employing only half a dozen hands came to our rescue. They were Mike Keele of Tring and Robin Fowler of Shepperton, and they worked themselves and their men right through the night to make sure that our craft was ready in time. Christopher Wright, a machinery merchant I knew, telephoned the carrier who took our stuff from Cardington to Southampton and told him to charge his account instead of mine.

Once, in a hurried moment, Colin took delivery of the beautiful light chronometer which Thomas Mercer of St. Albans was lending us and signed a safe return slip for it. I pointed out that we couldn't, for obvious reasons, guarantee its safe return, and Mr. Mercer told us to take it and consider it ours.

All this help was of great value to us, but almost as important was the tremendous encouragement the unstinting generosity gave us.

As well as the persons mentioned in the book our thanks are due to:

Nat Alcock; Sr. don Tomas de Armas Alonso; Tom Beasley; Sr. don Jesus Alvarez Beyro; Lord Brabazon of Tara, G.B.E., M.C., P.C.; Ken

Bryan; Group Captain Mungo Buxton; Sr. don Enrique Cañadas; Douglas Collins; Sir Harold Roxbee Cox; Sr. don Tomas Garcia Cruz; Rex Curley; Peter Davey; Frederick Davidson; Ian Davis; Capt. C. J. Wynne Edwards, D.S.C., R.N.; Lt. C. J. C. Wynne Edwards, R.N.; Sr. don Juan Pedro Durán Fernández; Robin Fowler; Eric Fox; Commander C. E. N. Frankom; Doctor don Gumersindo Robayna Galván; Sr. don Evaristo Gomez Gonzalez; Sr. don Santiago Galindo Herrero; Tony Horder; M. O. Imray; Sr. don Francisco Fuentes Iruraosqui; The late Sir Arthur Jarrett; John Douglas Kaye; Hamish Kidd; Sr. don Lorenzo Machado Mendez y Fernandez de Lugo; Wilfred Moore; Bruce Norton; Sr. don Gines Sanz y Garcia de Paredes; Col. R. L. Preston, C.B.E.; Sir Alfred Pugseley; M. W. Ritchie; Sr. don Manuel Rodrigues; George Sassoon; Derek Smart; General don José Maria Lopez Valencia; Peter Windibank; Tim Wood; George Zorolo

and to:

The Royal Aero Club
The Imperial College of Science
Bristol University
Fédération Aéronautique Internationale
National Physical Laboratories, Teddington

and also to the following firms:

Accles and Pollock Ltd., Oldbury, Birmingham. Tubular framework, safety rail and load ring.

A.E.I. Lamp and Lighting Co. Ltd., Leicester. All lamps and lighting.

Allinson Ltd., Millers, 24 Newman Street, W.1. Specially baked and packed bread.

British Cycle Corporation Ltd., Smethwick, Birmingham. Pedal unit for stabilisers, charging batteries and winching.

British Nylon Spinners Ltd., 68 Knightsbridge, S.W.1. All clothing and sleeping-bags.

British Oxygen Gases Ltd., St. James, S.W.1. 690 gas cylinders.

British Productions Ltd., 10A Trinity Road, London, S.W.17. All wood-turning, including winch pulley.

British Thomson Houston Co. Ltd., Rugby. Generator for charging batteries.

Buck and Ryan Ltd., Euston Road, W.1.	All tools.
Ciba (A.R.L.) Ltd., Duxford, Cambs.	80 lb. of Araldite for laminating Terylene to foam plastic.
City Display Organisation Ltd., 30 Uxbridge Road, W.12.	Accommodation and equipment for building car.
R. and W. Clarke Ltd., Cowes, I.o.Wight.	Rudder and lee board.
P. B. Cow & Co. Ltd., 12 Hay Hill, W.1.	Li Lo mattresses plus a donation of £10.
Dexion Ltd.	Slotted angle for car fittings, radio mast, etc.
The Dunlop Rubber Co. Ltd.	Shoes and rubber hose-pipe.
Elders and Fyffes Ltd., 15 Stratton Street, W.1.	Shipping of crew and equipment to Tenerife.
E.M.G. Handmade Gramophone Co. Ltd., 6 Newman Street, W.1.	Special controls for radio receiver.
E.M.I. Ltd., Hayes, Middlesex.	Minifon tape recorder.
Fortnum and Mason Ltd., Piccadilly, W.1.	All food and emergency rations.
Robin Fowler, Tamesa House, Shepperton.	Special engineering assignments.
G. Q. Parachutes Ltd., Woking, Surrey.	Safety harnesses.
Greengate and Irwell Ltd., Manchester, 1.	Proofing of gas bag.
Hawkins and Tipson Ltd., Marlow House, E.C.3.	Hemp rope.
Imperial Chemical Industries Ltd., Thames House, S.W.1.	Foam plastic, Terylene for gas bag, car and sail, also Terylene rope.
Industrial Tapes.	Speedfix Adhesive tape for all purposes.
Jack Holt Ltd., Putney Embankment, S.W.15.	Sails, fittings, pulleys.
Mike Keele, Brookside Works, Tring.	General engineering of small units.
Kelvin and Hughes Ltd., New North Road, Barkingside, Ilford.	Sextants.
Lea Bridge Industries, Southend.	Water-lifting bags and solar stills.

Luke Turner & Co. Ltd., Leicester. — Shock cord and shock absorbers.

Metal Box Co. Ltd., Baker Street, W.1. — Diothene film for food. Polythene containers for water.
Diothene for practice balloon.

Mica and Micanite Supplies Ltd., Barnsbury Square, N.1. — All synthetic-resin-bonded fabric and machining thereof.

Negretti and Zambra. — Barographs.

Peel and Campden, 83 Queensway, W.2. — Nev for hemp rope proofing.

Renold and Coventry Chain Co. Ltd., Gt. Charles Street, Birmingham, 3. — All chains and driving wheels.

R.F.D. Ltd., Godalming, Surrey. — Making up of Terylene balloon.

Siemens Ediswan Ltd., Charing Cross Road, W.C.2. — Radio transmitter and receiver.

Smiths Clocks and Watches Ltd., Cricklewood, London. — Wrist-watches and stop-watches.

Ultra Electric Ltd., Western Avenue, W.3. — Air Sea Rescue Beacon SARAH.

W. Vinten Ltd., North Circular Road, N.W.2 — Motion-picture camera.

Wace & Co. Ltd., 3 Eyre Street, London, E.C.1. — Printing.

"W" Ribbons Ltd., Croydon, Surrey. — Webbing for harnesses.